# It's your turn, chickadees

## Rosalie Fuscaldo Gaziano

# It's your turn, chickadees

Rosalie
Fuscaldo
Gaziano

PAROLA Publications, USA
Wilbraham, MA

Book produced by PAROLA Publications, USA

First Edition  Quebecor Printing U.S.A.
Laurel,Maryland 20705


Library of Congress Catalog Card Number
is available upon request

ISBN 0-9653750-0-5 Hard Cover
ISBN 0-9653750-1-3 Soft Cover


Cover Design - John Auge

Illustrator - Philip F. Gaziano

Typesetter - Jon Frost


First © 1996, Charleston, West Virginia

# DEDICATION

To my parents,
who introduced the joys of travel to me,

To my husband,
who lovingly journeys with me,

To the Holy Spirit,
Who inspires me to write.

❧ ❧ ❧

# ACKNOWLEDGEMENTS

A book, like a child, takes much love and many people to nurture its growth. This book was conceived long ago, and only brought to life with the support and love of my family, the expertise of special gifted friends and the daily prayers to the Holy Spirit.

I wish to thank my husband for his loving support of this project, my sons who began to share their new-found knowledge with me: Philip, both artist and computer expert; Michael, loving advisor of professionalism; Todd, astute teacher of terseness; Dominic, impetus for perseverance and excellence; Thomas, expert of 'things English' and memories untold.

To the experts who advised, reproved and contributed; to Barbie Dallman for extensive hours of patient editing and encouragement; to Stephanie Coleman Shultz, Lucy Baker, Helen Gango Fuscaldo, Henri Marler and Carol Melling for the many hours of proof reading, many thanks.

To the artists who enhanced the visible images; to John Auge, graphic designer, Jon Frost, typesetter, Dr. Philip Gaziano, artist, and Dr. Dominic Gaziano for slides and photographs, I am grateful.

To the many family members and friends who prayed faithfully, and encouraged the concept of telling the story, I am indebted.

# PREFACE

Wanderlust is a seductive passion. It calls in the night like a lover, hinting of places and people not yet seen. You wake in a hot sweat of desire, feeling that something within you is missing. It was that incompleteness that preceded seven journeys of my life.

Wanderlust can come at any age. When I was only seven, I saw America pass before my eyes from the backseat of a '47 Pontiac. In the heat of July, my family covered Route 66 from West Virginia to California. Travel across the country was slower then and without air conditioning.

Squeezed in between my two brothers, I was forced to look out the back window, but the wonders of the West were framed in that glass. From orange and yellow streaks across the Plains, to the ghost towns of the West and the gold and blue of the Pacific Coast, I could see the world opening to me for the first time.

Everything I learned in the third grade that following fall seemed muted to what I had seen. From that time on I dreamed of seeing the rest of the world.

When my oldest son was about the same age, wanderlust returned. Maybe it was the confinement I was feeling as a young mother, for there were four children and one more on the way. It seemed my own youth and all its opportunities were about to evaporate. And so without money, our family of seven set out on a work-study year abroad that would open the world to all of us.

The journey to England would be the first of many that came out of restlessness when I was trying to balance motherhood, marriage, and my own need for growth and adventure. Twenty years later, deeply immersed in the problems of mid-life, another journey enticed my husband and me—this time alone—to leave our mundane world and visit Jerusalem. It was after this mid-life odyssey that I realized that the insights from each journey had come at crucial times and had enabled a new understanding of the world and myself.

The recording of these journeys in my own journal was at first a very personal account, a story meant to remind our children of shared experiences. And then as I retold the story to other families, I heard familiar questions, which made me realize that our family's journeys were merely a metaphor for life's growth.

As a book evolved, I realized that there were seven chapters, each coming out of a particular journey and a special need for us at that age. Our odyssey began with a search for knowledge of the world and turned inward to the more difficult questions. The journeys brought answers and joy, and there were some unexpected gems along the way. All of this I wish to share.

# CONTENTS

# Chapter 1

# England With Children

*"The city is there, the one that has caught the rhythms of dreams and silence. I can go. I can find it."*

—Mary Lee Settle

The center of England has the stillness of silk, with gentle greens and lakes that gleam blue. In the north, low gray skies give an air of legend to castles that dot the hills, while Liverpool reverberates with rock music made famous by the poets of the '60s. At land's end, where Arthur and Guinevere might have lived, a craggy shell is open to the sky, and white cliffs jut into a fierce sea.

There are many Englands.

There are many ways of seeing England. I have seen her on foot and by car, as a young and almost penniless student and as a tourist returning. I have seen her many moods change with the seasons, her fields muted in autumn when the wildflowers mix with hay, her lanes snow-covered in December, her gardens dripping with the heavy scents of summer. I have inhaled the crisp air of spring and endured the damp chill of autumn when the rain penetrates even the walls within the homes.

My husband, Dom, and I lived frugally as students for a year in the industrial northwest of England a generation ago. With us were our five little sons, the oldest only eight years old. It is to that first journey that my mind most often returns.

There were many journeys to England in more comfortable times, but it was not until our youngest son invited us to see his corner of England in Oxford that I understood what England had given us. It was a cold December morning when Thomas, a struggling new Rhodes scholar at the time, met us at Heathrow. Tom had rented a gray van large enough to transport the gathering family to Oxfordshire.

"Are you tired?" he politely asked.

I straightened my rumpled skirt and brushed back stray strands of hair, surprised that he hadn't noticed how excited I was to be once more in the land of low skies and high teas. Tom helped us with our bags as we greeted each other, having come on different flights, each from a different part of the States. Our family had grown. Besides our five sons, there were two brides, a fiancée, and our first grandchild was on the way.

The M-40 is a ribbon of concrete that connects the hub of London with the villages and towns of the southwest.

"Oxford is just an hour away," we were told, giving us enough time to catch up on family news and adjust to the atmosphere. Once off the main artery, the small villages of Oxfordshire came into view and then the spires of Oxford, rising from the mist over the horizon as they have for a thousand years of learning. It was quiet as we entered the city, with most of the students and professors gone for the month. Only the ringing of monastic bells in early morning broke the silence.

*What an idyllic place to study*, I couldn't help thinking.

Tom pointed out the landmarks with pride: Sir Christopher Wren's Sheldonian Theater, the Bodleian Library, the Cherwell where he would punt in the spring, the meadows of Christ Church.

"There are 35 colleges, each with its own green," Tom explained.

We passed the 400-year-old market off High Street, and he pointed out that the goose ordered for Christmas dinner was waiting there for us.

"I thought of you when I shopped for it, Mom. You'll like browsing there. It's your kind of place. Wonderful cheeses, displays of vegetables, all manner of wines, and last-minute Christmas shoppers with holiday faces."

Tom turned the van into Turl Street, a narrow, cobbled road not built for 20th-century traffic. Pulling up to the gate of his college, he parked half on the curb.

"Exeter isn't as well endowed as some of the larger colleges, but I'm beginning to feel at home here," he confided. "I even know the cooks."

He pushed the heavy oaken gate open. Four ancient gray buildings housing dons, students, chapel and dining hall formed the quadrangle. The small grassy expanse in the center was a muted green in the morning mist. A few stubborn roses held up their heads with blooms despite the December chill.

"The buildings are mostly closed for the holidays. No females either," Tom mused as he nudged his closest sibling. Being the youngest of five brothers, he was ecstatic that for once he had something to show them.

"The best way to see what's here is on bikes. After you get settled in, we can ride by the canal." He closed the gate and we boarded the van, now headed for our rented home for the holidays.

Tom's transition to English schooling had not been easy. At Thanksgiving, he had called home for recipes. His solution to homesickness had been to talk the cooks into letting him take over the kitchen so that the American students could have a traditional Thanksgiving dinner. We promptly received pictures of friends with whipped cream in their hair, pumpkin pies baking, and an invitation to be with him at Christmas.

Looking for a place for us to stay, our son had drawn on stories of the house we rented for a year near Liverpool when he was a baby. I had offered to find our own accommodations, and my husband had offered to rent the car from the States, but Tom had other plans for us.

The van weaved in and out of traffic, and I realized he had conquered the transition of driving on the left side of the road well. As Tom deftly turned from the round-about into narrower streets, we were all glad he was in charge.

He pulled to a stop in a quiet neighborhood beyond the quadrangles of the college. The home we were to rent, he explained, belonged to a professor of Italian literature who was off to the Continent on his seasonal break. There was a single pebbled walkway leading up to the two-story stucco house, much like all the rest on Polstead Lane. Peering in the leaded window of the front door, I could see pieces of princely acquisition on the walls, old books mingled among small busts on the hall table, worn boots at the foot of the stairway, and a narrow hallway leading to two floors of English threadbare gentility.

"Is this like you remember, Mom?"

I smiled. "You've done well, Tom. It's nicer than I remember." And yet there was something very familiar about it all. The quiet lanes, the houses of the same substance all in a row, the winding pathway in the front, the door with leaded window.

Tom pushed open the door. He had put up a rather sparse Christmas tree in the parlor.

"We'll decorate it tonight after you've had a chance to unwind," our host said, fully in command of his new role. "Did you bring the ornaments?"

I had, indeed, tucked in a few familiar ornaments as we agreed, just as I had done on that first trip to England a generation ago. I hoped they were not broken. Tom continued his tour of the house. We peered into the kitchen. He stopped to fill the teapot with water from the tap. The sound against the tinny, hollow container was riveting. *We are in England*, I thought.

There were blue porcelain dishes on the ledge; the teapot with its crocheted cover was waiting. Looking out the back window, I could see the small, fenced-in garden. The glance was almost a rush of strange warmth on that chilly day. *Yes*, I thought. *I have been here before.*

"I've got your bags, Dad," Tom called out. And we followed him upstairs to the front bedroom. The other bedrooms were quickly claimed, and our bags were dropped beside an iron bed. Amid the chatter I looked for the decorations, hoping I had not forgotten any. My packing this time had been harried. I sat on the bed rummaging through the parcels, and I felt relieved when I saw the clump of little gingerbread men and the candy canes. But it was the old, flaxen-haired angel wrapped in tissue about which I was most concerned. I unwrapped her carefully. She was intact.

"Don't tell me you brought the angel again, Mom!" teased Mike, peering in the room as he passed.

"Why not? She travels well," I answered.

He seemed amused, and I wondered if he realized that the worn angel had represented more than a decoration for the top of the tree. She had been a form of security to him on our first journey to England.

I scanned the master bedroom with pleasure. There were pink and white roses on the coverlet of the iron bed and, next to the fireplace, an overstuffed tan chair, well worn and padded with tossed pillows. Tom had carefully laid out the wood. He took a match from the top of the mantel and lit the fire to take the chill from the morning, and I sat for a minute on the bed, the angel still in my hand, gazing at the flickering flame. There were five or six half-opened bags scattered around me, some light duffle bags and two compact roll-ons.

How different travel was when we had come when Tom was a baby. We didn't even own bags enough for a year's journey then, so I had picked up two unlined trunks from Goodwill before leaving for England. I had to think of a year's needs for five little boys a generation ago.

I felt my eyes blinking, and my memories of packing for both trips were becoming mixed, intertwined in my mind. Packing for our first journey to England had been harried, also, or had I forgotten? All the preparations had been filled with both excitement and some anxiety for the children. For impressionable children, myth and reality must have been hard to separate. We had told them we were going to England, a land my husband, Dom, and I had only recently introduced to them in fairy tales.

There was Philip, not quite eight; Mike, six; Todd, four; little Dominic, almost three; and baby Thomas to think of. For weeks the boys looked at the old trunks in our bedroom, wondering if their prized possessions would be safe in them. I had told each boy that he could choose only two favorite toys to take. It was all part of the decisions we had to make. Toys were dropped in and then often pulled out before the day was over. I showed them the familiar angel I would take and a spring-form pan for our annual lemon Christmas cake to assure them that we would have Christmas in England.

*The children deserve an explanation*, I remember thinking. The England of my own childhood had been filled with castles and mist and Beatrix Potter's prim cottages, a country defined only by its stories. I had always wanted to see that mythical land, even dreamed of seeing it, but like most women educated in the '50s, I had given it up for parenthood. There had been no trips with free-spirited friends after graduation for me or even the fellowship I could have pursued. There were four children and a fifth on the way when the idea hit to follow my childhood dreams.

By then, I had no aspirations to tutorials or dreamy spires, I was simply a young mother filled with the dream of touching the literary haunts of my favorite writers and the land of their greatest inspiration. My husband was just finishing his medical training and Thomas was on the way. Maybe it was "the confinement," as they used to call it. But something snapped that summer when I was pregnant with Thomas.

In the last months of my pregnancy, the sight of my shapeless body, and the weight of responsibility with no outside stimulation to balance the routine, was beginning to take its toll. That summer was oppressively hot, and I was growing restless as the swing of the screen door banged each afternoon, children coming in and out of the house, trailing sand from the sand box, needing help with water, help with the potty chair, help with loads of little buckets and shovels. As the sun went down, I watched my husband returning from the medical school on the hill. He seemed equally weary and restless.

Slumping in a chair after dinner one evening, I closed my ears to the gleeful shrieks of the older boys in the bathtub and reached for a book, hoping for an escape from the daily routine. I wanted to thumb through something pretty, see some exotic scene. But there were only piles of little, well-used books, all written in monosyllables. *Green Eggs and Ham, The Little Engine That Could*. I closed my eyes and began dreaming of the places I had never seen. I thought of my education, incomplete, and wondered if my brain was growing dull on its daily intake of Dr. Seuss.

Lying in bed after our boys had been read their last story, I began dreaming more and more of faraway places. There was always the mist, just out of my reach, and then I would awaken to "What's for breakfast?" and piles of diapers and dishes to face all day. The days grew stuffier, the August heat suffocating. There was a closeness in the air, hard to describe. I was beginning to feel trapped, trapped in my body, trapped in my home.

Then as the college students came back onto the campus, I found a little escape. With a student to babysit, I signed up for a night class in English literature. I left the house each Wednesday evening overwhelmed with guilt, tormented by the sight of four little noses pressed against the window pane. The eyes of Michael, then six, haunted me most, tears rolling down his little cheeks as he watched his mother drive off in the car.

But the class transported me to the wonders of the world I had left just a few years before. Joining the young students on the campus of the university for two hours once a week was a balm to my soul. I sat rapt, listening to a renowned professor of English literature. I still remember the sensation of pure joy one warm autumn night when Dr. Patrick Gainer was trilling those wondrous lines of Wordsworth:

> *"I wandered lonely as a cloud that*
> *floats on high o'er vale and hills*

*When all at once I saw a crowd, a host of*
*golden daffodils*

*Beside the lake, beneath the trees,*

*Fluttering and dancing in the breeze."*

The words had worked their magic. I could see the daffodils, and I could see England. There were the little thatched-roofed cottages and the lakes that gleamed blue, surrounded by hundreds of daffodils, bright and yellow in the sun.

*"For oft when on my couch I lie in vacant*
*or in pensive mood,*

*Flash upon that inward eye which is the*
*bliss of solitude.*

*And then my heart with pleasure fills, and*
*dances with the daffodils."*

Something within me had been tapped... unleashed. As I drove home that night I could hear the professor's final words of the class: "You will find Wordsworth's soul in the ever-shifting beauty of those peaks and valleys that inspired him. If you really want to know the poet, you should get to know the Lake District of England. You just might catch the spirit of inspiration."

"Inspiration, that's what I need," I told myself, and I wanted to see England. All of England. The vast glimmering cliffs of Matthew Arnold, the darkened alleys of Dickens, Victorian England, and even the dissident corner of England's latest poets, the Beatles. There was a world out there I had always dreamed of, and I wanted to see it, touch it, get to know it.

From then on, it was a pure case of wanderlust. Wanderlust can be a seductive passion. It calls in the night like a lover. You wrestle with its lore and wake in a hot sweat of desire. My husband saw it in my eyes as I came through the door that autumn evening and caught it in my restless tossing that night. Somewhere before dawn, he awakened me.

"Do you really want to see England? You know we could arrange a work-study year before we settle down."

"Now?" I quipped, with the weight of the fifth baby making it almost impossible to shift my hulk in the bed. We had turned down other chances to go to Europe. All of those lost opportunities rushed through my mind— the fellowship I could have taken, the Army assignment he could have chosen, the tours with friends, all given up for parenthood.

"There's a professor here from England," he continued. "He could help me find a place to work and continue my study of lung diseases in the hospitals of Liverpool. And you could study all the art, literature, and history you ever dreamed of."

In the morning, the reality of it hit. We would have to uproot our family and sell our house. All the security we had in the world consisted of a little equity in a small house in a university town, a car that would not start on cold mornings, and a washer that spun on its side with a heavy load of diapers. And yet those were the threads of stability that tied together our life. The children were faring well, felt comfortable in their school system, and had their grandparents nearby. Our world was ordered. And if we stayed, there would soon be relief from the burdens of my husband's training.

*But would there ever be a more suitable time to go?*

That autumn, I began to look at our hilly West Virginia neighborhood with new eyes. The hills were home, but limiting. The idea of adventure grew in me as Thomas grew in my belly. By January, I delivered Thomas. I rocked him in front of the wide glass window of our ranch house, feeling the warmth of a newborn in the midst of a snowstorm. By March an offer came from Liverpool. The stipend was frugal, meant to support only one. There were seven of us. An option to rent a house nearby in the village of Thingwall arrived. The house was described as semi-detached without central heat. We signed for the job and the house.

By June, we had sold our own home and bought seven tickets on Icelandic, the cheapest airline to England. Yet, the tickets represented one-third of all we owned. The day the trunks were sealed, Todd parted with Renard, a well-worn red fox who slept with him nightly. Renard landed head down in the trunk, and my pensive four-year-old leaned over and pulled him out. Renard would ride on the plane.

The children were sent to my mother's as I waxed and shined the house that had been nest to seven of us. The empty rooms bore no resemblance to the place where Batman jumped freely from the landings and people ate Cheerios together. Two friends from third grade came to the door, asking for Phil and Mike. I told them the boys were with their grandmother and that they would write to the third grade from England. I looked out at the open lawn. It was warm, and the fireflies lit the night. Down the street, three boys called, "Red light, green light," and I wondered what games little boys played in England.

## The Exodus

Thirteen patched, borrowed suitcases and odd parcels lined the curb the day we left the little Greyhound terminal in West Virginia. We had decided on an overnight bus, reasoning that the children would sleep during the night while traveling, and it would save us a hotel bill in New York. Placards lined the window of the terminal that July day in 1968. The heat was stifling. I stood sentry with the five boys as my husband purchased the tickets inside. I pulled out our other credentials. Passports could be done in family groups in those days. Our picture had seven people in it. I looked at it in disbelief. It was us, on a passport!

The bus rounded the corner seconds before my husband returned with the tickets, and I watched the eyes of the boys light up. The luggage was quickly tossed into the bowels of the bus, and the boys lined up for their last kiss from Grandmother. My mother, with tears in her eyes, handed over her youngest grandson. It would be a year before she saw him again.

Phil and Mike could stand the ceremony no longer. They darted for the steps before the hiss of the bus had ceased. Leaving their middle sibling uncomfortably behind, they scrambled for the only empty double seat, and we directed Todd to a seat about midway, next to a white-haired matron. My husband lifted three-year-old Dominic safely to the large seat that went across the back, and I placed Thomas next to him. Flanked by their parents, the youngest two were content.

High above the pavement I could see my family, who had come to say goodbye, framed by that tinted back window. Their images remained on the window as the bus turned the corner of Adams Street, my brother hoisting a West Virginia flag, my teenage sister waving frantically, my mother crying. It was not quite the send-off to Europe I had always imagined. There was no gangplank to climb, no Queen Mary tooting, no red roses and white handkerchiefs waving, but it was a royal send-off nonetheless.

As we turned onto Interstate 79, the pink sky lit up the horizon, and the hills in the distance were rich and full. As the road emptied into the Pennsylvania Turnpike, my husband's eyes met mine. There was an electricity between us. Our journey to England had really begun.

I watched Phil and Mike chatter through the night, glancing back and forth from time to time in quick, excited jerks. The pathfinders, discreet in their course, tried not to catch our eyes but nonetheless scanned the outline of their parents in the back. Todd sat bolt upright at first, next to his white-haired companion, fingering his only friend, Renard, the tough old red fox. He needed but a smile from his seatmate to begin a most profound explanation of what was happening to his family.

"No, not Liverpool, Ohio," I heard him say. "We're moving to Liverpool, England. You know, where the Beatles live! I'll go to preschool and see the Queen. You know, that England where the queen lives with her coaches and horses."

She smiled politely and fixed Todd's strap as he returned from the restroom in the back of the bus.

Dom and I took turns reading to Dominic and feeding Thomas. There were tales of Peter Rabbit and images of Lancelot and King Arthur, well-worn little volumes that I passed up to Todd. Thomas was changed many times and finally secured in his spot on the lumpy seat as the night turned pitch-black outside.

The smokestacks of Pittsburgh were barely discernible, but the tiny orange lights outlined their shape and I wanted to point them out to Dominic, who loved watching flickering lights, but his head was on my lap, his eyes closed, the ringlets of his curly head wet with perspiration. I took off his sweater and let him sleep. My husband and I dozed but did not sleep, jolted often by the blast of air that opened the door for exits and entrances.

The purple skies of morning met us ruffled, tousled, and weary. The boys' jerseys no longer looked fresh, and the elastic in their socks sagged. Their white shoes that I had polished meticulously the night before were cracked and graying, but dawn hid the details. The last hiss was a relief as we climbed down, sore and glad to see the Greyhound sign again in New York. It was 7 a.m. We were promptly delivered to JFK by cab. A long day stretched before us. Our flight would not leave for 13 hours. In the terminal nursery we all slumped into a short silence. Some may have dozed. When the boys began nudging each other with ideas of investigation, I pretended not to notice.

As evening approached, I cleaned the boys one at a time in the restroom and redressed them in wool Eton suits, polishing their shoes until they were white again and buffing them until they shined. Each had a white round-collared shirt and white knee socks for the trip. They would enter England properly, I had long ago decided, being prepared for that England of high teas and misty mornings.

It was sweltering at 8 p.m. as we walked out of the air-conditioned terminal onto the steps that led to the plane. At the sight of the 747, the boys shrieked with unabashed excitement, not one complaining about his scratchy wool suit nor his assigned load, endearing them to the harried crowd around.

For a moment I froze. With all the rush of pride, I suddenly realized what I had with me. These were my sons, the legacy of two families, and we were walking into the night to cross an ocean with them. What if something happened to them? An icy chill came over me. What were we doing it for, anyway? But then the crowd pushed forward, and there was no turning back.

On board, the boys found their numbered seats easily enough. Following instructions, they clipped on the safety belts, and then they touched and fingered every button on the seat sides. Dominic secured his favorite little car in the pocket ahead of him, and Todd placed Renard in his. Everyone but the baby was wound up, their questions shooting across the aisles at a speed I couldn't decipher. Poor Thomas, sopping wet in his wool knit infant suit, sobbed.

"The air conditioning will not come on until after take-off," the stewardess informed us, and Dom reached over to yank off the baby's top. The promised bed for Thomas was thrust at my feet. "The bed" was a cardboard box lined with a burnt orange wool army blanket. I fed my infant some cool juice, lined the box with a clean cotton diaper, and dropped his limp sleeping body in the "bed." He adjusted to the new crib with a sigh and was contented.

The other boys were not settling down. I handed out crayons and matchbox cars and sat back, hoping they would sort them out themselves. My whole body ached. I had not slept in 48 hours. I remember telling the stewardess how nice it was to be waited on and that I would take cream for my coffee. The rest is a blur.

Somewhere between Iceland and London, sometime between dark and daylight, that elusive time when pitch-black has turned to hazy gray, the time just before a pink streak over the horizon hints of sunrise, I awoke. My tray had been taken away, and I had a blanket around my legs. I peered out the window with the hope of seeing some cloud or a sign of where we were in the galaxy. It was hazy, but I thought I saw him through the pane. He was framed like the picture I kept in my wallet.

"Go ahead, Chickadee... it's your turn," I heard him say. His voice was as clear as the stewardess's when she had announced the air conditioning was not yet on. It was my dad. Not portly Frank with the cigar in his mouth, telling the men where to put the tires. Not the young father who had taken us, grinning, across the country when I was seven. It was Francesco, the immigrant's son, young and handsome, broad-shouldered with thick, curly hair. He was dressed in white slacks and a white shirt, walking down the midway of the Chicago World's Fair. Looking much like Jay Gatsby, he wore his clothes well. He had his arms around the shoulders of two cronies, but he clearly was the leader.

I had kept that picture in my wallet always, fingering its faded and rough edges many times. It was a picture that burned with excitement and wanderlust. On the back was written simply, "Summer of '33," but the story was all over Dad's face. His grin was wide and his eyes lit with the wonder of what he was seeing. Dad was only eighteen then. It was the year of his graduation, and he was expected to go on to the grocery business by fall.

The little grocery store was at the edge of the railroad tracks, and Dad had his feet planted shakily in two worlds. On one side was the warm world of pasta and Parmesan and a fiercely protective mama. On the other side were young girls in stiff white organza. Nightly, he listened to the train whistle calling like a lover. With the Depression hanging heavily over the world, the cattle cars coming from the West carried train-hopping migrant workers. In the morning the C&O returned to Chicago. Dad bartered for tales as the hobos jumped from the train. For a hunk of bread and some salami, he could listen to tales of the World's Fair being built in Chicago that year.

"A Century of Progress, they call it," the freeloaders had told him. "They put up a building a week, made of plaster of Paris, not to last, but it gives us work for a while. And, boy, do they know how to take it off—the girls, I mean. You ain't seen nothin' like it," they taunted. "The girls are straight from Paris!"

The idea must have sizzled in his dreams that spring, for one morning the shrill whistle proved too much. Dad and two cronies jumped the train and headed for Chicago. They ate junk food never allowed in an Italian kitchen and drank Coke from hourglass-shaped bottles.

"Travel and Transportation had it all," he later told his family. "I saw them put together a GM car in front of my eyes!" And to his friends: "And that Sally Rand... she knew how to hold those feathers just right!"

Life would never be the same for Dad after that summer. He never returned to the family store. He had seen the American Dream. It was tires and business and a long love affair with travel. Every chance we had, we were off as a family to see New York or Cleveland or Chicago. And those trips were the happiest memories of my life.

"Go on, Chickadee, it's your turn," I was sure he said. And I dozed again.

* * * * *

"Let the mother through," I heard with relief as customs was stepped up for our family. The clerk punched and signed cards almost without looking, his English clipped and polite. "And tell the little lad to get his hands off the pulley."

My eyes followed the red pole that three-year-old Dominic was twisting. High over our heads he was slowly closing the window in the huge terminal. I yanked him along, a little embarrassed, and proceeded to survey the revolving carrousel that was displaying our 13-odd suitcases that had been ejected from the plane.

"We've got to get some sleep, real sleep, in a bed, before we go on," I murmured.

"It's the middle of tourist season," Dom answered, "and we don't have reservations."

Out of the corner of my eye, I saw Phil and Mike inching away from the bench, Dominic was clinging to my skirt, and I couldn't stop usually placid Todd from pinching the baby. I knew we were all overwrought and exhausted.

The boys were soon to learn the look of an innkeeper when Dom gave them his budget and the number in our group. "What's the difference between a 'hard-up room' and a motel?" I heard one of the boys ask his dad as he led us to the accommodation in London.

"Plenty!" I thought, as we descended the stairs to the basement quarters Dom felt we could afford. The 'hard-up' room was a dormitory with a row of seven small beds.

Flowery wallpaper was unevenly hung, cracks covered the ceiling, and one single light bulb dangled overhead. At least the linens looked clean. Todd looked around, as a sergeant casing the barracks, and candidly remarked, "And this is London???!"

London looked brighter a few hours later after sleep. Red double-decker buses swirled around us; urbane businessmen hurried past. We realized for safety we had to initiate a military plan. To cross the thoroughfares, Dom instructed the middle boys to grab him by the hands when he called: "Group!" At that moment, Todd and little Dominic took his hands and seven- and eight-year-old Mike and Phil flanked their younger brothers. They walked five abreast. I followed, carrying Thomas. The air was crisp, and their wool suits were now comfortable.

After three days of unrelenting travel—a Greyhound bus from West Virginia to New York, an overnight flight to London, and another flight to Liverpool—it was a relief to be met at the airport by a young physician, who had recently been through a similar experience with two children while studying in Baltimore. Our host, Dr. Meecham, a gentle, well-bred Englishman did not flinch at the sight of five boys and 13-odd parcels. Without missing a beat, he tossed the luggage in the back of his car and around us, and we were whisked through Liverpool. His wife had searched through rentals for us, finding a place in a quiet village near their home, across the Mersey River from the industrial port.

The images of London's poorer cousin in the north have faded like a dear, old photo. I remember streaks of graffiti on barred windows, debris on the ground under a gray sky, but once out of the tunnel that connects Liverpool to the Wirral Peninsula where we were to live, the green of the grass in rows of semi-detached houses with prim little gardens awakened every sense in my tired body. It was July, but smoke ascending from the chimneys reminded me that we were indeed in the north of England.

All our correspondence had confirmed that we were to be housed in a semi-detached (duplex) home with a small garden in the back, situated in Cheshire in the village of Thingwall. Thingwall, a Viking hold in the sixth century, was in 1968 a pleasant little village of tree-lined streets and small homes with fenced-in gardens.

Ours was an average stucco home, distinguished from the others in the row by a leaded window that sealed the privacy of the hallway. There were painted morning glories climbing the walls of the dining room, and some of the fresh roses of the garden had been brought in and placed in a jar on the table in the hallway.

Glancing into the living room, I saw that the furnishings were post-war "English modern," with large floral images on the carpet and streamlined chairs and sofa in the living room. All our luggage was neatly placed at the foot of a stairway leading to four bedrooms. With the proper British gesture, Dr. Meecham excused himself, "You will no doubt wish to be alone to settle in. We'll look for you for dinner on Sunday."

The boys quickly tested the bannister, fingering the smoothness of it going up and the speed of it sliding down. A glow from the lamplight filtered into our bedroom that first night. We tried to induce sleep. There may not have been sleep, but there was, at last, relief. In three days our whole world had changed. Gone were ranch houses and open lawns. Gone were fireflies and "kick the can." The glow of the northern light at 10 p.m. made it seem a midsummer night's dream.

\* \* \* \* \* \*

And at times, over the last 'twenty-some years,' it still seemed a dream. The images have faded in and out over time, sometimes mythical and sometimes startlingly real. My head jerked as Tom called out, "Tea is ready!"

The fire had almost gone out, and the chill of the room had returned. I had always remembered that first year in England with a touch of romanticism, but the chill vividly reminded me that things had not always been easy. Like childbirth, labor is easily forgotten when new life comes. Little did I know during those early years the new life our journeys would bring.

## Village Life

The land around Cheshire was simple and undramatic, explaining the personality of the country squire better than ten volumes on the subject. We quickly put away pre-conceived ideas and books on the English. There was enough to learn in the very act of living in a village. And in every corner of the island there was grist for the imagination of small boys.

There would be leafy lanes to follow and picnics by sand dunes. There would be stone walls to climb and walled cities where layers of English history could be unfolded. There were castles where King Arthur would come alive. But settling in would be our first adventure.

The house itself was investigated excitedly from bedroom to garden. French doors from the back living room led to a small, enclosed, overgrown garden. French windows upstairs revealed a green expanse so rich it seemed unreal. Beyond the field sat Thingwall Primary. School was still in session, and from the windows our boys caught their first glimpse of boys their age, wearing gray short pants and stripped ties, playing games our boys did not know.

The kitchen had undergone many changes. Once a coal bin, it was covered most recently with a thin layer of tile and was cold on entering. In a corner was a three-tiered wire vegetable rack and a tiny fridge, a single Bendix washer, a cooker with electric elements, a tea kettle, a few pot holders, and a crocheted cozy over the teapot.

There were coal grates in every room, none of which were usable. The living room fireplace did have a small electrical unit, which, when turned on, gave the appearance of burning logs but produced very little heat. It had been a bright spring in West Virginia when we signed for the lease. The rhododendrons were in full bloom, and it was warm. A house without central heat seemed a small sacrifice to make to see England, we reasoned. Now as we surveyed each room, barred by heavy doors, the July chill sent out its warning.

The boys noticed little closets under the stairway which could be great escapes from one another, and they noticed the tellie with its barrage of new images. Within a few days, a maroon "Cadillac" of a pram was placed at our door. "Me mum got it out of the attic," announced nine-year-old Ian Hamilton, from the stucco home to the left of ours. "I can tell you where the best tree houses are, if the boys 'ceere' to know."

My husband learned the rudiments of travel to work- a walk to the double-decker bus taking him to the river's edge, a ferry across to Liverpool, and yet another bus to the hospital. I soon learned to place Thomas in the center of the pram and pile groceries around him as the local village women did.

Shopping in the village of Thingwall was like going back in history some 40 years. The shops and stalls around the corner formed the center of the village, a pleasant walk for the boys and me—after five were dressed, prodded and enticed away from the maze around the stairway.

The nearby row of shops provided the basics of life. Chickens hung from hooks in the unrefrigerated windows of the butcher shop. Vegetables, encrusted with the soil from which they had just been taken, were piled in bins at the greengrocer's, and creamery butter and beautiful local cheeses could be had at the dairy. We could order milk in glass bottles to be delivered to our door, with fresh eggs upon request. At the chemist's, all kinds of medications and sundries were available, along with candies in visible jars easily discernible to the boys.

The rhythm of life was to be regulated by the timing of the opening and closing of the shops. For an hour and a half at lunch, the shades would come down. Without planning, on our first excursion to the dairy, I saw the blind go down, only to be reopened when the shopkeeper noticed our disappointment. Her kindness endeared her to us as she explained there was no more butter, but she would be glad to give us some of her own. We had to forego pick-ups on Sundays, as the shops would all be closed. Our life would take on a new cadence. Marketing more frequently would sweep us back to an earthy pace, a day-to-day thinking, in some ways a simpler kind of approach.

We also noticed that a community bulletin board was a great resource for second hand wares, a system we quickly used to find a crib for the baby. Adding up the barest of new essentials, we soon realized we could not even afford cleaning help on our stipend. But we did use the bulletin board, requesting some help with the children. The ad eventually brought Stella, a perky sixteen-year-old, to our door for some timely assistance with the "wee ones," as she quickly named them. The neighbors, who were used to older nannies, chided us for even thinking of "the young watching the young." But using my better judgment, I thought a teenager could be of some help in taking the children out for walks from time to time, and so I advertised.

Stella was more than a freckle-faced young Irish teenager looking for work. She presented herself at our door, with a warm smile and a willingness to explore areas of the peninsula with the boys. Her family often backed her up when they saw the size of our little group. We were learning the diversity and warmth of the British Isles, with Scottish neighbors next door from Glasgow and the Irish clan who assisted Stella.

The restrained, orderly style of the British who first inhabited the island was reflected as well in the symmetry and privacy of the village neighborhoods. Each home on the Wirral was enclosed by a fence, hedge or wall. Each garden spoke of the private world of the British.

One evening, soon after our arrival, when all the boys were asleep, I sat in the small overgrown enclosure that was our garden. In July, there was still light until 10 p.m. in that part of the hemisphere. The reverse, of course, followed in December, when dark came as early as 4 p.m. In the early days of our stay, a glow from the street light came into the space. The garden had taken on a peacefulness with fading light, and I realized that it would be refuge for the pram in the morning, space for children to play by day and a corner for solitude with my journal at night. That evening there was pure joy with the new setting. My education was about to unfold by living in another world. And with me was my own little world, my family.

Our jaunts into the lanes of Thingwall took us past mounds where the Norse Parliament met in the sixth century, and to the home of Lady Hamilton, where in the 19th-century whispers of her affair with Lord Nelson stirred this little peninsula. The village secrets, its ancient and recent history, unfolded day by day as we wandered out into the gentle landscape of Cheshire.

The Wirral, for the most part, was unspoiled. Far enough away from the sea and the docks that had industrialized Liverpool, it remained a peninsula of little villages and quiet lanes. In the British tradition of walking, "scrambling" with a stick and just rambling, we continued our investigation on foot. There were treks that took us into the wonders of the English countryside and English life. There were leafy lanes and field paths, heather-clad commons and an irregular coast-line. Country churches and parsonages often summed up the image of the country squire with his deeply rooted love of tradition and his acquiescence to a quiet, private kind of life. The landscapes were indeed soaked in personality.

Besides long walks around the Wirral, it was possible from our location to branch out into one-day trips that unfolded the countryside in wondrous little packages.

Often we would spend an afternoon in a nearby village or churchyard in the country, just musing in the beauty of the landscape or the peacefulness of ancient ruins. One day in a priory, some 300 years old, we meandered through its grave-yard first and noted that we were examining the names as if we knew the families. Inside, regimental flags that hung tattered and worn from the ceiling of the little parish church were as sacred as old family pictures on a piano. The boys, who had scampered outside like pups, squeezed through the narrow entrance. A reverent hush came over everyone as we read the warning inside the door:

"Many find God in quietness. Do not unthinkingly disturb them in their quest."

Our little group kept the silence, eyeing the arched ceiling, feeling the carved pews reverently. 'Were we becoming like the British?' I asked myself. *'caught up in the past of ragged banners and ancient ruins?'*

And then as we left, the plaque at the exit spoke to us: "Time that thou spends humbly here shall link thee with men unknown who were once of thy race."

A connection was unfolding: "England is our Nation's Mother Country," I reasoned, and I found myself growing fond of this kingdom by the sea.

As the summer wore on, we purchased a small blue Cortina mini-wagon. With a sense of wonder and four wheels, it was to be our summer of discovery. Loading in five little boys and a picnic and taking to the road, we found that the "kingdom" was made up of many villages, each with its own character. There were quiet, sleepy hamlets with dry-stone walls, medieval lanes and a modern roundabout  leading inward. Nearer Liverpool, there were turn-of-the-century deserted seaside amusement centers such as Southport, where the eerie remains of once-thriving parks were silent skeletal reminders of a nearer age.

## Walled Cities

Many of the villages by the  sea are still polished gems. Situated on the River Dee not far from Liverpool, 40 miles from Thingwall, is the city of Chester, a larger village founded by the far-reaching Roman Empire some 50 years before the time of Christ. Chester is a city with an Elizabethan face and a Roman substructure. An oasis to 19th-century Americans who came to the industrial north by ocean liner, it remains a beautiful city.

The walls of Chester are the finest and best preserved of any city in England, still intact, undulating as they do over and under current streets and grassy expanses. Rising in height from 12 to 40 feet, they offer magnificent views in some places and mesh into city life in others. The old city was destroyed twice; the remains of a Roman bath and heating system can be seen below ground, but the impression of a camp still surrounds the Tudor city. You can circumvent the city in an hour, walking briskly.

With children, it was an adventure of jumps and climbs. The wall, as it circled the city, narrowed and widened, meshing into the Tudor structure and skirting the 20th-century car parks. The walk revealed layers of history as well as natural jump-off spots just for the sport of it. Amid the fun, we were realizing that children truly do learn best on an experiential adventure. They chattered as we walked along, sometimes asking questions as they saw for themselves the kind of encampment that the Romans had established.

Our boys loved this kind of rambling adventure. Along the way we abandoned our neighbor's huge pram and let Thomas ride on his father's shoulders as the other toddlers skimmed ahead. This kind of brisk exercise with the pace set by the older boys, Mike and Phil, pleased everyone. The views were fun, a crooked alley that spoke of Elizabethan life, black-and-white timbered houses hanging irregularly over the street, storefronts with patinas softened by the weathering of the years, and the old English abbey at the city's edge.

Chester's 12th-century red sandstone cathedral, first built for the Benedictine monks by the Earl of Chester, was a landmark we were told not to miss. Its choir, its cloisters, its original 9th-century nave, introduced us to medieval history through stone architecture. Inside, there was a sweet, cool

dampness. It was a nice break from the Roman camp and our first real introduction to English Gothic. Outside the abbey, gardens provided a fresh, grassy retreat and a chance to see the tower at close range.

In the distance we could see the Elizabethan city, now effectively incorporated into a double-tiered shopping mecca. After a reasonable break in the garden, we headed for the Tudor buildings in the center of town. Here again, our little boys would ramble through the narrow lanes for a glimpse into another age.

For a long stretch, two tiers of shops form what came to be called "the rows." The rows are an architectural phenomenon, best appreciated by wandering through both layers. There was bustle and browsing in these curious arcades. We were told that as the first-floor level had burned, new stories were built above, and in the end a covered walkway connected the four main streets. The walkway circumvented the streets, with half-timbered upper stories providing the roof.

We climbed up to the top row of shops, where mostly chic clothing, curio, and silver shops were housed. The boys skipped along as they did on the Roman wall around Chester, their pace somewhat slowed by crowds of people shopping. It was a traffic-free walkway, but we had to keep an eye on the group as the crowd of Saturday shoppers grew more dense. This upper layer has a running public passage, and flights of stairs took us down to the lower layer at each of the corners.

As we eventually wandered down one stairway we could see that the lower shops were dotted with pubs, antique and art emporiums and Tudor coffee houses, and these were teeming with shoppers. Each shop, with its thick-paned windows, held wonders of ancient history, maps, silver and curiosities that were collected from the many ages of Chester and indeed England's history.

The history we had touched on the outside parameters was both Roman and medieval; the inner city was Elizabethan with some Victorian additions. Across the main thoroughfare was a laced metal arch with a fine Victorian clock, reminding the famished boys of lunch time. Tea rooms looked cozy but not affordable. The pubs and shops were enticing, but even-

tually we settled on some English meat pies from the bakery shop window, with the promise of a round of chocolates from the candy shop. Everyone enjoyed the day, the rambling, the browsing, the history. Chester was a gem, introducing us to 2000 years of twists and turns of English life.

## Castles of Wales

Encouraged by the success of the first day-long venture into the English countryside and excited by the wealth of English history around us, we began to drive farther in our little Cortina. We set out every Saturday in some new direction. From our home in the northwest, Ireland, Scotland and Wales were within easy reach. Wales being the closest, we decided to cross that border first. With a picnic and a plan to touch its four major castles, we headed to the northwestern corner of Wales.

Welsh history predates Christian times, but most remnants we saw were medieval castles, largely left barren. There was legend, history and myth entangled in the stone. Adventure was high as we set out to see what was mythical and what was real in the landscape.

As we crossed into this corner, we realized immediately that Wales was different from the rest of Britain, struggling into the 20th-century to maintain her own language, culture and identity. Some 700 years ago King Edward of England had begun a span of building that would long outlive him. He commanded the construction of massive structures, 17 in all, to subdue the fiery Celtic people and establish his own domain. His goal was to put an end to Welsh independence.

The fortresses remain a testimony to that struggle, dotting the landscape with some remarkably beautiful sights.

As we set out, a gray sky penetrated the borders, muting the shades of green which were ever present in the British Isles. Borders of hedgerows in deeper tones formed a pastoral patchwork so gentle that its very lay quieted us as we entered the smaller northern corner of Britain. There was a brooding, poetic nature to the Welsh land. Our drive took us through valleys where we saw cities of a Celtic world, their ancient titles announced in voweless Welsh.

Bettws-y-Coed, the "Chapel in the Wood," with its fairy glen, and Snodonia, with its mountains and streams, spoke of the wild beauty of the land. But Ffestiniog and Dolgellau spoke of Victorian drabness exemplified in the many little mining villages throughout the valleys, gray and isolated from one another and the world. In many towns, only the smoke ascending from the little bungalows assured us of life inside. All was quiet for miles. Mine was a melancholy appreciation for the plight of the miner and his subterranean world.

But for adventurous little boys, the promise of castles was grist for imagination. The National Trust did a wonderful job preparing pamphlets for each castle. We had done our homework with stacks of books, but that day in Wales we learned that, although we could read every detail about the castles as we prepared to go in, the real joy of this excursion was seeing

everything through the eyes of the children. King Arthur and Lancelot were destined to run through the ramparts and cross the moats. We began a series of car tales, each boy contributing his ideas as we drove, which heightened the anticipation of each new territory.

There was a sense of distant presence, the looming height, a different climate, even a different sort of structure of earth and sky as we drove further into Wales. England wears her history like a comfortable old coat, but Wales seems to entangle legend and mystery with her far-reaching ancient history. Her temperament and terrain are varied, and each castle had to be approached differently.

Likewise, the four major castles that Edward built with the help of a French master clearly showed us the variations of protection. Each was built to deal with the existing terrain, on hills, by the sea and in open plain. And so we saw in Caernarfon, Conway, Harlech and Beaumaris examples of moats and drawbridges, stone ramparts and dungeons designed for the 12th-century. In our 20th-century car, we covered the land in a day. Although our British neighbors were appalled at the idea of "doing Wales in a day," it proved to be the best architectural lesson we could have had, comparing quickly one with another, touching them all.

Harlech stood impregnable on a hill, as foreboding as any rider in the morning mist could imagine. Perched on a steep rock, right up to the base where waves used to lash, it was protected by its natural cliff. The corner towers were massive; I could see the gleam of a climb in the eyes of our seven and eight year-old boys even before the car doors were opened. The fortress was a mere shell of residence, its turrets and dungeons thick, rough and massive.

"To the tower!" went the cry of our group. The winding 153-step climb to the top was nothing to Phil and Mike, but carrying seven month-old Thomas was more than I bargained for. I passed him off to his father as we wound the stairs to the top, and each of us stepped back with awe as we came out into the light. A breathtaking view of the rolling green Welsh countryside unfurled in four directions. Patchwork formations of the palest green and blue green against a cloudless sky faded into the mist beyond.

"Down to the dungeon!" the group echoed and plunged, darting and squatting as they descended the dank steps. Leaning against the cool walls, we adjusted to the dark and then tried to survey our limited space at the bottom.

"Some spent their last days here, wishing for just the sight of the sun one more time," I heard a guide say. Our group was silent.

Caernarfon Castle held a different story. the castle sprawls massively over the edges of the modern city of Caernarfon. There was a livelier sentiment in the air. Tradition had given Caernarfon a visible role. The largest of the Welsh citadels, it was once the seat of the king of England when in residence. Flags waved that day as they had done to declare the king's presence. The ceremony which welcomed the first Prince of Wales has continued through the generations, leaving a festive aura to Caernarfon.

Again, the tradition went back to the time of King Edward, when every bit of cunning was used to keep the local Welshmen subdued. At one point, the English King wittingly promised the people of Caernarfon that they would have a ruling prince from their own soil. Slyly, the King brought his own wife, Queen Eleanor of Castile, into the castle. He failed to tell anyone that Eleanor was pregnant. When she gave birth to their son in 1301, Edward presented the child to the people of Wales, proclaiming him the first Prince of Wales. The ceremony was equal to none that the Welsh had ever known, in spite of the ruse.

This tradition has continued through the centuries. The first male of a reigning monarch bears the title, Prince of Wales. Prince Charles was crowned in 1969, carrying out the 700-year-old tradition in front of 300 million people who witnessed it on TV. Another side of the medieval mind remains: a clear taste for pageantry. The royal trappings within the keep were being prepared as we walked through.

The boys wandered through the castle, climbing into the ramparts, and the language of siege, defense and counterattack was played and replayed. In the keep, they sized up space for people and animals, fingered the cannons, and seemed to understand.

Near Bangor, the graceful span of the Menai Bridge, the first suspension bridge in the world, took us across the Menai Strait into the Isle of Anglesey. It was a land of quiet, rocky bays with sandy beaches, restful villages and streams. On flat land, we approached yet another castle, Beaumaris, built by Edward between 1295 and 1298. We spread out a lunch before investigating. The boys were more interested in another mode of protection. They had built castles themselves, carved in the sand of the moat; it was as if reality had elevated their imaginations to a new level. While we studied, read and looked at guide books, they lived history. With their enthusiasm, castles came alive for us, too.

Beaumaris was gray and thick. In contrast to the others, it was protected by a moat. The boys leaned over the small connecting span, forged ahead, and sized it up. The city and sprawl were now an enchanting reminder of the 13th century, the Welsh, and a world of power through fortifications.

There was a storybook feeling of Conway Castle with its long drawbridge visible for miles. The castle was white, and against the blue sky and the Conway River, it offered a mystical contrast to the gray cities we had just left. Up close, the castle's keep and tower were merely shells of its great past.

Edward had completed this massive castle and town wall in four years. It took a force of some 11,500 men from all over Britain and an architect from France. This castle had an air of lightness and the mystique of medieval legends. The city, however, with its fishing boats and farms, seemed to take us back in one leap, past all the forces of Edward and the Roman legions to the innocence of man and his sea and soil.

On our way home, the road wound through a different corner of Wales, closer to the sea, thicker in hedgerows and dotted with stone walls. Through Colwyn Bay and Llandudno we saw glimpses of the sea through the foliage as night came on. The roads we chose were narrow, and the little lanes jutting from them seemed private and yet inviting. We made a few abortive tries to find a private road to the cliffs and eventually found an unmarked narrow lane that took us directly to a cliff overlooking the sea. The sun was setting, and we walked in contented silence, wholly removed from the castles, the villages, the world. A single sailboat, pulled gently by the wind, passed before us and, except for the rustle of the leaves and the whisper of the sea, our cliff was a silent setting for our evening meal.

My thoughts were washed over by the brooding sea, bringing me back to the day's amazing revelations. The boys, with the spirit of children, had shown us castles. With their eyes, the medieval world had come alive; history was rich and never to be forgotten. After a satisfying meal and a full day, Dom looked again at the map spread out at the edge of our picnic blanket, surveying what we had covered and the road that would take us back to Cheshire. I knew my way had been mapped long ago by the words of Wales' finest poet:

> *"It was my 30th year to heaven;*
>
> *Woke to my hearing from harbor*
> *and neighbor wood;*
>
> *And the mussel pooled and the heron;*
> *Priested shore;*
>
> *The morning Beckon;*
>
> *With water praying and the call of seagull*
> *and rock and the knock of sailing boats on*
> *the net-webbed wall;*
>
> *Myself to set foot that second;*
>
> *In the still sleeping town and set forth."*

—Dylan Thomas

## Ireland and Its People

The castles of Wales were bound in history, their ramparts physical reminders of battles and treaties. But it was the people of Ireland who told us that country's story, the people who remained in spite of war, famine, and the whims of the sea. I had been schooled by an order of nuns, mostly Irish, who had directed my education through reams of Yeats, Synge and James Joyce. My best friends in parochial school filled in my education with legends and lyrical ballads that we sang faithfully on St. Patrick's Day. I once had a starring role in Synge's masterful "Riders to the Sea," and I had already felt the desolation of the crags and moors, where the sea claimed its due for a meager livelihood.

The departure point to Ireland from northern England was the rocky city of Holyhead in Wales. A ferry daily transported visitors to the land of Eire, as it did us that day. As we drove from the ferry to the port of Dunlerry, a fog encircled our car, making the identity of that island, already bound in legend, even more intriguing.

"Turn left if y're intendin' to visit," we were instructed over the loudspeaker and, with the lyrical cadence of the speaker's voice, the Ireland of scholars and poets came back to me. "Queue up for customs," he continued, "and we'll check your car." As we followed the lines forming on the left, I could see clear orders on the signs ahead. "No arms, no meats, no plants allowed," they read. Our car, now scrubby with the diapers, toys, and books between and around the boys, also had a picnic basket with our frugal allotment of food for the weekend: canned hams, crackers, fruit. The customs official surveyed the car, the basket, the family and then waved us on, hams intact. "Drive carefully," he instructed.

We were not far into the gentle hills the next day when we began to feel the quietness of the land. Fortified with the only hot meal we would have, a breakfast that came free with our B&B, we set out to explore the western tip of the island. Passing simple cottages, sparse and white, we could see hamlets here and there, small houses built from the natural stones that surrounded them. The brilliance of a blue sky was interrupted with clouds that emptied gentle rains from time to time.

Many had fled Ireland because of its famines and its religious conflicts. Yet we had no delusions about being able to get to the core of the country's socio-economic problems in one short visit. We wished only to partake of her special character, the beauty and simplicity that had captivated those who had stayed despite the pulls of nature and politics. The mist of the night before had lifted, and the day was gentle. The Wicklow Mountains soon unfolded a hundred still-life portraits as we drove into the countryside. The children were quiet as the rolling hills lulled them into a subdued rest. For our short stay we made a pleasant, unpressured itinerary that included Blarney Castle, County Cork, and Trinity College in Dublin.

Driving along the gentle rolling hills early in the morning, we competed only with the goats. By afternoon there were some carts on the road and we saw bands of tinkers (Ireland's gypsies, formed at the time of the historic potato famine of the 19th century). These itinerant wanderers had not emigrated but had remained, surviving by tinkering or repairing pots and pans, establishing their camps wherever they could.

While searching for a spot for our afternoon picnic, we came upon a green tent, a pony and a young freckle-faced girl of about twelve, gazing at our car as we curiously eyed her. A friendly interchange revealed that she was left to watch the pony, the tent and the brood inside.

"And how many are there inside?" I politely asked.

"Eleven, and I'm the oldest," she answered nonchalantly.

"Eleven!" I repeated.

Quick as a dart, she surveyed our car, with boys peering out all windows and the baby climbing over my arm.

"You don't do so bad yourself!" she retorted.

We shared our picnic and she shared the rights to petting the pony.

"Are you heading for the castle?" she asked as we turned toward Cork and the mountains that surround Blarney Castle.

"Watch out for the fairies," she reminded us.

We assured her we would. To miss the lure of Ireland's unique people would be to miss Ireland.

We were all relaxed as we headed to Cork where a stop for something to drink and directions seemed in order.

"How many miles to Blarney Castle?" I heard my husband ask the barkeeper at a pub outside the city. The boys and I, not wishing to interrupt the male bonding at the moment, had remained outside, enjoying the people passing by.

"Not far. You wantin' to kiss the stone?" the bartender replied in a rather testy way.

My husband, not so sure where this man stood, elbowed in as if he were one of the natives and hedged his bets a little.

"We were told the castle isn't really Ireland. It's maybe a little bit of a tourist trap, but," he said, pointing to the car and the boys, "they love castles. We'll just have time for a quick stop."

"I wouldn't hurry if I were you," the bartender insisted. "The stone at the top is really what you want to see. You've come all this way, you know, and the stone has powers. You know the stone was carried through Egypt, Spain and Sicily."

"'Tis the same stone of Jacob of the Old Testament, you know," said another old man in the back of the pub.

"You're dead wrong. It's from Solomon's temple. It is holy, used as the death pillow of St. Columbus," argued another.

It seemed we had started something and, even at the door, as the boys and I were watching, we could feel the heat of repartee. Dom looked at the men inside, the boys outside. Feeling obliged to buy a Guinness, he ordered the expected and then said loudly, "Five Orange Crushes to go."

The red-faced barman grabbed hold of a glass, gently pulling the spigot. The glass filled slowly, and a column of bronze foam spilled over the top. The bubbly, sudsy froth looked so good, even the dark foam that had spilled over dissolved into a kind of nectar.

"The real truth about the stone on Blarney Castle is that we don't know where it came from," the bartender said authoritatively.

"We do know for a fact . . . ," he continued.

And I grinned to myself. "And what is a fact, in a pub in Ireland?"

"We know it was the builder of Blarney Castle who placed a monument of faith atop the strongest Irish castle. It remains there today. And it is said to work wonders as it did for Cormac MacDermod McCarty. They come from all over the world to kiss it. Winston Churchill owes his eloquence to it. After he lifted his hulk up those stairs and leaned over to kiss the stone, he was a different man. He could barely squeeze through, they said, but it changed his dialogue. He being English, he needed it."

He leaned over and whispered to Dom as if this could only be shared with a male. "Now for us Irish, it isn't always necessary. We have the gift, you know."

Outside again, we watched the children of Cork return from classes and our boys felt heady with their freedom. I was heady with the inspiration all around us.

Blarney Castle was not too many miles away. "What do you think?" My husband put it to the group. "Shall we see this castle and kiss the stone?" The discussion continued in our car. To kiss the Blarney Stone was to partake of the legendary lure of Ireland's special grace. Few countries had legends as rich. And so we drove along the quiet road toward Blarney, passing beneath overhanging ilex trees and evergreens. This stretch of land was fertile; the trees lining the streets, some hundreds of years old, were gnarled and monstrous, almost mythical, holding in them the stories of generations of Irish life.

We knew we would stop. If the banter in the bar had not whetted our appetites, the sight ahead would have: the Bogorragh Mountains in the distance, the emerald-green elms in the foreground, and a regiment of bagpipers lounging at the base of one of the huge trees. At the end of a winding lane, grown over with craggy moss, stood McCarty's Blarney Castle.

The younger boys darted in and out of the lane, but the discussion was focused, the older boys intent.

"What's the difference between blarney and baloney?" Phil asked.

"Only a politician would know," my husband answered.

Not being totally satisfied with that answer, Phil turned to me for some discernment. I could see his mind was ticking. Here was an interesting turn of words.

"Some say blarney is the varnished truth," I tried to explain. "Fair words, they say."

Long ago during the reign of Queen Elizabeth, the one they called Bess, this part of Ireland was separate but under her rule. Ireland's lords were divided in their loyalties. McCarty was one of the wealthier Irish land owners. The queen wasn't sure where his loyalties lay. She ordered that he give over this castle's bounty to England. He pledged his loyalty and told her he would but had a million reasons why he was not ready to vacate. He had kissed the stone long ago, forewarned by a fairy, and he waited as did the queen. Finally, she got tired of being put off, remarking that his procrastination was a trick.

"'Tis all blarney," the queen exclaimed. "He says one thing and means another. If it's the truth, it's the varnished truth." There were, in the end, many fair speeches back and forth, but sentiments were stirred against the queen and she finally had to let him go.

We climbed the winding stairway, surveying the beautiful country, but the boys were unflinching in their resolve. Phil and Mike headed for the spot where I was supported by a guide, who politely covered my skirt with a blanket. They watched quietly as I leaned backwards to kiss the cold rock. Dom took his turn, and the boys drew closer, now aware that the rock on the outside of the castle must be approached from a precipice several stories high. It would be difficult not to look down while doing so. Still convinced they could do it, both of the older boys took their turns quickly one after the other. Todd, terrified by heights, heard his brothers taunt: "Go on, Todd, don't worry. It's only 500 feet down! On a freezing day, you might crack, but the ground isn't that hard today."

He froze, and I ushered the little ones toward the exit. At the last moment, our four-year-old had a change of heart. Whether it was sheer wonder over the magic in the stone or the fear of being mercilessly teased by his "superior" older brothers, he dashed back to the site without looking and

kissed the very stone said to carry with it such powers of magic. To this day, Todd—a Truman scholar, debate champion and lawyer for the Justice Department and Congress—remembers with me that sweet moment of victory.

We would have only a brief stop in Dublin, where we wanted to see with our own eyes the Book of Kells. Encased in glass in Trinity College, the beautiful script that the monks copied in the sixth century was Ireland's masterpiece of ancient scholarship. It was completed as an act of faith with attentiveness to recording the words of God for meditation and worship. Without knowing the impact of their dedicated work, the monks had made a rare contribution to Western civilization. The tedious work done in the hidden glens of Ireland was the thin thread that had kept a form of history of mankind alive while books, buildings and knowledge were being destroyed all over the rest of Europe in raids of the Dark Ages.

Ireland's golden age had few other testimonies, except for the wonderful glens where these monks once lived. We would see those later. Peering into the case, with its gold and brilliant symbols, even the boys recognized we were looking at some-thing very old, something very special and they were quiet in our only indoor stop in Ireland.

Tired, we headed for a recommended B&B in a quieter corner of the county. It was on a farm road that our faithful lit-tle car began to issue steam. A few squabbles—the kind that come out of exhaustion—erupted in the back seat, and steam hissed from under the hood. My husband got out to take a look. There was no visible problem but, when he got back in the car, the motor would not respond at all. The night was pitch-black. We settled into a slump, calming the boys with stories and a last snack until we heard the hum of a car behind us.

With the lights of the car streaming on us and the cinder drive to our right, we could see a farmhouse ahead. The car pulled up beside us.

"Is thar' a problem, son?" the driver asked. Surveying our car, there was compassion as the elderly couple looked over our group.

"My car is overheating, and it won't make it to our destination tonight," Dom reported.

"We've used the farm for tourists, but we're closed this weekend to rest ourselves. But I'll see what the 'missus' can do."

Within minutes, we were in the kitchen having milk and cookies, and his wife had put up the crib for Thomas. By morning, a mechanic from down the road had fixed the car, serving us a bill for merely a pound and sixpence (less than three dollars in those days). There was no guile in this family, and we had felt much at home. I was never sure of all the legends of Ireland, but as for the saints....

## Scotland and the Festival

At the border of Scotland, the sun glints on the hills, giving light and shade to the little villages that lead to Edinburgh. Unfinished abbeys, lying bare to the sky, mingle with the gold of the newly cut hay and purple of heather growing close to the roadsides. On the last weekend of summer, we followed the road with hopes of seeing yet another Celtic branch of the British Isles. It would be our last fling before the children began the fall term.

Informed that the largest festival in Europe takes over Edinburgh on this last holiday of the summer, we booked in a B&B recommended as reasonable and "convenient to festival." With no other preconceived images of the city or scope of the festival, we set out early on the fall Bank Holiday with our usual picnic and supplies for five young children. At dusk, after eight hours of driving, we reached the gray, handsome city on the hill, Edinburgh. Winding upward to the heart of the city, we saw a proud and stern castle. It seemed to be a magnet for light, the moon casting shadows on the stones, and the spotlights making it a floodlit beacon.

Edinburgh's massive stone castle dominated the city. In the light of the moon, bright that night, the castle seemed more myth than reality. The group in our car, though tired, was excited about what we would see in the daylight.

Searching for our home for the weekend was not simple in the dark. Among the Georgian homes with newly put up B&B signs was a two-story whose numbers were barely discernable in the waning light. At last we saw that they matched those on our confirmation letter. The silver-haired widow Mrs. Wright received us late Friday night with all the warmth of a grandmother glad to have her family home for a visit.

Hers was a well-appointed home with polished mahogany furniture and brass accents, each reflecting the patina of care. We were tired, and her offer of tea was a benediction to our day. We bedded the boys in their weekend room and laid out their clothes for the next day. Mrs. Wright had put us at ease. She was a gentle soul who offered to babysit if we should require it, "for seeing the festival at night." We all slept like babes, with prospects for a good weekend.

Banners proclaimed the festival as we approached the center of the ancient city the next morning. There was an eclectic feeling, with movement and sound, art and music bursting around us. We had come to see the city and to learn a little of the history of Scotland and its capital. However, we soon learned there was a juxtaposition of modern festival over historic sites. Edinburgh's past was intertwined with the lively arts of many nations.

Flags waved and colorful umbrellas dotted the parks. Little clusters of red geraniums, pink and yellow pansies and myriad roses added a cheerful welcome as we wound around the cobbled streets that led to the historic landmarks.

The fervor of the festival was all around us, proclaimed in handouts and street gatherings. A literary salute to Burns and Scott was advertised in the library. Art from Bodin to Picasso was displayed in the museums and under tents. Groups of students from Oxford and Cambridge had brought their shows on the road. They were performing on the streets and in the playhouses. Every hall and building seemed assigned to bringing some form of art to the city. Marquees announced opera, drama and symphonies.

The festival, organized in 1947 to pick up a war-torn city, had grown to be the world's largest. Its participants took over the main artery of ancient Edinburgh, which bore the name Royal Mile. That normally austere cobbled area was dotted with musicians, mimes, and jugglers, beckoning visitors to view the vignettes and to see performances inside the halls.

"Get your tickets here for the Military Tattoo," the barkers touted. "Front row seats, only a few left. You will never see a spectacle like this! Scottish bagpipers, regiments from all over the world, more than a parade or a review. You will see Celtic dances, the Queen's own guard, all in review on the esplanade of the castle. Matinee almost sold out."

"Seven, please," my husband quickly answered. And with that purchase, we began to enjoy the city around us, entering some of the historic buildings on the Royal Mile, with an eye for its past. We started at the lower end, first visiting Holyrod Palace, where Mary Queen of Scots was first received from France as a young princess. The guide was quick to point out the room where the Queen later entertained her music-loving secretary, and he also deftly marked the spot where that same secretary was murdered.

The secrets of the Stuart family unfolded all around us. The story was one with many twists and turns of power, with love and intrigue remembered most dramatically in the royal residences. More of the epoch was revealed as we climbed the Royal Mile in the center of ancient Edinburgh.

Midway in our walk toward the castle, we passed St. Giles, the gray Gothic church, said to be the site of long, doleful words of the Reformation. Outside, vignettes of morality plays were hissed and booed by many a passersby; light musicals were drummed out in the courtyard as the festival-goers threw down coins in appreciation.

We broke from the path mid-morning to rest on the grass of Prince Street, a lovely thoroughfare that divided ancient from 18th-century Edinburgh. It was all beautiful, I thought, the city, ancient and present, the festival, the monuments to the past. I sat smugly with Thomas in his stroller, half asleep, while the other boys climbed the monument to Sir Walter Scott. The sun was bright but the autumn air crisp. I put a sweater over the sleeping baby and relaxed on a bench. This is better than taking a class, I thought, smiling to myself, and

I have my family with me. My complacency was to be tested before the day was out.

As we headed back to the Royal Mile and the castle, it became more difficult for the group to navigate. The fervor of the festival had picked up considerably. There was an expectancy in the air. One single regimental piper lagged behind his group. Our boys stopped to look at his instruments. We pushed the children along and realized that the Tattoo was assembling as the crowd poured into the narrow cobbled arteries leading to the castle keep. We had to abandon our usual system of grouping older boys beside younger ones. Soon we were a line of Daddy duck followed by four little ducklings, with Mama and stroller bringing up the rear.

At one turn, as I straightened the stroller, I did my usual check. One, two, three, f-o-u-r. I could not see four boys. Squinting, I caught sight of Phil, Mike, and Dominic, but where was Todd? The intensity of the mob pushed in on us. The reality hit. We were in the middle of an international festival, with myriad tongues babbling around us, and I could not see our four-year-old son.

I felt flushed, hot, then an icy chill crept down my neck. "Where is Todd?" I yelled. "I can't see Todd!"

The other boys stopped. Dom counted.

"Don't move!" he ordered with dramatic composure. Drawing the other boys around me, he attached their hands to the stroller and searched the path behind us.

The boys did not make a peep. Frozen, they clutched the stroller as ordered, glancing only at my terrified face to be reminded of our bond. When Dom returned, his face was sallow, too. Todd was not with him.

"Grab that Bobby!" I yelled, panic-stricken. "We need help! Todd is gone!"

"Stay here." Again my husband took hold. He pushed his way forward to the box office at the base of the castle. When I saw him waving us on, I pushed forward, the boys right at my heels. There, on the castle wall, was our four-year-old, waiting with the day's other lost-and-found little boys. Dom plucked Todd from the perch, and the other boys touched their brother in ritual jabs of affection. With the sleeve of his sweater, Todd wiped the tears that were forming on his cheeks and then happily pointed ahead. "The Tattoo! It's starting!"

The terror of losing a child had drained me, but the resilience of the children was a healing balm. They were undaunted, caught up in the joy of martial music and the pageantry. We found our assigned seats, huddled a little in the brisk air, bought hot chocolate for nurturing, and made a few new rules. Names and address were carefully repeated, along with a plan to stay put if one ever strayed from the group.

The sound of the brass sparkled, and we were all caught up in the wonder and specialness of Scotland and its castle esplanade. From all over the world pipers had been drawn to this center with a commonality only in their instruments. They spilled over the edges with color and sound heard through the millennia from these peaks.

The word "Tattoo," we heard the announcer say, "is just a snappy way of saying 'tap to.' " In the 17th-century, when the beer taps were turned off, Dutch regiments going back to their barracks turned on their heels with a fancy step. Steps grew into routines, and the first formal tattoo was a combination of regiments doing their planned routines.

Regiments came from all parts of the world, including massed fife and drum groups, bagpipers, and the Queen's own guard. The pageantry was dazzling, with stunts and demonstrations crossing in front of us and appearing on the ramparts of the castle. Kilted dancers and choruses brought Scotland's fondest regalia to its most dramatic setting, ending with strains of "Auld Lange Syne" and finally "Amazing Grace" unifying an audience from all over the globe.

The next morning the sun beamed on a quieter Edinburgh, and a hearty breakfast fortified our group for one last look at the city. There are times and places that imprint on the mind an indescribable essence that comes from the blending of elements. Sunday morning in Edinburgh was one of those happenings.

Edinburgh, like Rome, is spread over seven hills; the finest view of the city that morning was indisputably Canton Hill. Climbing Canton Hill, we met Sunday morning regulars with their papers spread out before them on the grass, and tourists meandered on the top, taking pictures of the wonderful panorama before them. As we reached the top, we looked down upon the Royal Mile, where we had walked the day before. Edinburgh's history was acted out on that mile. Her golden era under the Stuarts was well remembered in every step of the way.

Finally I could put the story together. At one end, there was the Edinburgh castle, where Mary Queen of Scots gave birth to James, who would become the only monarch from Scotland to rule all of Britain. At the other end of the mile, I could see Holyrod, the palace where Mary was received as Queen and where her secretary was murdered. When the Stuarts ruled Britain, it was a brutal epic of history, and its leading lady, Mary Queen of Scots, remained one of those characters of history who continues to fascinate people to this day. Her intrigues eventually led to the dungeon, at Frothingay where her head fell to the executioner.

Sunday was quiet and peaceful. On that early August morning, with just a hint of the autumn to come, a breeze chasing the clouds, the children were content to wander about in the open fields. It seemed a wonderful way to touch the past. Enriched with her plots, Edinburgh's life was an open book, and the overview cost us but a climb.

On our return, the borders of Scotland seemed mellow, ripe with the summer's fullness. The hills blowing with hay reminded me in some familiar way of the hills of West Virginia. It was easy to understand, looking out over the mountains, why so many of the Scotsmen had settled in Appalachia. Looking for some semblance of home in our hills, a place to pipe their tune, to find and keep their fierce sense of the mountain revelry, they had come in great numbers.

We pulled over at one point to enjoy the view that had been inspiration to the works of Sir Walter Scott. The River Tweed and mountain peaks tempered by rolling hills were another point of recognizable beauty.

Further along the way were abbeys unlike any we had ever seen, their stone walls laid bare to the elements. Dissolved by Henry VIII, they were now overrun by briars and ivy, but their once-vaulted ceilings, now open to the sky, seemed almost more beautiful, surely as prayerful.

With this last excursion, our summer sadly came to an abrupt end.

# The Rhythm of Autumn

The rhythm of life once again changed with the ringing of the school bells in September. The pageantry and history of the far corners of the British Isles was sublimated to the routines of life in the village. Settling in had taught us that village life centers around market, school and priory. With the beginning of a new term, we were to learn the depth of attention the British gave to the world of letters and the preparation of each student for the process.

There was bound to be an Anglo-American comparison in education, both on our part and that of the British. Three of our boys would be entering the British system. The local primary was directly behind our house in Thingwall, its green abutted our garden. I would not have to deal with car pools, but we were not sure where the boys would fit into the system or how they would fare in the transition. Their abrupt introduction soon after our arrival had not given them any security.

School was still in session when we arrived in July, and from our second-story French window in the back, the boys had watched children their age at recess. Each day they anticipated the timing of recess and found their places against the window, fascinated that their counterparts, wearing such formal outfits, could kick the ball with such great facility and terrified that they couldn't. The anxiety in Mike's eyes was clear. He did not know the game they were playing. Mike, Phil, Todd, and Dominic stood glued to the window each of those first mornings after our arrival for the duration of recess.

Taking advantage of their fascination, I put the baby in our newly acquired "secondhand" crib, and left the other faces against the pane as I continued to unpack in the front bedrooms. I could hear the distant rousing noises of the games on the green and the muted chatter of our own boys at the window.

When the noise in both the bedroom and playground came to an abrupt halt, my mother's instinct told me to check. Running to the back bedroom, I saw the windows were wide open, the curtains blowing in the wind. Todd, the more cautious of the boys, stood clutching the curtains from the side of the window. The window led to a slanted roof, a second-story position that revealed the garden below and the green of the primary in the distance.

Edging closer, somewhat panicked, I could see the population of the whole school—students, teachers, janitors—frozen, looking up at our window. Immediately below were seven-year-old Mike and the pathfinder, Phil, their eyes also turned upward. On the edge of the roof was a single red tennis shoe. Somewhere in between, I surmised, was three-year-old Dominic. I held my breath, knowing better than to scream a warning. When his curly head bobbed at the bottom of the drain pipe, a round of applause went up from the school yard, and I imagined that the teachers were drawing straws for the placement of the Yanks.

A few days later, as we were ushered into the headmaster's office, there was a wryness in the tone of the information. "The daring one can't come," warned red-haired Mr. Kay, the schoolmaster. "Our system starts the semester before the fifth year. This child is not old enough. The three older ones will fit into first, fourth and fifth forms. It should be an interesting Anglo-American experience."

I agreed. Dominic curled into my lap, and we gathered up the papers instructing us on dress code.

As the days grew shorter and the September air grew cooler, we settled into the heart of village ways and faced the adjustments to our adopted life. For all of us, it took more than a stretch of the imagination to adapt. It was clear: The honeymoon was over. Besides the warmth of welcome came the inevitable, competitive fervor of the colony and Mother Country. There was pride and interest in our culture, but it was a depressed year in England's economy. We were seen more often as the son who had outdistanced his parent in goods and prosperity. On the tellie, the common image of the American tourist was a fat American wife dragging her husband in a flowered shirt all over England picking up pieces of

junk. Americans were those gauche people who lived a shallow lifestyle.

The English educational system was backed by every form of support in literary heritage and serious attentiveness. The "11 plus" examination divided the college-bound students from the labor-bound citizens at age 11. Reading began a year and a half before our system. Our boys were three semesters behind their peers in this area. They were, however, far advanced to the Brits in their concepts of math. Were these all to do with the systems or the children? Some of both, we reasoned. The academic variances were clear. The social and emotional adjustments were deeper for all of us.

For our one-year stay with our stringent budget, we purchased the minimum of uniforms and sent the boys off in their American black-and-white saddle shoes, which were thought to be B-E-A-U-T-I-F-U-L by the girls in their form and a bit of a joke by the boys. Todd, not used to any previous nursery school, decided to spend his lunch break with us, coming around the corner for peanut butter and jelly instead of eating Brussels sprouts and English meats. Dominic and Thomas were content with a quieter home and their mother at hand.

For my husband, the myriad of differences was beginning to creep up in his work, a constant Anglo-American comparison put on the mark every day in the medical world. He learned to enjoy the transit system, a bus, ferry or train to Liverpool, and the shorter hours and longer lunches, but technology was at variance and approaches to patient care a constant revelation.

The real test of the season for me was in dealing with the weather. By mid-September the rains began, gently at first, little drizzles each day, and then they seemed torrential. While I was used to bright autumns in West Virginia, where color runs wild in the hills, the endless rains began and persisted to monsoon proportions. It was a rain that changed the atmosphere. The day could start out bright, the sun pouring into our back garden, and within minutes the whole house would turn pitch-black. I could be ironing or focused downward, feel a darkness surround me, switch on the lights, and lift up my head to a garden window where I would see prisms of sun on the little leaded windows, the gloom temporarily relieved.

Never had we experienced the amount of dark at that time of year or the pattern of constant rain. Looking back at my diary, there were close to six weeks when my journal began: "It rained today." The stucco house without any heat grew damp and cold. We turned on the oven in the kitchen, steamed the bathroom, ran through the cold halls for any room with a semblance of heat. I pinned down blankets on the crib to make sure Thomas was warm. We piled blankets and even coats on the beds of the boys, took hot baths ourselves before bed, and still the icy sheets were difficult to endure. Even the walls of the hallway and the commode began to feel cold.

My work was grueling with no help, having given up on the possibilities of a nanny or even a little domestic help on our budget, but the atmospheric changes seemed to take the biggest toll. Again I went to my books at night and found solace. The faces of the children coming home from school and the joy around the table when our family gathered was light enough, I reasoned. Besides, this was the climate that the great English writers had endured.

It was time for me to get on with my real passion beyond the family, the literary world of Britain. As the rains began to settle down in mid-October, we decided to venture out again, to the countryside of England, this time heading to the midlands and the heart of great prose and poetry. I could see the beloved land that had inspired the greatest of English gifts, the masterpieces and simple stacks of literature that had long ago inspired my love of Britain. It was time for the first of many treks to the land of the great writers.

## Literary Pilgrimages

The literary pilgrimage, that form of travel based on the principle that homage should be paid to genius or the land from which its inspiration came, was next to be explored. The pilgrimages became my class that autumn in Britain. I thought of my beloved professor, Dr. Gainer, and his insight: "You will find Wordsworth's soul in the ever-shifting beauty of these peaks and valleys, in the place that inspired him. If you really want to know the poet, you should make a literary pilgrimage to the Lake District in the northwest of England. You just might meet the author or at least catch the spirit of his inspiration."

Leaving Liverpool, we passed through the doom that the prophets of industrial revolution had predicted. There were rows of little gray slum houses clutched against the embankments, monstrous slag heaps, crumbling chimneys, broken windows, piles of scrap, and paths of cinders crisscrossed with blackened debris. Where was the England of my

dreams? Was the England of the romantic poets a dream in itself, lost in the age of urbanization? Or worse still, was it only in the minds of the poets?

With five little children in the car, we set out for Cumbria, the land of Peter Rabbit and the Lake District, home to Coleridge, Tennyson, and Wordsworth. "Children who live in cities must travel to the country in their imagination, if not in person," Beatrix Potter had proclaimed. Her stories had exposed my children to many wooded scenes and the plight of errant bunnies. This was the land of Flopsy, Mopsy and Cottontail, the world of whitewashed cottages and winding country lanes near Lake Windermere.

Ms. Potter herself took up residence in her beloved Cumbria at age forty. Convinced that she, too, would get a fresh start on life in the country, she purchased a piece of the beloved land and continued to live and write in the peaceful surroundings.

As we drove closer, there were, as I had pictured, meandering stone walls and hedgerows, lovely fells and farms, but within minutes it was all muted by a slow drizzle that penetrated the atmosphere. I remembered Beatrix Potter revealing the secret of her art: "I spent a wet hour," she observed, "inside of the pigsty drawing a pig while composing *Piglet Bland.*"

The sky grew gray, shrouding the car with its dismal tone. The temperamental moods of autumn on the island shook us often. Darkness crept into the car in the middle of the afternoon, coming and going throughout the day.

Looking at the map again, I was not surprised to see that we were near that northern corner of England that had inspired the descriptions penned by the Bronte sisters. The lonely winds of darkened skies, with horizons bleak as far as the eye can see, are as mood-evoking a reality as they were in *Wuthering Heights.* We began a habit that would soothe the long silences, pulling from our books the tales that had come from the area. The imaginative embroidering of the well-known stories began to change as the atmosphere changed. Even the car tales of Flopsy, Mopsy and Cottontail ceased to be light. The plots took on a narration of heavy mystery and drama with a new twist.

But then, as is typical in England, the rain, as if exhausted, fell again into a drizzle. And we beheld the land of little thatch-roofed cottages and lovely gardens. It was truly the stomping ground of Squirrel Nutkin, Jeremy Fisher and Mrs. Tittlemouse, and, to our great delight, we saw that this idyllic land was copied faithfully.

Rain came and went as it is wont to do in England, but our arrival in the beloved Lake District stirred our hopes of discovering the poet's favorite panoramas. The mountains and woods seemed covered by the mist and a maze of dripping woodlands, but shyly the sun came out as if to greet us and at once the scene was familiar.

*"The long light shakes across the lake, and the wind cataracts in leaps in glory,"* Tennyson had told us long ago.

As the clouds parted, little prisms glimmered on the water, and the sight of Lake Windermere was both placid and bright. Here indeed was the splendor, the stillness and solemnity of lake and land. England's landscape seemed to incorporate everything in manageable bites ... mountains, lakes, forests, and wildflowers. As Wordsworth had said, " 'Tis the sense of majesty and beauty and repose, a blended holiness of earth and sky."

This was the land where Robert Sotheby, Coleridge and Ruskin, as well as Emerson and other American writers, had found inspiration. Nearby, Wordsworth and Tennyson had sought and found refuge from the ugliness of the industrial revolution. Wordsworth had explored every inch on foot, walking as many as 30 miles a day. Its sights, sounds and colors, along with humble cottages, were reflected in his verse.

I felt that odd sense of being where a great person has been, where, through nature, God had inspired the poets to paint for us a lasting picture. With five children, I did not expect to experience the bliss of solitude, and I knew that the experience would be different for each one of us. But for all of us there was a peace in the pure gentle country with long, uninterrupted panoramas and a landscape so pleasant that it quieted our spirits.

The lakes themselves are mirrors in which are repeated all the changing beauty of the year and the movement of the sky.

For the children, the inspiration of the journey was mainly in the stories they had heard, not the landscape. They had gotten into the spirit of adventure as Beatrix Potter had so imaginatively described. I saw them edge near the lake as we stopped to circumvent what would have remained peaceful.

Little pebbles were plunked in and the ripples spread beyond their reach. Then, as if in imitation of the rabbit they loved, they edged closer and closer to the water, in spite of warning from us that it could be cold, until finally I saw Phil splash in and Mike, his closest sibling, follow. The chill of wet clothes made them spitter and sputter and shake to dry themselves. What next, I thought? We had been given an invitation to a private home in the Lake District, but would we be welcome with wet children?

We were to be the guests that day of my husband's medical mentor, who had a small cottage on Windermere with some attachments to Tennyson. With two little wet boys, we headed to the cozy cottage of our host.

Dr. Ogilvie's mother, who had not been afforded the chance to be a grandmother by her bachelor son, welcomed the opportunity to be one to our children, as she offered the boys scones and clotted butter, fresh jam and even camomile tea. All was well and, once the boys were outside in the paths beyond her wisteria-hung cottage, she shared her personal connection to the poet Tennyson. I sat bolt-straight, knowing the hidden treasures of literary pilgrimages can often be discovered by talking to a caretaker who actually knew the writer.

Our hostess continued with that knowing authority that precedes a juicy story: "This cottage has been in my family for three generations, decorated by an Italian mistress of one of those fine gentlemen living in the area. When my grandmother took possession, she kept it just as it was. She even kept the parlor maid, who knew Tennyson's maid. The maid was quite chattie."

"I can tell you honestly, Tennyson was a true gentlemen," Tennyson's maid had related.

'You know it is traditional to put a sixpence in the chamber pot under the bed for the one who has the unseemly job of emptying it every morning. When the maid would go round to collect it, she would smile because Tennyson always put a sixpence in it, whether he had used it or not. *Whether he had used it or not!*" she repeated in her sweet Scottish brogue.

With her tale, I felt I had touched the poet.

After our first trek into the countryside, we knew that literary pilgrimages would open up the literary world of Britain in a personal way.

Traveling through England, I often felt that I was entering the pages of my favorite novel, poem or story. Everywhere I went I recognized certain towns, villages, moors, hills and dales, bits of coastline, great houses and other landmarks because they recalled some literary incident. Driving through Welsh mining towns, I thought of Dylan Thomas; in Exmoor, of Lorna Doone; West Dorset, of the Hardy novels; Norwich, of Jane Austen; Yorkshire, of Jane Eyre. In many places I saw the secret gardens and English provincial upper middle class cities remembered in *Pride and Prejudice*.

In London later, walking down Wimpole Street, it was Robert and Elizabeth Browning that came to mind and on Baker Street, it was Sherlock Holmes. In the Cheshire Cheese, the tavern off Fleet Street, it was easy to picture Dr. Samuel Johnson and Dickens sitting there.

The whole of England began to open up to us. Later that fall we headed to the Midlands. The center of England has the stillness of silk, painted in soft pastels just as I had known it would be. In autumn, wildflowers mixed with hay to create muted colors. Everything was touched by the mist. And although I had hated the incessant rains in September, the grass was still green in late October.

It was in that month that we headed to the small city on the Avon where Shakespeare grew up. It seemed a nice Saturday excursion with children, a small city easy to get around, we were told. In fact, Stratford was still a market town. Going without the crowds of summer, we found it quiet, pleasant. Foxgloves, feverfews and buttercups dusted the air, making rambling a visual lesson in cottage and garden beauty.

The black-and-white timbered birthplace of Shakespeare and the idyllic little cottage of Anne Hathaway, his bride, would sweep us into the world of the 16th-century. But the tree-lined path leading to the church where he was both baptized and buried would touch the man in a more profound way.

With children, it was not possible to listen to a Shakespearean play in the famous theater by the water, but a picnic by the idyllic Avon was a wonderful break. The landscapes were teaching us much about what had inspired the 18th-century romantic poets and the 16th-century bard.

## Modern Poets of Liverpool

Our little home on the Wirral Peninsula was surrounded by waterways that led us to new worlds. On the left, the River Dee gently flowed, leading us to Chester. On the right, the Mersey loomed, reaching its muddy port in Liverpool. The gray and huge city, home to those modern-day poets, the Beatles, gave us a chance to understand the pulse of writing and the music of protest of the '60s. I had visualized Penny Lane and dark caverns wild with rock music as the Beatles came to popularity, and the boys had wondered about the city where their father worked. For all of us, a visit to Liverpool was a modern pilgrimage into the heart of the mod world of the Fab Four.

Liverpool echoed with activity in a bright conglomeration of colors painted on the sidewalks, music blaring from the cafes and clubs, young girls strutting the streets in mini skirts and young men watching, quick to comment. From the quiet peninsula where we lived, the double-decker bus, the dark subterranean ride, and then the world in front of us were all an adventure for another Saturday in late autumn.

We knew when we emerged from the train station, which had been center to Merseysiders since Victorian times, that we were suddenly and surely in the middle of the world of John Lennon, Paul McCartney, George Harrison, and Ringo Starr. There were also protesters of the war, draught beer and life in general.

Liverpool in the 19th- and early 20th- centuries was refuge to a large population of Irish whose families escaped the potato famine and an industrial home to villages from the surrounding peninsula of Cheshire. There was an interesting blend of the King's English and Liverpudlian scouse, where "Yes, Luv" and "No, Luv" was heard in every transaction. A flag of Ireland and the banner of Guinness flew side by side; pop art on the sidewalk bordered shops of the finest china. These happy interchanges and more formal dramatizations in the nearby playhouse were a visible part of the gift of the Irish and the Merseysiders endowed with the art of storytelling.

But the heart of Liverpool was never in the pedestrian walk or the Cavern, where the Beatles once played. The city's heart was in her docks. The gravitation to the docks was a natural one and a happy one for adventurous children. A customhouse and seven miles of dry docks attested to the slave trade and the industrial life of the city through the ages.

For a few shillings it was possible to board the "Ferry Across the Mersey," just as the Gerrymanders who documented the crossing in their song of that title did and to look as the young protesters of the '60s did to the receding image of Liverpool. This we did as we boarded the four-penny ride in 1968.

I sat with Thomas on my lap as Liverpool faded from us. The other boys ran about with the authority of Lord Nelson, while I watched the sun go down on that smoke-filled city. There was a stern reliance in her demeanor, a beaten, downtrodden economy, a city stained with smoke from the harbor, the wars, the protests, and yet there was something so homey. It was at the docks that I felt closest to home, and by late October we were becoming a little attached to that diverse kingdom by the sea.

By November, the larger city of Liverpool and the village of Thingwall were preparing for their ritual bonfire in remembrance of Guy Fawkes. Guy Fawkes, it seemed, was a 16th-

century traitor to the crown, and to this day his effigy is burned in bonfires all over England.

On the way home from work, just as he entered the subway leaving Liverpool, my husband was introduced to the tradition by a small child with his hand out begging. "A penny for the Guy," the child pleaded in a thick Liverpudlian scouse.

"Who is the Guy?" my husband asked,

"Ya know, the Guy, we've got to burn the Guy. Just a haypenny, p-l-e-a-s-e. We have no rags to burn."

It was our own boys who explained the local tradition to us in more detail and prepared us for the annual trek into the neighborhood.

"Remember, remember the fifth of November, gun powder, treason and plot," they repeated as they skipped home from school, fully caught up in the tradition of English schoolchildren. Each village had its own bonfire formed of old furniture, clothes, rags and any burnable junk. At the top was an effigy of the infamous Guy Fawkes, who had plotted against King James.

On the night of the fifth, we set out with our boys to the ritual remembrance. There were chestnuts roasting, caramel apples and treats along the way. Neighbors greeted one another, much as our neighbors did on Halloween, and everyone sighed when the torch lighted the massive pile of debris, the cloth effigy soon to be devoured by the flames, and the night filled with crackling sounds in the crisp air.

It was fun to be in the rhythm of the village rituals, as if we were by the seasonal changes slowly being baptized into British life.

And then one day, I wondered who I was. While reading to the small ones in the darkened parlor one morning, I was started by the trill of our doorbell. Literally no one came to our door. There were few salesmen and we knew so few of the British at that point. So, as I headed down the hall, watching the outline of a bobbie in our leaded window, a disturbing chill went down my back. "Is someone hurt?" I wondered.

The official was curt, cold. "Is this 12 Berwyn Lane?"

"Yes," I answered, the toddlers at my skirt equally unnerved.

"R. and D. Gaziano?"

"Yes . . . ," I waited.

"You must come down to the station to register. All aliens must register."

Aliens? I thought as I closed the door, promising to do whatever we were required. I thought we were just students, guests, even visitors, but aliens? Well, it took days to release that gloomy feeling.

A neighbor, hearing my story, felt the bobbie's words to be a bit cold, too, although, she explained, "The British are caught up in rules and rituals. The rules are meant to keep order, for the most part. You know our bobbies don't even wear guns, like your American policemen do, now do they?"

As if to compensate, she invited me to an "assize," showing the ancient respect to the passing of laws in England. This had a different flavor.

The assize was an occasion of celebration, a ceremony performed yearly to open the courts. With all the pomp that the British do so well, the Lord Mayor, in full regalia, arrived, bearing his miter and granting permission from the Queen to impart justice to the people. I stood by bearing witness to an ancient system, one that had given us civil law as we know it today.

And as the village had invited us to its rituals, we in turn invited people to taste pumpkin pie and turkey, as Americans annually enjoy on Thanksgiving Day. There was an unspoken homesickness creeping into our house as November came to an end, in spite of all the Anglo-American sharing. As the days darkened, we continued with some of our own rituals, but the test would be the time most dear to our family, the fast-approaching Christmas season.

## A Dickensonian Christmas

Dusk comes early to Britain in December. The children

arriving home at 4 p.m. were barely discernible in the waning light. At school the children began making paper crackers and foil holders for candles for the tree. The lights were as welcome as the solstice.

Now the security of the boys was to be tested. The tall, lanky Father Christmas was everywhere, but our boys were not convinced he would be as reliable as the portly familiar Santa with a Coke in his hand. Clement Moore's creation was beloved and familiar to them.

Neighborhood stores were advertising suet for plum puddings, berries and minced nuts. Holly was stacked in bins, and stout, short trees in dirt lined the back of the outdoor stalls. The familiar scents and smells for us four weeks before Christmas were Italian pita piatas baking in the oven and lemon fruit cakes slowly rising. I suddenly realized how important it had been for continuity at Christmas time for my poor, alien ancestors from Italy to continue the baking of traditional pastries with whatever they could afford at Christmas time. We would do the same.

The boys had not realized when we packed the trunk before leaving America that the pan for our annual lemon fruitcake and the angel for the tree would be so meaningful for us at this time. As the days grew close to Christmas, I went to the trunks, which were safely in the garage, and pulled out the cake pans and the flaxen-haired angel, who always sat atop our tree. When the boys returned from school that day, the smell of the pita piatas baking sent them jumping around, sure that we would, indeed, have Christmas in this strange

land. And when Mike spotted the angel on the table, his eyes lit up. He fingered it and then literally jumped for joy around the table.

Our excursions were limited to trips to the nearby villages for ingredients for our celebration feast. The market was teeming with seasonal items. A sign in the butcher shop reminded us: "Order your Christmas goose now. Fresh kidneys also available." I had a good time watching the people handle and test and the grocer weigh a carefully chosen head of cabbage or a bag of chestnuts.

Mike pulled me to a space behind the store where Christmas trees, still with their roots and dirt, were anchored in a long row. His pleading eyes were serious. Ritual was going to be tested again and again this season.

Our tree was heavy, and we had to secure it with a bucket. But when it stood decorated in the parlor, we knew Christmas had come to Thingwall. There were foil coverings for Victorian candles and some English twinkle lights. The decorations were both homemade and sparse, but atop the pine was the angel who had been there every year of their little lives.

Christmas in England. The very sound of it had magic. We began reading installments of Charles Dickens' *A Christmas Carol*, as we always had at home. Of all the English writers who had affected our vision of Christmas, Dickens had been with us since childhood. And as our house grew colder, the Dickensonian images needed little verification. We hovered around the little grate in the living room, made sure that the heavy doors were closed, and kept a jacket nearby to run through the halls. A Victorian Christmas might be as gay as the scene from the newspaper that depicted Prince Albert and the children all around, but most of the English were feeling the cold of the season, just like the beloved Cratchits had.

Christmas in England might be all doused in snowy scenes in the Christmas cards, but it was damp and cold inside our home on the Wirral. The excitement of the season prevailed, however. I was eager to learn from the neighbors how to use suet in the preparation of a plum pudding, and each day the boys came home with a new interpretation of the seasonal fun. Puppets for plays were a part of the English tradition. One day I heard the boys playing magic show and realized Todd was inside the box they intended to saw in two.

It was a bittersweet season. With every new gesture, there was a remembrance of something or someone left behind. We were beginning to miss our Italian clan. Without realizing it, the children were talking more often of their cousins and grandparents. They had never experienced a Christmas that was not filled with family members and friends. The British, a more private people, were all turned inward for the holiday season.

A few snowflakes began to fall as we put the boys to bed on Christmas Eve. It was quiet and almost lonely, so when the doorbell rang, I ran through the hall, willing to greet anyone coming to see us on this night of family ritual.

Opening the leaded door, I was surprised to see Stella, our babysitter. Snow was fluttering down and caught in her little eyebrows.

"Mum has sent some of her soda bread, and I have but one gift. I know you always go to Midnight Mass. The boys told me so. So I've come to sit for you. Aunt Mary will sit for Mum and Dad, so we're all set."

Dom and I dressed quickly and walked into the crisp air, feeling the spell of the holy night in Cheshire. A wet, white snow, the kind that flutters down gently and sticks, had covered the village. The moonlight and the amber street lights reflecting on the new covering gave a glow to the village, the houses sending out puffs of smoke, and the little stone church waiting with its amber light shining through the window.

Inside there was a hush as the well-rehearsed sound of little boys in their red cassocks and white surplices announced the birth of Christ in choral perfection. There is no counterpart to the sound of an English boys' choir at Christmas. The choir of St. Anselm filled the little chapel, leaving us with the sounds of "Glory to God in the highest and peace on earth."

Stella's parents came by to pick her up, and we ran through the halls, warming a kettle for tea and sharing our Italian pastries with them.

The chill of the house did not daunt the boys' Christmas morning. The older two had given Thomas his morning bottle and carried him down ahead of us to show him what was waiting. Father Christmas was deemed reliable, even though the tokens he had left would be considered simple by most American standards. There were small matchbox cars, coloring books and silly putty. The older boys had been told their real gift would be a trip to London. Tom was happily crawling amid mounds of ribbon and paper by the time Dom and I joined them in the parlor.

Dinner was a festive combination of red pastas, green salads and our first lighted plum pudding.

"A speckled cannon ball!" I heard the boys mimic as I walked into the room. By that time we had been thoroughly indoctrinated into the local tradition. The sixpence in the pudding went to Mike, but Dominic was ecstatic just to watch the glow of blue flame covering the round ball.

*What little it takes for children to be happy*, I thought. Our family was aglow, sitting in front of the little fire with the last installment of *A Christmas Carol*. I was convinced our house was colder than the Cratchits had ever experienced, but we bonded in a special way that Christmas in England.

"Boxing Day," the day after Christmas, is an official holiday in Britain, started in medieval times as a remembrance of the feast of St. Stephen. On that day, in the massive, cold

cathedrals, money that had been placed in the boxes for the poor was dispensed.

In Victorian England, boxes were distributed to the hired help on the 26th, rewarding the staff with tokens from the lord and lady of each manor. They were also given the day off. To this day, Boxing Day remains a special holiday in Britain. I wasn't quite sure what category we fit into, but we were to be the lucky guests of our unofficial hosts, the Meechams. They had lived through a similar experience in America with two small girls and knew what it was like to be a little homesick during the holidays.

A crackling fire awaited us, as did boxes of tiny matchbox cars for the boys under their tree. Sizzling sausages, applesauce, meatballs and minced pies were set upon the mahogany table in the dining room. But the desserts, created by our hostess herself, Margaret Meecham, dazzled the eye and introduced us to the Victorian creations that had been passed down to her.

She had ordered double cream from the milkman. I know no counterpart in America. Mounds of it topped her English trifle. Tiny raspberries and confetti turned it into a work of art. The boys were mesmerized by the fruitcake she had decorated. Carefully sculptured, firmly set white icing covered the traditional Christmas cake, and in the center fairyland skaters were poised gracefully on a miniature glass lake. Tea time would not only endear us to the civilities of the British but to the warmth of the Meechams as well.

Nor were we to be forgotten by our neighbors on Berwyn Lane, the Hamiltons. On New Year's Eve, the Scottish rite begins with a gathering of the clan and ends where the spirits take it. The "first footer" (the first person to cross the threshold on that auspicious night) is expected to bring a lump of coal as he enters the party. The coal had been placed in the hearth, and the nose of our host was growing red by the time we arrived. It took us a while to convince the children to unwind after the excitement of the days before. Mike and Phil were told to feign sleep while the toddlers nodded off and then to join us next door for the celebration.

Nine-year-old Ian, their bosom friend by January, was already in happy reverie by the time the boys arrived. On the threshold of early adolescence, his face reddened with mirth. Ian, it was soon clear, had been sharing his worldliness with our boys as they sang together boisterously bold verses of "Lily the Pink," introducing us to lines we had never heard.

By the time midnight struck, there was a blend of sounds, Liverpudlian scouse, southern American, and Oxford English, as poems of Bobby Burns were read. A hush fell over the gathering when the head of the Hamilton family recited the full version of "Tam O'Shanter" with a Glasgow glow. And with the fervor of a true Scotsman, he led us all in a final round of "Auld Lange Syne."

# London After Christmas

The village of Thingwall was our safe port, but London was to give us the English Christmas we had always read about. That is where Dickens had created *A Christmas Carol* and Prince Albert had introduced the Victorian Christmas tree to the world. After the image of Queen Victoria's family dancing around the table with a green fir alit with candles appeared in the *London Telegraph*, everyone in America and England had wanted such a tree. A Christmas in London would take us to the heart of the most romantic of celebrations and, with only a few plucky shoppers headed for the after-Christmas sales, we would have London virtually to ourselves, we were told. The off-season rates were the last enticement for what we had termed our "real gift" to each other, three days in London. We would see the city dressed for the holidays.

We had planned to beat the traffic, but too much "Lily the Pink" and the icy bedrooms made it difficult to get an early start the day after New Year's. We found ourselves on the road with five little boys, snack food and paper diapers, sharing a crowded M-6 with other tired, hung-over drivers.

It was clear from the beginning that this post-holiday trip was not going to be a snap. To start with, the traffic was heavier than expected. The toys tucked in were not good choices. The little matchbox cars were fine, but the silly putty was a gross mistake. As we approached the city limits, we had to call cease-fire on the silly putty balls that were being tossed back and forth and make an all-out cry for help in finding our B&B for the night.

The neighborhood of Kensington has probably changed little from Victorian times. Its brick houses, beautifully proportioned windows, handsome chimney pots, ironwork, twinkling brass letter boxes and door knockers all seemed a warm welcome after the harrowing drive from Liverpool. When we finally found the right number, I reached in the back to help the boys with their jackets, only to find globs of sticky putty everywhere, between wales of corduroy and matted on sweaters. And when the boys got out of the Cortina, I saw it on the seat of their pants and, of course, in Dominic's curly hair. Dom gave everyone a load to carry, and we forgot the putty for a while.

The four-story house had a pleasant enough front, but it was soon apparent we were not yet out of the "hard-up" category. This time we were sent to the attic, trudging 72 steps upward (Phil counted). There were 20 steps down to the toilet (Todd tested immediately) and 90 steps to the breakfast room (no complaints on that one).

The large attic room was lined with three double beds, a simple table, lace doily, and green shaded lamp. It was immaculate but cold. It seemed we could not escape the cold on our budget. On closer examination, we saw a small sign attached to a heater in the corner: "Six pence every half-hour for heat." The children never minded the cold as we did, but they were in constant motion. At one point, as they got rid of their pent-up energy, a lamp toppled over and a pillow landed on top. My husband's eyes met mine from across the room. Were we going to gain anything this trip?

Our Scottish neighbor had looked at us from her front window with unbelieving eyes as we left.

"You're taking five children to London?" I remembered her asking. Then she had muttered some proverb about a frugal Scotsman spending half his money on food and saving half, but a poet spending half on travel. Were we poets, I wondered, or fools?

I washed five little faces and dressed the boys as if they were Victorian children, tight leggings for the cold, mittens and caps. I had bought warm wool coats and leggings, adding one a year for the last five years. The last ones were a little threadbare but, zipped in, the boys were warm and dressed for the streets of London.

The early January day was cold and clear. The air was crisp as we drove through the boroughs around the city. There were no long lines to daunt us, and soon we knew what a gift of wonder London at Christmastide could be for children and their parents. It was discovery and much elation as London unfolded around us. There were Dominic's eyes, alight with excitement as the soldier came straight toward him at Buckingham Palace. There was the Tower of London with its jewels and gleaming armor. There were trees lighted in the portico of St. Paul's and changing horses in Whitehall. For small excited hearts there were "boat trains" gliding down the Thames, with Big Ben in the background.

Red double-decked buses swirled around Trafalgar, and tree lights twinkled under the statue of Lord Nelson. There was a mammoth tree, an annual gift from the people of Norway, as a token of their thanks for British help during the Second World War. Abundantly covered with red and green lights, the tree rivaled the tall pedestal of Lord Nelson and Westminster Abbey with its triune bells and choir boys at evensong.

There are many parks in London. There is Kensington Park and Hyde Park, where on Speaker's Corner any Briton can speak his mind on a Sunday morning. We started with a combination of a park for the little ones and a walk through a museum for the schoolboys. London Museum, at the time, was in Kensington Palace but it was later relocated to a home of its own. The replicas within provided a wonderful way for children to start their tour of the city. Laid out in miniature was the city when it was known as Roman Londonium, with all the walls and fortifications. There were visual reminders of busy London in medieval times with its trades and shops on the famous London Bridge.

The story of the great London fire of 1666 was visually re-enacted as well as pictures of the planned rebuilding of masterpieces we would later see. A miniature of St. Paul's and beautiful, huge gilded coaches with plush, red lining were

also housed within the city's museum.

Out in the streets, the crisp, clear air edged us on to the palaces and towers we had seen in concise miniatures. Buckingham Palace and the Tower of London were wonderful places of escape. While I contemplated the fate of such notorious captives of the historic sights—seeing Anne Boleyn and Sir Thomas More—Dominic caught sight of a barge. "A boat train!" he bellowed, and all eyes went to the Thames.

Westminster Abbey, that dark gray English Gothic church with its profusion of busts, thrones, monuments to poets, knights and warriors, was elegantly decorated for the season with a tall tree in the nave, covered with silver triune bells.

Outside, as we headed back from our first day of touring, the lights of Piccadilly came on and the boys again were awed. My husband and I knew that there would be no night life, no plays on this trip, but we were more than happy to collapse into bed, amazed at what we had covered in one day and with our children.

Each morning of our three-day visit we fortified ourselves with an English breakfast, reminding the boys that we would probably have only have enough money for sandwiches that evening. They ate heartily the cereal, eggs, jams and milk. The boys stoically passed by vendors with pretzels and chestnuts, knowing we couldn't afford such extras. And in the evening when we silently wished for money for a hot meal and some extra shillings to put in the little heater in our room, we gathered the children together for a bedtime review of what they would see in the morning. Too exhausted to think about the cold, we all fell quickly off to sleep.

There were times when we wanted to be alone with our revelry. For Dom it was in the masterful halls outside the House of Commons, where the great hulk of statesman Sir Winston Churchill was remembered in bronze. The guide reminded us that the great lion had lain in state in the halls of parliament, and I took the boys out, allowing Dom time to enjoy the beamed halls and the history that had enriched it. He allowed me my time and my solitude in St. Paul's Cathedral. As we drove up Ludgate Hill, I strained and stretched to see it all. That beacon had excited me, and Dom could see it. To this day I do not know why St. Paul's touched me so. Perhaps it was the light that poured in or the impact of history.

Dom ushered the children back to the car where they huddled for a car quiz and a tale of London's old life, while I immersed myself in the church that Christopher Wren had rebuilt after London's great fire. The black-and-white marble was classically simple, the stunning Balachino poignant, I thought as I approached the high altar. But it was behind the altar that I stopped, remembering the war that had been introduced to me in newsreels as a child.

Directly behind the main altar was a monument to the war dead of the Second World War and a chapel dedicated to the goodness of the American people who died for Britain. The bond between our two countries was deep.

Looking in my guidebook, I read of the raids and bombings on this very spot. In one paragraph I felt the determination of the people on both sides of the Atlantic during Christmas of '42. While this church of the people, this master-

piece of Britain's history, was under fire, Winston Churchill, in America at Christmas, had sent this message to us. I read it slowly as I walked around the church:

"I spend this anniversary and festival far away from my country, far from my family, and yet I cannot truthfully say that I feel far from home. We're together in a common cause of great peoples who speak the same language, who kneel at the same altars and, to a very large extent, pursue the same ideals; I cannot feel myself a stranger here. I feel a sense of unity and fraternal association which, added to the kindness of your welcome, convinces me that I have a right to sit at your fireside and enjoy your Christmas joys.

"Let the children have their night of fun and laughter. Let the gifts of Father Christmas delight their play. Let us grown-ups share to the full in their unstinted pleasures before we turn again to the stern tasks and the formidable years that lie before us, resolved that by our sacrifice and daring, these same children shall not be robbed of their inheritance or denied their right to live in a free and decent world. And so in God's mercy, a happy Christmas to you all."

Our bond had been sealed by blood spilt here, and my own five children were now safe in London with my husband. As a last part of my private tour, I proceeded to the crypt. There, beyond the marble tombs, was one small stone in a remote corner. On it was the epitaph to Wren. With typical British understatement, it read: "If you seek a monument for this man, look around you."

Outside, the children were eager to move on. Our itinerary was stringent. We watched the changing of the guard not only at Buckingham, but at Whitehall, enjoyed the earthiness of Soho and Covent Gardens and made a pilgrimage in honor of Victoria and Albert, visiting the museum bearing their names. The parks provided wonderful breaks. In Hyde Park, Phil, our chatty eight-year-old, stood on a crate next to a tattooed zealot, both taking their turns to speak their minds, in the old tradition on a Sunday morning.

On Fleet Street we looked for the spots where Dickens and the people of the *Tribune* had clerked and written. We peeped into the Cheshire Cheese, that sawdust-filled pub where the writer was said to have bantered with friends well into the evenings.

By Sunday afternoon, we had but one tribute left. We wanted to see where Dickens had lived, the house where his growing family had bustled about. The number 48 Doughty Street, Bloomsbury, was what the guidebooks said would bring us to Dickens.

We passed Euston Station to a district of old houses coming down and apartment blocks going up. There were a few small grocery stores taken over by Indians and Greeks, a barber shop and a few fruit stores. Was it here that young Charles was inspired to write of the social injustices of his time? He could have wandered past the clothing store, through the maze of these streets. We, too, were lost in the maze as we kept missing Doughty Street, but the shabby tenements seemed to speak of the spirit of his London. Remembrances of his descriptions of tenements and Victorian working conditions were all we took with us as we headed to the M-6 and Liverpool. We were never able to find his home.

The boys were hungry. It had been a most frugal post-holiday excursion. We had packed in a lot of sightseeing and had depleted a rather meager allotment to do so. Dom emptied our remaining coins on the dashboard. "This is for petrol and lunch," he said.

Petrol was expensive and, though the tank was full, our stomachs weren't. In total we had a little over a pound. A little neighborhood Indian grocer showed meat pies in the window for a shilling apiece. We gave him our last pound and he gave us a meat pie for each boy. There was not even a penny left for fruits or drinks. The children held out their hands as Dom passed out the sparse meal. It was their portion for the day.

They bit into the crusty pies with eager gusto, and then I saw them gulp and wince. One after the other, tears came into their eyes. The little pies were highly seasoned, not really a good choice for the palates of little boys. But not one of them complained.

"It would have been flat heresy to do so," Dickens would have said. And besides, we had feasted on London at Christmastide.

# Chapter 2

# The Grand Tour

*"When April with his showers sweet,*
*The drought of March has pierced to the root,*
*And bathed every vein in such liquor,*
*So then people long to go on pilgrimages."*

—Geoffrey Chaucer, *Canterbury Tales*

Rain poured down the downspout outside the window but, by the time I got to the front door, the leaded glass windows had only the tiniest drops on them. I opened the door to see how the packing was going in the front of the house. Relieved that the rain was at least letting up, Dom and the boys put down their umbrellas and stuffed the last boxes of diapers into the open back window of the wagon.

"Leave room for one boy to sit in 'the bucket,' " I heard him tell Phil, who had taken command of packing the section behind the back seat. Wanderlust knows no end once it's in your veins. It was late March 1969 during the children's spring break in England when we set out for the Continent. Our goal was to be in Rome by Easter. It would be our family's Grand Tour, three weeks in our little blue station wagon, crossing the continent of Europe.

The Grand Tour of the 18th-century established a new mode of learning for the wealthy. The sweeping, whistle-stop visit to major art capitals of the world was a rite of passage for them, a finishing to their education.

Those well-born British young men and occasionally well-chaperoned young ladies set out for the Continent accompanied by tutors, carrying works of Cicero and Sophocles. It gave them a chance to broaden their horizons, to learn languages, to sharpen their manners and to find out a little more about foreign affairs of state before entering their social, business and diplomatic worlds.

They saw it as an art tour—the romance of the sunny climates of France and particularly Italy held a seductive enticement. Some historians have said that many of them just wanted to get away from the damp chill of England.

We bore no resemblance to that image. We were working students with a very big family, but we wanted what they had wanted: a finish to our education. The Cortina, all packed, would be our caravan. There were no chaperons or nannies. On the dashboard was *Fodor's Guide* and that bible of budget travel, *Europe on Five Dollars a Day*. We did, like our English predecessors, know firsthand of the penetrating chill of England.

After our trip to London, we had settled into a routine of survival in our Thingwall home without central heating. Daily, I planned my marketing in the morning to give the sun time to come through the larger windows, bringing some light if not heat to the house. Returning mid-morning, I often left Thomas in his snowsuit so he could crawl on the cold floor comfortably. I centered my work in the kitchen, where the oven heated the room just a little, and in the living room, where an electric log pretended to give heat. I kept a coat handy to run through the halls. At night we added blankets and old coats to the beds and drank hot chocolate and tea, trying to deny the cold dampness that penetrated the house.

As winter wore on, we began to think of our spring trip in much the way the celebrated Grand Tourists did, as "an escape from the chill." Spreading out the maps on the living room floor, we made our itinerary. We planned to cross at Dover, drive over the Alps, positioning the car to enter Italy from the northwest, visit Venice, Pisa and Florence and be in Rome by Easter. By my bed were biographies of many artists, a few novels and a review of Kenneth Clarke's *Civilization*.

Sir Kenneth, as I had begun to lovingly call him, had become my hero. Actually, he was curator of the British museum at the time, an expert who had begun to use a different forum for teaching. Watching his new 13-part series on the art of the world on the BBC, I felt I was again in the presence of one of the world's exceptional teachers. His excitement was infectious.

The pitch of our life rose as we thought of what lay ahead to see. We were excited, counting down the days for our tour but, as usual in travel, at the last minute there was resistance. I had dreams of being lost on strange roads and I worried about our safety. The old balancing act began anew. I was, after all, a mother, fiercely protective, yet still a student with hungry desires to study. Determined to have both family and growth, we planned carefully, thinking through as many dilemmas as possible. We put things in and took them out, keenly aware that we would be locked into a three-week trip together.

"Everything's in and we're ready to take off," Dom called to me. I went to the highchair where Thomas, now a wiry one-year-old, was trying to climb out over his cereal, and wondered how he would be cajoled into staying in the car-seat for the long trip ahead. I lifted him out with a kiss to his forehead.

"No matter what it's like in the car, it beats staying at home fighting the daily chill," I thought. Thomas wiggled in my arms.

I quickly strapped the baby in his carseat and let Dominic find a space between Phil and Mike, who had each claimed a window in the back. Todd had drawn the bucket for the first shift and seemed snug in his niche. As we drove from our chilly, gray stucco home, our Scottish neighbor Marion, who always seemed to know our comings and goings, peered out her door.

"Are ya sure ya're gonna be all right?" Her eyes betrayed the closeness she felt to the children. "Ah well, go on ... you're young." And I clearly saw a bit of longing with the loving benediction. "We'll be here when you get back."

The village of Thingwall, with its prim gardens, soon passed out of view. Through the Mersey Tunnel and past the graffitied, empty storefronts of a dissident Liverpool, we saw the last familiar scenes, and then the road reached out onto the M-6.

"I'm hungry," little Dominic cried.

"Not yet, Dom," my husband snapped, "we just had breakfast." Our lunch remained untouched in the back, but I did pass out little cartons of juice. We ruled out silly putty and games with lots of pieces, leaving us with the one car game that worked for everyone. We began to create car tales that were inspired by the changing terrain.

The storytelling was a simple diversion, a trick as old as man, one that our predecessors had used before the Grand Tour, before the fine carriages of the 18th and 19th centuries, a trick used by the medieval pilgrims. Let the imagination help pass the time. Let the travelers tell their own tales. It was Chaucer who really came to mind as we left on that dreary day in March, Chaucer and the pilgrims trying to reach Canterbury by Easter. Chaucer and his tales of strangers hoping to pass the long days of March on a dusty tilt of road from the north of England to Canterbury.

"We'll be in Canterbury before dusk," Dom interjected, as he checked both his map and the speed limit.

Canterbury is a famous pilgrim stop. We can see the cathedral and then drive to Dover by dark. "Chaucer's pilgrims," I explained to the boys, "made the trip on foot, taking many days. They camped nightly in hostelries that squeezed as many as 100 into bare rooms on the ground. They ate poorly preserved rations along the way."

It took us but one long day from Liverpool to Canterbury in our little blue car on a long, gray ribbon of cement. For the medieval pilgrim there was much hardship. For us, there were sundry squabbles, many diaper changes and the high-pitched whining of tired children by mid-afternoon.

We relished our thin English sandwiches and the last of the Cheshire cheese from our fridge, washed down with Orange Crush in bottles—our one extravagance for the day. The last few miles tested the patience of each of us. "Will we make it for three weeks in the confinement with five young children?" I wondered silently. The stories gave way eventually to the eternal question: "How far?"

"We'll be there in 30 minutes," my husband promised. Within seconds we passed the first announcement of the city of Canterbury. The black and white sign sent a rush of new excitement to me, another connection to the ancient world of letters and history. As we wound closer, the sight of the fifth century city of waddle huts, of Augustine the bishop, of the assigned archbishop's seat of Christendom in England, gave way to a singular image.

It was that mellow time of the day, just before the sun sets, when the light has become effusive. In front of us the Gothic spires of Canterbury Cathedral reached up, a shaft of the sun cutting across the front of the honey-colored stone. No more tales were necessary. When legend and history meet geography, there is a new marriage, a new-found love. Timing has much to do with it.

There was no description to frame the encounter. Canterbury Cathedral caught in a thicket of poetry and illusion was directly ahead of us. The beams of the evening sun were spread across its spires, giving a mystical grace to the towers. The stones of history were reframed in our pictures. We knew what lay ahead for us, what a Grand Tour was. No longer would we know Europe imagined or described through the eyes of famous writers and artists or composers. It was ours!

The boys were like puppies released, glad to get out of the car but more than that. They saw my husband's relief at having navigated so well the first day and they felt my excitement for what was in front of us. In my mind it was poetically perfect. The children responded to the happiness of their parents, and relief mingled with fun. We knew we were subtly passing on a kind of respect for the world and its treasures. They pranced up the steps, but they knew, too, they were in the presence of something special.

The cathedral remained unchanged in a world of constant change, undaunted by the vehicles of the 20th century swirling around, the centuries of warring tribes, pilgrims, visitors, even the modern tourists who had taken their turns climbing the front stones and opening its massive doors for a peek. Yes, it was unchanged, I thought, and beautiful.

For us, as travelers, pilgrims of another age, the challenge was invigorating. Each arrival, each new sight was like birth again; and we soon forgot the labor. We felt a great sense of satisfaction and joy for coming, for having occupied the boys on the long road behind, our first of a planned adventure. Our reward was obvious. We were present at Canterbury at sunset.

We quickly parked the car and ascended the steps of the church. It was two weeks before Easter. Preparations for the feast were apparent. Arriving at early evening, we were by chance the guests of that uniquely British expression for the end of day. It was Evensong in the cathedral. In the choir stalls was a male choir, facing each other, singing praises in perfect harmony. The echo from the vaulted ceiling was a sound I had never heard. Ancient psalms filled the vaults with joyous praise in the style of the monks of the sixth century. Candles flickered in the shadows, reflecting on the brass. Interspersed were lessons, read softly in the waning light. The sounds we heard that March day in the late '60s were a blend of psalms and lessons designed to connect man with his God at the end of day. In Canterbury, this Evensong seemed a perfection of harmony and praise, a true blessing to our long day of travel.

For 350 years Canterbury has been one of Christendom's chief places of pilgrimage, surpassed only by Jerusalem and Rome. For the medieval pilgrim, this site of the slaying of Thomas á Becket was the end of the journey. For us, it was only a beginning.

# The Channel

Evening descended on the city of Canterbury as we left the cathedral. The children did not have to be prodded into the car. They remembered the plan and they trusted us. We were their parents, weren't we? We had promised Canterbury at sunset and they expected to reach Dover by night. The channel crossing would be their morning adventure. Outside the windows of the car, the March winds moved trees and caused people in the street to tug at their jackets. Both modern and medieval villages passed by our window, weaving a contrast of England that we had grown to know. It was misty as we neared the sea, and the air felt damp.

Even in the semi-dark, the whitewashed houses and the lay of the towns told us we were near the coast. The children were quiet, content, almost soothed by the distant waterway. It was a cloudless night as we ascended the hill to the bed and breakfast recommended by our handy guidebook. The famed white cliffs bordering the sea were a powerful icon. A million references came to mind. In the distance was Harold's Castle and the spearhead of the Battle of Hastings and, indeed, the site of enemy bombardments throughout the centuries. There was no roar of bombs; only sea gulls kept sentinel over the shore.

Sleepily, we trudged up the stairs to a gabled attic room where our squadron of seven was lulled to sleep by the coziness of the angular room. After my weary children surrendered to heavy slumber, my thoughts reeled back to the coast we had just passed and images of it from newsreels. I was suddenly no older than Todd, our four-year-old, when, in the darkened theater of my hometown, I saw naval vessels and bursting bombs where now there were merely gulls. The staccato words of a correspondent interjected the positioning of Allied forces. The Second World War was with me still, brought back by its very battleground. I don't really know if I slept, drifting in and out of semi-conscious dreams. But I felt no tiredness in the morning. The anticipation was overwhelming. Across the channel was the continent of Europe.

No alarm was needed to awaken the boys; the promise of a ferry ride was enough. By the time I returned from the toilet, the boys were already dressed in the clothes I had set out the night before. Mike buttoned little Dominic's strap in an attempt to move things along. As soon as Phil headed for the winding steps that led to the breakfast room, his younger brothers followed. I grabbed Thomas, who was heading for the stairs.

English evening meals of boiled beef never stirred my soul, but the first meal of the day was a different matter. The British always sent us off with proper breakfasts. I have come to realize that it was not only the bountiful courses of cornflakes, eggs, gammon, toast and marmalade that comforted us so much, it was also the lovely style of serving that made it so pleasant. No matter how humble the circumstances, the china was as important as the portion it held. The teapot, with its cozy jacket, said something to me that morning as we left Dover. Mother England had hugged us, sending us off warmed and well nourished.

Braced for the sea air, we headed for our crossing, entering the queue of cars waiting to be gobbled by the ferry and sent below the deck. Once aboard, the children were set free to survey the upper decks, quickly spotting the vending machines and chairs along the edges. They examined every loose trinket on the ground and seemed unaffected by the myriad languages that were immediately audible. England grew dim in the early morning mist.

## Calais

Our doorway to France was through Calais. That small border town, like Dover, had dealt with siege and invasion, was often cut to the bone and rebuilt, strived to forget and

later to remember. Not to forget its siege by the English in 1347, when for a harrowing year its people lived in terror, the city had commissioned France's greatest sculptor at the time, Auguste Rodin, to remind the world of a sacrifice of six burghers who had given their lives to save the city. A masterpiece came from the commission. Known as the "Burghers of Calais," it speaks of more than the siege.

I had read of the siege—not one of history's well-known stories—on one of those cold nights in England while the maps were spread out on the parlor floor. We looked at the map often, pointing out mostly major art capitals—Venice, Florence, Pisa, Rome, Paris. And then we spotted the smaller cities along the way, where we knew some gem was tucked. As Irving Stone's *Agony and Ecstasy* had given insight to Michaelangelo's life, *Naked Came I*, the novel of Rodin's life by David Weiss, not only gave me a graphic picture of the struggles of Rodin but the story of Calais' siege.

As we neared the city, we debated the value of stopping. We knew we couldn't visit every little town along the way, but the boys were captive as I took my turn in the story time, relating the frequency of border town battles between England and France and particularly the siege of Calais that prompted its masterpiece of art.

"During the rule of Edward III of England, the city of Calais was held captive for nearly a year. The English king threatened to burn the city and kill all the citizens," I began. "To save the city, six noble men with nooses around their necks, carrying the keys of Calais, offered the keys and their lives for their fellow citizens. The king accepted the offer. The city was saved."

"No more siege?" Todd repeated.

"No more siege," I answered. "The people and this city were spared. As often happens it was years before these heros were honored. Centuries later—in fact, in the second half of the 19th-century—France realized what a sacrifice these men had made and commissioned August Rodin to recreate the heroic figures.

"Rodin accepted. But when he received the commission, the request was clearly limited. The group had requested only one symbolic hero to be sculpted. He screamed back. 'Were there not six men who gave their lives?'"

" 'We have money for one,' they retorted. He went into his cold studio, racked with rheumatism. Each new job was painful in the last years of his life, but the idea consumed Rodin. Nothing would stop him. Years passed and he had to put his own money into the project to make it work."

I was inspired by the story of Rodin's persistence, his need to create as he saw it. The boys wanted more knowledge about the siege. "My history is limited, but I would like to see what the burghers look like," I said. My husband could see that all of us were curious.

"Check your *Fodor's*," Dom suggested. "If it isn't hard to find, we'll stop. Calais is a small town."

"According to this book, it's right in the center of town. Shouldn't be too hard to find."

My French was rusty, but after circling the main square three times, we pulled over to ask a pedestrian. "Oú est la Statue de Rodin?" I struggled.

"Right behind you!" an American student grinned, pointing to a rusty fence. We had passed it three times. Pollution, the green mold and an unpretentious fence were distorting our view. We stopped nearby to get a closer look. The boys were still caught up in the story of the siege. They clambered up to the rail, peering through like little monkeys. Clustered behind the grille, unheralded, reddish-brown in color, were the once-bronze figures of six haggard old men. A key hung from the hand of one, a lamp from the hand of another. Mike turned to me with tenderness. "Look at their eyes, Mom. They look like they want to cry."

Neither dirt nor time, not even the noise of vehicles whizzing by, could interrupt the connection he was making. We all began to examine the individuals and the composite, the stooped composure, the eyes, the pathos of six doomed burghers. It was clear there was a sad fate, a sacrifice. Rodin had shown it in the stance, the eyes, the gestures of the men. Little Dominic reached out to touch the bronze figures. Despite the elements of the outdoors, they were lifelike. Their story was real. The sacrifice of the men would not be forgotten. Rodin was also a real hero. He had told the truth. Even the children could see that.

## Crossing the Alps

Bavaria belonged to the boys. It was their kind of art, formed by the hand of God. It would provide a new kind of adventure. The Alps were nature's untamed surfaces to be conquered as we drove. We passed through Belgium, enjoying

the crisp air of the mountains and entering the increasing altitude with a new vigor. The farther we distanced ourselves from the familiar terrain of northern England, the higher the spirit of adventure became. With "Rome by Easter" still our goal, we had but a few days to cross the Alps. In spite of a brilliant sun, a cold wind swept away the clouds. At long last the dampness we felt in England was leaving our bones. The clean, white snow covering the pines of Germany and Austria was an energetic lift, a kind of a tonic to the spirit.

Dotted with well-designed, stone picnic tables, the German autobahn was a pleasant sight, and the promise of a winter picnic kept spirits high. After such picnics, the younger boys even learned to nap with the help of a droning car. They were adjusting to their confinement better than we had hoped. We continued the creative game of "Car Tales in Europe," remembering characters from Grimms Fairy Tales. Of course, each tale was retold with new twists.

A stop at a German gästehaus just outside of Aachen opened new doors. The boys eyed the eiderdowns with wonder and experienced them in many ways after the stern matron showing us to our rooms had left. They crawled under and hid and then jumped on them like trampolines, resting well in the end, warm and snug for the night.

As we approached Ulm the next day, we saw the blend of art and nature that belongs only to an alpine city with a medieval history. The spires of its Gothic cathedral matched the natural grace of the snowy pines. Ulm's cathedral was built in a competitive verve of creation in the 13th-century that produced the explosion of spires that began to dot the continent. The city fathers had hoped Ulm's cathedral would be the world's largest, but it has been credited with being the tallest in Europe. I looked upward to the intricacies of the stone. The boys were still mesmerized by the grandeur of nature. They saw only the Alps in the distance. As we left the city, there was a changing panorama of ancient villages nestled in the mountains, medieval castles perched on steep rocks and onion-domed churches firmly planted in the heart of every little village.

As we drove farther into Austria, ahead of us rose a range of mountains so vast and beautiful that we had to get out of the car and physically absorb the flawless harmony between the pinnacles and sky, the sweeping vista of surrounding villages, and the higher peaks yet to be reached. The fervor of our new conquest was high. Standing at the edge of the road, we pointed to the snow-capped peaks in the distance with the clouds and mist lying low.

"There they are! The highest range of the Alps! How shall we cross?" my husband asked adventurously. "The Brenner Pass will take us up and over, or ... or ... *and it's up to you* ... a car-train can zoom us through a dark tunnel." Dominic's eyes lit up. Tunnels were magic to him. Phil and Mike pushed forward for another look. They were ready for the out-of-doors. Todd had the answer, "Can we do both?"

And so a pact was sealed. We would ascend by the Brenner Pass going and return via the Gutter Pass.

Quietly we re-entered the car, everyone eager for the climb. The snow continued to fall as we wound around a higher peak. We could feel the wind seep into the car. We adjusted to the chill, pulling a blanket around little Thomas and zipping winter jackets on the others. The road grew slick, and the boys were totally transfixed with the wonder of the Alps. The light car swayed and slid once toward the edge. All banter ceased, and the only sound that each of us heard was his own heartbeat. We felt the wind pushing our light Cortina.

Our faithful car had never been challenged like this on the tranquil island of England, nor had we. The older boys peered with wide eyes over the side of the mountains. Todd began to fidget with his hands, refusing to look out, and Dominic snuggled against Mike, hiding his eyes. Cars passing us had chains, and without saying a word, Dom pulled over at a petrol station to invest in a set.

Phil and Mike got out and watched. It was serious business. We did not have to warn them to keep squabbles down as the older boys took their seats again. "Let's shift all the weight we can to the back of the car," Dom ordered, and his sons looked for boxes that could be moved. Problem solving had excited them. They knew they were a respected part of the teamwork. Two boys piled into the back compartment. All canned goods and extra items filled in the space around them.

We inched away from the station, wholly absorbed in the climb.

Finally, at the top of the peaks with snow outside, the children burst into applause. The reward was a new vista of the exhilarating mountain range, villages dotting the distance and the pinnacles rising majestically behind us. Dominic passed around his clutched bag of animal crackers in celebration.

Our Cortina wound through villages of picture-perfect cottages and onion-domed churches, distant castles and chalets with wonderful carvings. In the Black Forest, near the River Nicer, we caught sight of Heidelberg Castle in the distance, and wished our itinerary could be extended, but we had to be content with the distant view. The Bavarian Alps and the ordered highways in between had presented a hundred different winter scenes that we would not forget.

Beyond the last snowy peaks of Tirol lay a different world. The snow-capped mountains gave way to hillsides of brown earth, castlettos and clustered cities topping the hills. On the descent, we saw valleys lively with fruit stands, streets bustling with people in the late afternoon sun. The boys shed their jackets and pushed away the blankets.

The orderliness of Germany passed into a more cluttered terrain. Precipices jutted out into the road, and little towns clung precipitously to hillsides. At the official border, enterprising tourist stalls overflowed with gaudy displays of beads, towers and crosses. It was a different world indeed. On the snowy slopes we had observed roadside pilgrimage spots marked mostly with simple wooden crosses. Now Madonnas with small jars of flowers were placed in the miniature sanctuaries at the edge of the road. Children ran in the streets, uninhibited. The action was livelier, louder. At a petrol station, a group of teenagers argued over a card game. Winter was over for us. Rain and snow and clouds were gone. Light poured into our caravan. We were in Italy.

# Venice

All the splendor and mystery of the East, the romantic gaiety of a masquerade, the shrewdness of bargaining merchants

were mingled in a carnival atmosphere the day we saw Venice. We could feel it as we approached the city from across the lagoon. From a distance, Venice seemed exotic. There she was, the reflection of her Oriental domes twinkling in the water, casting a spell of sheer breathtaking enchantment. There was no time to analyze, scrutinize and understand every problem and paradox of the cities we visited. Venice, especially, was going to be a day of fun.

Coming in as we did from the back door, our first close view of Venice was like that of a delivery man. We followed the maze of alleys and side streets lined with small, private dwellings and artisans at work. Grocery shops were laden with every kind of herb and grain. The scents were a mixture of East and West. Launderettes and pizza shops were tucked in among centuries old villas. Despite the erosion of time, the vanishment of power, and the waning of her wealth, Venice remained Venice.

We joined the fun, listening, watching and talking to the merchants. The markets were part of the continued tradition of trade with the East. I bought a wooden fork that was larger than our youngest son and a Venetian hand-painted tray. The swarthy salesman assured me it was "lingua" (wood), but the plaster began to chip before I got it home. It was still beautiful and part of the fun. There was a richness of humanity in the hustle and banter of the open booths near the canal. Colorful stalls along the bridges and streets were laden with lace and Venetian glass, only a mimic of the trade from centuries gone by.

When young Marco Polo grew up in Venice, the trade routes were teaming with silks and scents that were to give Venice her importance in the Adriatic, Aegean and Mediterranean seas. The thriving city republic controlled trade routes that gave her unbridled power for a few centuries.

What we saw as we wandered through the Venice of the 20th-century was a wonderfully incongruent mixture of classical lines, baroque palaces and Byzantine churches glimmering in the water. We did not view the city from the usual ride down the Grand Canal. Dom's practical side couldn't justify such an expense for seven. We walked and walked and walked.

With the boys trailing behind, we wound past rows of faded, shuttered palazzos where once the courtesans of the 18th-century had entertained the likes of Casanova. Finally, somewhere between past centuries and our own, we found our way to the threshold of the Piazza San Marco.

The mid-afternoon sun was perfect lighting; an orchestra was gay, performing splendidly in tune. People were sitting and standing about the cafe terraces; little groups of school children led by their masters were crossing here and there. The Holy Week crowd was picking up, tourists mingling with the faithful. A thousand pigeons, unaffected by applause, fluttered about playing their parts with utmost naiveté. The gold of St. Mark's glistened in the sun.

Dom and I stood for a moment to inhale the scene, but none of the boys was so patient. Thomas wiggled free from his strap in the pushchair and, with a thrust of his fat little body, wobbled to the middle of the square. Amidst the pigeons, the boys ran about in uninhibited prances and skips, not for one moment stealing the scene from the tame birds that had owned it for centuries.

We allowed the boys to enjoy their freedom in the safety and the sun of the piazza as long as we thought their rapturous bodies wanted to. They danced about happily. Then we moved them slowly toward the great architectural embodiment, which was the backdrop.

The basilica of St. Mark was an anomaly in Italy. Every idea it embodied had been confiscated from the East. Even the body of St. Mark the Evangelist was taken from Alexandria to be enshrined in Venice, giving the little city republic its own patron saint. We glanced up at the four bronze horses, which were mounted high above the main arched doorway. They had been looted from Constantinople in triumph of Venice's growing imperial hopes.

Inside the Basilica the gold and marble were but a frame for the art that had come to be known as the Venetian School. Entering, the boys caught the sensuousness of burning candles and the richness of images; they were quiet at first, as much as boys can be. Thomas didn't like the dark. He wiggled out of my arms, wanting to head back to the sun and the pigeons. My husband followed him with the rest of the boys, allowing me the pleasure of wandering alone through the Byzantine wonder. I entered the palace of the Doges next to the church, where the massive halls of Renaissance Gothic were a reliquary for a few of the city's countless masterpieces. The palace was a light and lovely pink and white marble foil for the remembrances of all the best of Venice's creativeness. The empty rooms spoke of the fall that had begun in the 16th-century and eventually whittled away Venetian power.

The past requires a way of seeing. The Venice of my memory, sweet lines of poetry and reremembered lines of history, surfaced and I almost heard the sounds of people in the empty halls.

There was yet one other face of Venice that I remembered from romantic novels and vignettes of historic allusions, accepted with the mystique of the special city. It was the Venice that perhaps the Grand Tourists were drawn to, that romantic lady of masquerade and romance. Long after Venice had lost her place among the powers of the world, she continued to live elegantly. In the 18th-century, the novel and the wealthy, the young and the frivolous, were looking to Venice to hear her music, to play at her casinos, to join in her masquerades and carnivals and to be a part of a naive, spendthrift society.

It was this Venice of the 18th-century that we thought of later that evening when all the weary pigeon watchers were refreshed with dinner. Evening brings the magic and charm of Venice's moonlight life. The sound from the casinos and opera houses filled the night. We could almost hear the laughter echoing in the alleys. I saw a young man, surely a great-grand-nephew of Casanova, and I imagined the many courtesans, their masks discreetly in place, frolicking in the streets.

These scenes and the fading picture of a singing gondolier in his striped tights were there, reflecting their mirth in the moon-touched water of the Grand Canal every evening. Under the arched bridges, gondolas were slowly passing. The tempo was melancholy, the reflections entrancing as they swayed on the lulling ripples of the quieted canals. The night was filled with romance when we turned from Venice.

## Pisa

The distance between Venice and Pisa was but a half-day trip by Italy's autostrada. It was difficult to drive through the area without flashbacks from newsreels seen in my early childhood. I knew this part of Italy best from movies. The shaded countryside was once in the direct line of Hitler's raids. As we experienced air raids at home in our corner of the eastern U.S., I could see fiery explosives from celluloid, and in my nightmares this very area was being wiped off the map. In fact, over 50 percent of the land from Venice to Pisa had been obliterated by the blazes of that war.

There were no signs of the losses as we wound around the Tuscan countryside. Rolling hills, quilted with soft olive

groves and cypress trees rising in glad-onyx flames, guarded the way. It was early afternoon as we came into Pisa. Small and self-contained, Pisa was a pleasant community, I thought. With minimal traffic, we were immediately set at ease in the city limits. If Venice was carnival, Pisa was going to be rest. Without much difficulty, we found our promised pension.

Everyone piled out of the Cortina. Each boy was given a load. We learned that teamwork got us to our destinations as quickly as possible.

A pale, rosy marble marked the vestibule. Green plants sprouted profusely. It was cool, welcoming in the warm afternoon. Upstairs in our large, comfortable rooms, beamed ceilings caught our eye. The little pension had been described as evocative of the area. We were pleased.

There was even a bonus not mentioned. In the bedroom on the second floor were doors that opened into a front balcony. We wasted no time checking out the view. When the shutters were flung open, framed in all its glistening white Romanesque glory was the Tower of Pisa, cutting the horizon with its special tilt.

None of the poetic allusions, pictures or descriptions of this bizarre phenomenon matched this view of it. Against a brilliant blue sky, the intricacies of the white tiers were etched in sharp contrast. My imagination was stimulated in a creative series of possibilities. It was a tiered wedding cake with its own bell, an intricately carved ivory tower, a finely crafted lace design, a jewel box set on a blanket of velvet. From every vantage point, it was something different.

It didn't take us long to dab a few dirty faces and tuck in a shirt or two. We left the luggage just where we had dropped it and headed for a closer view. The late March day in Italy was warm. No one needed the jackets that were zipped tightly just three days before. The boys felt free; we were but a few blocks away from the Piazza del Miracoli, a walk that everyone seemed to enjoy. The burnt oranges and rich browns of the tiled roofs on the unpretentious dwellings gave an earthy contrast to the fantasy that we had viewed from our balcony.

The Square of Miracles, the heart of the city, like St. Mark's in Venice, was exciting to the boys, and they raced ahead. We let them run. They were safe in this well-kept grassy expanse. Three perfectly unified buildings of white Tuscan marble—baptistery, Duomo and bell tower—are set against a blue sky, creating a most extraordinary spectacle. Seeing ourselves in new pictures was part of the fun of this tour, and thus we were framed in Pisa.

For a few moments, the boys were caught up in the freedom of the grass, but they were easily enticed into the mausoleum-like structure ahead. It was there, in the round baptistery that in the 15th-century Galileo had come, like these curious little boys of ours, his head filled with imaginings ripe for conjecture. Within these walls he had made discoveries that would change the course of science.

We entered the baptistery first. Inside the round building, a guide pointed out that if sounds were emitted in special sequence, they would blend together to resemble a chord from an organ. The mere suggestion was enough; each boy conducted his own experiment.

"Hello, hello!"

"Helllooo, hellooo," it answers.

The Duomo was another matter. The church's interior was one glorious display of fine carvings in marble and bronze, softened by painted frescos and subdued colors. Within the

cathedral were works of Ciambue, Sodoma, del Sarto—art spanning five centuries. Our eyes wandered around, as did the boys'. We all approached the pulpit, a masterpiece created by Giovanni Pisano in the 14th-century. The faces of children, at all angles, wide-eyed, vulnerable—as emotive as our boys running around—stared at us. Pisano had brought to life one of the world's most macabre events, the massacre of the innocents. I left in silence.

The boys were ready for the bell tower, the oddity that had put Pisa on the map. As we headed for the exit and the promise of entering the famous tower, I turned to get one last glance at the cathedral as a whole. Phil had taken a stance directly under a votive lamp, trying to follow the sway and the rhythm as Galileo once did. He had not missed what the guide had pointed out, that Galileo had deduced the laws of oscillation in that very spot.

Just at the end of the day, we came upon the famous oddity, a campanile leaning dramatically. The boys released all the pent-up energy of the day's travel by bounding up the 294 winding steps, almost without stopping. My husband, with Thomas in his arms, and I took a more leisurely climb, looking at the city of Pisa at each new tier—the Apuan Alps in the background, the Arno stretching through the vista.

It was another curiosity to enjoy the inside phenomenon, that one angle of the climb was steep and on the other side there was hardly a climb necessary. At the top we were caught up in a lively discussion about Pisa's sandy soft subsoil and just what could be done to stop the tower's sinking. "We have until the year 2150," Mike noted, having listened carefully to the guide. "Return and see," we challenged them.

No one talked on the way down. Our energy was spent; our day had been full. It was a quiet, satisfying stroll to the pension, and we took one last look from the balcony as the sun went down over Pisa.

We had no trouble inducing the boys to sleep after such a climb. Halfway through their nightly travel tale, they were out, and my husband and I enjoyed the end of the evening from our balcony.

# Florence

It was with renewed vigor that we drove into the Queen City farther along the Arno. Florence seemed ordered, serene, sophisticated and beautifully laid out. Still endowed with perhaps the most dazzling reliquary of art per square mile, she housed her gems in quiet confidence.

"How do we explore this sophisticated city, center of art in Italy, with five children? Divide and conquer?" we asked. "Let them go to the zoo? Get a sitter?" Our instincts told us to feel at least the essence of the city and to hit the highlights on foot, hoping somehow the spirit of the Renaissance would speak to us.

We settled into an apartment suggested by Fromer's. We wanted to experience something of life in the great 1400s by living in an old palace like Elizabeth and Robert Browning had done a hundred years earlier. Our apartment was on the second story of an old palace. The Brownings were nearby from 1848 to 1861, we learned.

The palace we chose was not in perfect repair, but it had been lovingly decorated with large vases of flowers and a few antiques. Even in its sparseness, it had a palatial essence. The antique beds in our second-story suite were comfortable, and the small sink made it possible to refresh the children and

wash their white knee socks. We slept well in the quiet surroundings.

In the morning, a bell invited us to breakfast in what had
once been a fine dining hall. All that remained of its former
wealth was a chandelier and an ambience of graciousness.
There were tiny bouquets of fresh flowers, crisp white linen,
and a silver pot on the table for coffee. These considerations
were costing only five dollars a night. Florence by foot was
waiting.

Italy's most sophisticated city was spread out before us
like an ordered painting. Our eyes scanned the lay of the land,
and we breathed in the crisp, fresh air with a renewed energy.
The light of the sun glistened on the Arno. We saw the Ponte
Vecchio, that exquisite medieval bridge that was spared in the
bombings of the Second World War. We walked, a lively but
convivial group, to view the well known quadrangles and
their facades. The old city, looking much like it did in the great
Quatrocento, still had energy and vitality. People passed by
briskly, with purpose, even those going to see the sights.

We headed for the Piazza della Signoria, the square that
had been the center of civic activity for 600 years and then the
piazza del Duomo. The sights were dazzling: the Duomo of
Santa Maria de Fiore with its vertical-striped marble, its bell
tower designed in part by Giotto, and the dome by Filippo
Brunelleschi. But it was the doors—the brass doors with their
biblical stories—that took Ghiberti 40 years to create, that
stopped everyone. Here, even the boys could appreciate the
Biblical representations beautifully executed. In spite of the
impact of seeing such masterpieces, however, we sensed the
limits of children. Their need for freedom of movement
stopped us from viewing the art indoors. It was time for a
gelato.

There were nominal admission fees to the Uffizi, where
art was lined in profusion, and the Academia, where the statue of the David could be viewed alone. We reasoned that if we
took money from our food budget, we could pay to see the
sculptured treasures of the Renaissance. At a small market, we
purchased cans of sardines, some tomatoes and a round loaf
of bread, leaving us less than the allotment for seven tickets to
both museums. Everyone wanted to see Michelangelo's

David, so the entire family entered the Academia. Our money was well spent and so was the attention span of the younger boys. Dom volunteered to watch the trio while I took Phil and Mike to the Uffizi. Everyone was happy.

With our pockets empty and our stomachs full, we turned to enjoy the free treasures of Florence. In the garden of the Pitti Palace, late in the mellowness of the afternoon, as the sun set in the ordered rows of umbrella pines and the orange-tiled roofs in the distance, one of Florence's human masterpieces came running through the garden. She was a child of about four. Her features were fine, a perfect little nose, big oval eyes, black silk hair cut subtly around her cheek bones. She stopped, pulling her dress demurely under her, and picked up some pebbles on the garden's pathway. Thomas and Dominic shared their pebbles with her. She smiled and laughed with them, her grandfather ever watchful from his bench, ready to shield his princess from any possible unpleasantness. I could see her as a woman, beautiful, well groomed in an understated way, self-confident as a Medici, a Florentine in spirit.

She was part of a heritage of wealth and a tradition that had come about in the Quatrocento, the remarkable 1400s. Once the Renaissance had scaled palaces and gardens to the wealthy merchant, a new kind of self-confidence had followed. Humanism was born and modern man made himself the center of the universe.

Manners became a passion of the wealthy, who lived their lives in strict accordance with *Il Cortegiano*, the bible of manners that formed Italy's notions of proper behavior. All of this was a part of the philosophy that man should be graced with gentlemanly behavior, speak quietly, and play games without cheating or kicking others in the shins.

The eyebrows of the elderly man arched as he watched the diminutive black-haired beauty brush the pebbles from her skirt. No one would know she had stopped to play. She stood exquisitely straight as Dominic and Thomas waved goodbye. She grabbed the old man's hand, and the two sauntered down the ordered streets of Florence.

As our family walked from the Pitti Palace, we saw the Ponte Vecchio and the city, golden in the sunset. I loved just being in Florence; the sophisticated style and majestic traditions had endured for 500 years, affecting even the way little girls play with pebbles.

# Rome

It was early afternoon on Good Friday when we left the autostrada and headed inward to the maze of circles and sirens of the city limits of Rome. Traffic was compounded by the holiday. Rome was preparing for her greatest feast. She invited the world to celebrate Easter with her. She promised her guests a festive spirit, a welcome by her Holy Father the

Pope and the sun of Italy, But, like any hostess with last-minute preparations, she seemed anxious. Arriving just before the pageantry was to begin, we saw Lady Roma vulnerable while she dressed, nervous, not quite ready for her guests.

A chaotic convergence of people was descending on the city. Pompous pedestrians crossed indignantly before us. Firm-chested carabineri, waving and ranting, seem to do no good. And then we were introduced to that moving macho symbol of Italy, "Man on Motorbike," buzzing in and around without warning or consideration. We were glad we had booked ahead in a pension, but our Italian was inadequate in asking directions. I waved a slip of paper in front of a group of pedestrians as my husband, whose grandfather had lived with him as a child, began in his dialect. Half in English, half in Italian, a friendly gentleman offered his suggestion of a direct route.

Before he finished, an overbearing young man, with his foot still on the motorscooter at the stop light, contradicted the plan, giving his shortcut. A passing matron warned me not to listen to either of them. Hands waved and voices grew louder, finally attracting a passing carabaneri. Traffic was backing up, and I smiled at the drama around us. I quickly took to the relative quiet of our little Cortina, and we followed the carabineri's lead to the first turn and waved him off.

Closer to our destination near the Spanish Steps, the drama of international interplay unfolded. I watched a variety of clerics in their robes and veils float along beside sure-stepping, mini-clad beauties. Julius Caesar's Rome could have offered no more diversity than we experienced that weekend.

The strip above the Spanish Steps was a good place to find cheap, pleasant lodgings, our manual said, but our room on the third floor of an old stone apartment seemed confining until I leaned out the window. The activity was in the piazza below. A grandiose setting for theatrical effects, the steps were lined with spring flowers. About midway, a black-haired teenager with an oversized guitar entertained while people seemed to wander up and down in procession. Here and there, young mothers, totally absorbed in their babies, pushed prams back and forth. A parade of people unrelated to one another passed by our window. I felt I was peering into a happening, so friendly, so natural and yet so exotic. Life was as bubbly as the fountain in the center of the scene.

Was this the lure—this exotic life, warm, passionate and vibrant—that had attracted those Grand Tourists of the 18th- and 19th-centuries? To the right of my open window was a house turned museum where Keats once lived. To the left was the English tea room where he and the other English poets had gathered, their home away from home. Mrs. Babbington, famous the world over for her homemade scones, helped the English adapt. The romantic poets stayed and stayed, some to be buried in Italy, so intoxicated were they by this warm, uninhibited city.

I loved it too, this exuberance, this vitality and passion around me. The air seemed to breed action; there were proud and passionate encounters all around. But I also had a penchant for some kind of order to come out of the chaos, at least in the preservation of the past. We had grown to respect the English preservation of history in the form of well-ordered greens surrounding well-kept landmarks. As I looked from my window in Rome, I stood in awe of 2,000 years of imperial history and every epoch of artistic excellence jammed into a reachable radius. But the history was almost lost in the chaotic use of ancient buildings and beautiful parks.

Everything seemed mad and joyous, even in the most serious historic landmarks. As we entered the piazza and walked throughout Rome, I became a little critical of the descendants of the Holy Roman Empire.

I noticed on a statue of most significant value, a coat hung. And at the fountain, I caught sight of a young Italian urinating. Our children had been reminded throughout our excursions to respect the history and value of art that had survived the centuries. Our admonishments appeared absurd here, where no one seemed to care. I was honestly a little embarrassed. The English poets could laugh and love it, I reasoned, but I was a descendant of this culture.

My youthful and erroneous conclusion was that Romans had no interest in, nor respect for historic landmarks. What eventually came to fore was that the Romans, and for that matter most Italians, loved the past as one would love an ancestor, an uncle or a grandfather. Respect in England means maintaining one's distance. Italians must embrace their loved ones, both living and dead. Respect means being loose enough to relax. I should have realized this. No one thinks it wrong in Italy to picnic on historic grounds, to pick the flowers of the gardens, nor to tromp in the water spilling around the many fountains.

The festive spirit was easily infectious. By Friday night, in spite of the solemnity of Good Friday ceremonies, we began to feel the openness of a Roman holiday. We watched a procession of mourners meander throughout the coliseum, lit only by the moonlight and the candles carried by the faithful. The empty shell was stark and tomb-like in the pitch-black night, a backdrop of mourning. In the summer, the pageantry of opera filled the same amphitheater. Life in Rome seemed passionate and incongruous. Piety and gaiety were often intermingled.

We were becoming accustomed to the mixture. On Saturday, we meandered through medieval streets, observing baroque buildings, classical civic structures, Renaissance facades, domes, spires and modern motorcars, all creating a unique interplay of urban living where art explodes.

It was, first and last, Easter weekend; we were in the mood for celebration but, within our time limitation, we wanted to touch the ancestors of Rome's imperial past as well.

We planned our daytime judiciously, half for the civil and half for the ecclesiastical history of the city we were visiting.

At Capitoline Hill, the world of Julius Caesar opened up among the ruins. After four years of Latin, laced with the history of the Gallic Wars, the monuments of triumph and imperial power were real to me. It was exciting to come upon familiar scenes first described in beloved books.

We continued among the ruins in a quiet reverence for a government that spoke of power extending farther than any empire before or since.

"At the time of Julius Caesar," I heard my husband tell his sons, "Rome and her imperial legions had conquered Carthage, Greece, Macedonia and Egypt. Her boundaries extended to France, England and northern Europe. After the empire fell, she was Europe's battleground. How could this great Empire recede, topple and fall?"

What happened was the ultimate history lesson. It took Gibbon 30 volumes to present it, and I mused that it had been on a trip such as ours that he had been inspired to write his meticulous study of the rise and fall. The boys listened and climbed over the pebbles with more serious expectation. I found myself lecturing to them: "People will always come to Rome to try to put the pieces together because it was not only the story of a lost empire but the central tale of all power. Traveling in historic paths often brings to light deeper issues. We try to understand, or at least think about the events, seeing the actual sites."

We walked among the ruins in a pleasant stride of examination and pleasure. As the boys followed little paths that were once streets of 2,000 years ago, a gentle drizzle came down. The weather put an end to walking but not to the enjoyment of Rome. We headed for the car, deciding to drive along the Appian Way, that famous road that had survived legions and centuries of traffic.

Mike's eyes lit up with mention of the Appian Way. After some registered smugness, Mike reminded me of a remark I had made in England regarding the less-than-GM-sturdy English Cortina. "How are we to travel to the Continent in that?" I had quipped. "It will probably break down on the

Appian Way!" Children remember everything, I thought, and promised to guard carefully my remarks. Making our way to the next point of interest without incidence, the boys gained renewed faith in our caravan.

As the rain continued to fall gently, we descended the steps to the underground catacombs. Lesser dungeons had intrigued the boys. These were filled with mazes of twisted turnings and fascinating symbols to be deciphered with discretion. The relics of the tenacious time in the history of Christianity were all around in the semi-dark. The boys fingered the narrow passageways with tender respect, tiptoeing past carvings of fishes and scratchings of a new-found code of those in hiding.

By afternoon the sun reappeared, lighting the freshly cleaned domes of the city. The monuments we had seen thus far had been built by the power of the empire. It was time to enter those built for the glorification of God.

As we headed for St. Peter's, the colonnades of the largest basilica in the world trumpeted from a distance. The Pantheon that we had visited earlier might have been a prototype when the first basilica was built in 330 A.D. But, by the time the center of Catholicism was reconstructed in the 16th-century, the greatest artists of the Renaissance had collaborated on creations that would outdistance any round-domed construction from the past.

Instantly we merged with the droves of spectators in the massive basilica. It seemed more like a museum than a church, at first. The art seemed grandiose, theatrical compared to the primitive buildings we had seen earlier. I felt more like part of an audience than a pilgrim. As we approached, with the light pouring in among the twisting of the gold, I understood a little better the Italian personality, the need for drama in expression of emotion. This reaching for beauty had its own style. No puritanical strain could touch the heart of the artist, as passion ruled his declaration of beauty.

We stretched more in the Sistine Chapel, our necks twisting as we gazed upward at the touch of God's hand in the creation of man, the ecstasy of Michelangelo before us. Later, as

we left the main basilica, we saw Michelangelo's rendering of the great pathos death and a mother's love in marble: the Pieta.

My son Dominic, much alive and saturated with this menagerie of people and dwarfing, cavernous cathedrals, pulled me out into the sun. "When are we going back to America where there are just houses?" he innocently asked.

The little ones had seen enough of the cultural achievements of man. With such wonders spread before us like a Thanksgiving dinner, we had gluttonously devoured more than our share of art. We called to the vendor passing and sat against the pillar of St. Peter's, tasting the rich chocolate gelato. It, too, was magnificent.

Travel-worn but satisfied, we trudged up to our second-story pension, where the children enjoyed a little freedom in the homey atmosphere. The large old apartments were spacious. A few overstuffed chairs around the desk in the outer hall gave them a little place to play as I enticed them one at a time to have a bath. It was, after all, Saturday night at the end of a day of sightseeing.

Down on the street below, I found a local laundromat. Passing by the beautifully displayed chocolate creations of eggs and fruit, I was reminded of the pagan Easter Bunny who came to our children annually at home. I knew they would not forget. Rituals were important to the security of little ones, I reasoned as I cut into our food budget to purchase some choice delicacies of Italian design. I hid them in the laundry as I returned.

Dom was lulling the listeners to sleep with the usual bedtime tales. He spoke of chariots and Roman figures. The older boys, acting very cosmopolitan, darted in and out with the curiosity of young Italian males on Saturday nights.

I polished their shoes with special care. New clothes were always a part of the Easter ritual. "We start fresh inside and out for Easter," my mother had often said. I placed a crisply pressed navy Eton suit, a pair of clean white knee socks and a white shirt by every bed. We would attend the Feast of the Resurrection in fresh garments.

Easter Sunday morning was brilliant. The children were mystified to find by their beds chocolates of beautiful shapes and marvelous flavors. I'm sure they harbored fears that Easter bunnies might not inhabit Rome. We persuaded them to hold on to the chocolate until we had our usual breakfast of hard rolls and coffee. I hated the syrupy coffee laden with sugar that we were served, much preferring the English breakfast. But this morning there was a special bowl in the center of the table. It offered hard-boiled eggs with the rolls. It was Easter.

Rome was brilliant this fine morning, even at 7 a.m. The sky was a tapestry of blue and the fountains sparkled. There was an infectious spirit of exaltation. People walked briskly in the morning sun. The fervor picked up by mid-morning. People breakfasted at the cafes and leaned from the tops of roofs. Everything seemed open, outgoing, even the flowers in the pots were in full bloom.

The boys in their Easter finery paraded with more pomp than the Swiss guards at the Vatican. As the throngs gathered in the early morning, we reinforced our regimental rules. Remembering the Edinburgh Festival, I counted continuously the little blue Etons and repeated often the reminder "to stay put if lost." No one needed reminding. Only one little blue cap was lost that day as the crowd grew into the thousands.

With the dawning of Easter, Rome was at her best, her buildings, her people all dressed for celebration, and she knew how to celebrate! The front of St. Peter's basilica was decorated with potted yellow flowers, and the arms of the great edifice designed by Bernini to embrace the world, waited as regiments of the Swiss Guard, the Italian Army and Navy, prepared to stand guard. Students from all over the world carried banners proclaiming their proud participation. Little dark-haired girls strutted in long, lacy communion gowns; clerics in swaying robes added color and drama.

The windows outside the basilica were draped in red for the Pope's appearance. The crowds strolling the avenues and side streets around the basilica grew denser toward noon, when the Pope was to bless the people. We were surprised to notice that our children had become one of the natural scene stealers. To the Italians, we could not have been more blessed. "Tutti Maschio!" I heard over and over again, and then I heard them add, "Benedicti." Blessings on the Mama and Papa. Suddenly I did feel blessed. We had our family with us and we were in Rome at Easter.

## Paris

Paris seemed to sprawl over miles of tiny lighted arteries, and traffic was intense. We approached it late and without reservations in early April. Life immediately seemed serious, sensuous and stupefying. To get directions we approached a

gendarme mounted on his well-groomed horse. The horse's tail swished back and forth as the policeman stared with contempt at our feeble command of his language. Feeling self-conscious, I kicked the diaper box out of sight, along with the papers and scraps from our simple picnic meal. I hated admitting the preconceived notions of people, but it was obvious that the idea of tourists spanning his city was odious to this officer.

Furthermore, it didn't take long to realize that children were not welcome, even in the recommended low-budget pensions. "Why don't we skip Paris?" my husband said as he returned from the third place on our list. "We could come back later, on a second honeymoon without the kids."

I didn't answer out loud at first, but finally said, "Not see Paris? It would not be a Grand Tour without Paris."

We had been systematically turned down in every recommended pension in the Sorbonne section. "I can't believe this," I said. "You would think that toddlers with their parents would be as acceptable as students alone."

"Not so," Dom answered.

"Let me try one of the unrecommended hotels," I pleaded. Something had started my adrenaline. Either it was the fierce protectiveness, my mother instinct surfacing, or I was reasoning that Paris should not be kept from me. Somewhere in my subconscious I had believed what Toynbee said: "The cultural treasury of great cities belongs to all of mankind." We had a right to see Paris.

With renewed determination, I got out of the car and began knocking on doors. Finally, on the last door of a long row, the little hotel welcomed us, knowing there were five children to bed down. It ended up being a very charming hotel with thick floral carpets and warm hot chocolate each morning for the boys.

We enjoyed the gardens of the Louvre, passed the Pantheon and, in crisp striped suits, the boys strolled the Champs Elysees hand-in-hand as if they belonged. We continued the happy, lyrical walk on the Right Bank, first past the Palace of Justice with the blossoms full along the Seine.

Travel always has surprises that give new perceptions when it becomes one's own odyssey. I knew of the Paris of Hugo's *Les Miserables*, that melancholy site of poverty; the land of wine, garlic and artists lunching by the river in bright cafes. I also knew Hemingway's city of sprawling trees, autobuses in round squares, purple flowers and the sudden drop of the hill of the Rue Cardinal and, of course, site of the Arch de Triumph.

The wonderful trees seemed to blossom in perfect blends of colors, but the Arch de Triumph evoked no emotion from our group. There was, however, an unmistakable awe when we descended the stairs in the Palace of the Invalids. The majestic tomb of Napoleon, set on black onyx, took us by surprise. Somehow the light pouring on it told the history of his valor better than the factual stories of his conquests and the architectural wonders of the arch outside. The boys felt they were in the presence of a giant.

Out in the afternoon air, a striking corps of ladies, molded in fuchsia uniforms, their hats tilted romantically to the left, passed by. They were a corps of census takers. "Oh, to be counted by them," my husband remarked.

Near Notre Dame, diligent artists took advantage of the warm weather and bright spring sun. We browsed after our pilgrimage took us into the cathedral, feeling the spirit of spring and the triumph of centuries along the Right Bank.

From the smart shops to the narrower streets where overcrowded markets reeked of brie and Roquefort, we wound our way to lunch. While I selected cheeses for our lunch, Dom picked out fruit and we let Todd buy some crusty baget rolls, fresh and hot from the vendor on the street. We caught sight of a little girl snatching a roll, and we added a coin to the vendor. No one should be unhappy or hungry on this April day in Paris.

As the sun reached its zenith in the Paris sky, we approached the happy symbol of the city created by Gustave Eiffel for the exposition of 1889. Its strange, gaunt frame was intriguing to the boys. We didn't care how naive we seemed.

To each of the boys, the Eiffel Tower held a different appeal. Thomas, who was just beginning to walk, wobbled and tumbled under the arched base of the tall girders. The middle boys raced from one giant leg of the tower to the other. The older two boys begged to climb to the top. I looked up at the somewhat rusty skeleton and decided it was all right. Two and one-half million rivets held it together, I read as I looked down pensively at my guidebook.

Driving slowly back to our pension that final evening, we watched the sun go down on the Seine, transfixed by the

beauty of the lovely city. The trees were in full bloom, bursting with buds. In the somber purple and pink, the sun descended behind the magnificent Palace of Justice, streaking the sky with deep purple, fuchsia and pink. The pastel blues and mauves moved in the moonlight of a spring full of passion and peaks and spires. All of Paris seemed lyrical and lovely.

Notre Dame, the Louvre, the Panthéon—full of art and artists—would be muted when we thought of the city itself, fresh that spring. Millions had painted her, described her. But to feel Paris, to breathe the spring air around her monuments and museums was to experience another kind of art. It was to treasure the haughty, beautiful city. Spending six months getting to know every museum and every avenue could not have given the joy we had walking those avenues with our children that spring weekend. I was glad we had not been discouraged. I would savor my taste of Paris long after youth and our pictures had faded.

# It's Your Turn, Chickadees

# Chapter 3

# The Root Search

*"Tell me where a man comes from,
and I'll tell you what he's like."*

—Saul Bellow

**W**hat is it in man that compels him to return to the land where his seed began? Visiting Europe was a wonderful refresher course in the history of Western man, but the generalities of our race were not enough. Our ancestors were part of the mass population that left Europe in economic exodus at the turn of the century. The history of our own families was obscured in poor records and poor translations. For us, the story was half told; our own past was incomplete.

As an aside from the tour for art, we planned a root search. From England, it had seemed a worthy idea, but as we left Rome, a different emotion took over. The north of Italy was well mapped and described in all the tour books; its art, the pride of Western civilization. The south was an anomaly, not recommended by anyone, least of all the northern Italians. Tourism had not yet opened in the southern provinces, and we had little reliable information from our own families. It had been three generations since my family left Calabria, a province on the southern tip of the boot of Italy. There were no remaining contacts. My husband's family had been in America for only one generation; a few distant cousins remained in a small village in Sicily.

Tour books of Italy made no recommendations for accommodations. The only resources available were the dated impressions of the English writers, such as Norman Douglas and Edward Lear, who had ventured into the south early in the century.

"Why do you want to go anyway?" my relatives questioned before we left. They were yet too close to the pain of poverty their parents had left behind and the degradation of ethnic rejections. "For three generations your family has worked to fit comfortably into the American culture. Why dig into a culture that failed its people?" Settling in the poorest sections of town, our families had risen, step by step to pleasant lives. There were a hundred "Little Italies" in America where life had continued as it was at the turn of the century. I could still witness the festivals and feast days. How would Italy be different? What could I learn from this land that I did not already know?

Nothing would stop my curiosity. I had read what I could get my hands on, digging into anything with a reference to "southern Italy." I found material going back to time unrecorded, where Italy was described as a land rising from the sea, shrouded in myth and speculation. There were records of Italy's 3,000 years of history and of the many peoples who had put their stamps on the area by the sea; the Greeks, the Romans, the rule of Barbarosa, the Norman period, and even the recent finger pointed by the Fascists.

Classics like *Christ Stopped at Eboli* had been given to me by a librarian. The book was an autobiographical account of Carlo Levi, a doctor from northern Italy who was banished during the Second World War because of his non-fascist views. Levi's punishment was banishment to Eboli, a village in the south, below Naples. He aptly described the superstitions, poverty, and abandonment of the people of the south.

"The South," by his testimony, was so remote it was the "other world." He described it as "hedged in by custom and sorrow, cut off from history and the State, eternally penitent, a land without comfort or solace, where the peasant lives out his motionless civilization on barren ground in remote poverty, and in the presence of death."

"We're not Christians," the people of the area say. "Christ stopped short of here at Eboli." Christian, in their way of speaking, means "human being." It is with this hopeless feeling of inferiority that they live.

Reading these books had revealed much, and now the people of Rome were confirming my fears. "The South?" they would say, "You joke! You don't want to go to the South. All the art is here in the north." For their part they would easily let the south secede. The mafia was an embarrassment. The provinces below Rome were underdeveloped.

My husband's view was different. His information came from family. His father and mother were both born in a small village in Sicily and had married by arrangement in America. They were nostalgic about home, sure that Sicily was part of Eden, and that American life was much inferior to their Italy. They held firm to the cultural subtleties of their native land, not yet trusting the American style of thinking. They had written to distant cousins telling them to expect a visit from us in Sicily. Were they caught defiantly in a pride of place that would disappoint and embarrass us as well? Whatever was true, we wanted to see for ourselves.

As an aside from our Grand Tour, we left the eternal city of Rome on Easter afternoon for the Bay of Naples to put together the missing pieces of our own past. But before we plunged into the unknown, we promised the boys a stop along the Amalfi coast for a day of rest, "a day by the Mediterranean" was how we billed it. The thought of the sea took all the sting out of fighting traffic and our anxieties as we left Rome.

Entering the Amalfi Drive at dusk put sport back into the car. The narrow road to the city of Amalfi hugged the sea as it wound in hairpin curves; the drive was not only complicated by sharp twists and turns, but daredevil motorcyclists and buses that came rumbling around the curves, taking up more than their half of the road. Behind the wheel, Dom became a new kind of hero to the boys.

Contented not to be driving, I enjoyed a wondrous view of the sea by moonlight. I saw houses clinging to the cliffs with the tenacity of century-old vines. Cascading flowers and shrubs spilled down the mountainsides to the blue sea. The glimmer of the distant moon and the light of the villages

sparkled and reflected in that same sea. The cracks and crumblings of the ancient homes, so gaudy from the outskirts of Rome, were now barely visible in the waning light. The panorama was sultry and exotic. In the distance we saw Amalfi.

With a worn "Five Dollars a Day" book on the dashboard, we entered the city limits. The recommended pensions were full, but the book still served us. An innkeeper, recognizing the bible of budget travel for Americans at the time, offered to match the deal.

"You got five-dollar-a-day book," he murmured, rubbing his chin. "We got five-dollar-a-day place. My cousin's . . . ." He led us to his cousin's house, a rundown apartment on a darkened side street. With the help of the moon, we could see we were a few meters from the sea. The inside was less appealing. We took the rooms, dour as they were, glad to be out of the car for the night.

By morning, the smells and sound of the sea poured through the narrow slits in the old building. In spite of the exhausting night's drive, everyone was easily awakened. Light poured through the door, a brilliant almost blinding light, obliterating the garish colors within the apartment. Opening the shutters, we realized that we were situated on a steep hill midway between the top of the cliff and the sea.

Amalfi is a beach town with flowers growing in the sand, and houses painted pink and worn by the sea air. When we saw it, its little markets were open to the air, and the fish were already in the stalls as the streets were being washed down by shop owners.

There was an easy air about life in Amalfi, and our tired little group began to enter the fun. We realized in the morning light that the buildings were frayed and worn. But amid clusters of overhanging bougainvillaea, cascading down into the Mediterranean, everything seemed brighter. We glanced behind us as we walked to the beach and eyed the striped facade of the cathedral in the center of this hillside town. Its ceramic bell tower, we were told, was built by the Normans.

The amazing structure, intact since the 11th-century, fascinated me, but the boys could see only the Mediterranean. We found a spot along the public beach, quiet on that April day. We realized that we were early even for the locals who picnicked there. Our boys doffed their shoes and let the fine grains of sand sift between their toes and then ran uninhibitedly toward the sea. Even fifteen-month-old Thomas got into the act. He half crawled and half ran in the soft, gritty substance, tasting a little here and there. Zipping into winter coats to cross the Alps seemed epochs behind as they yelped and pranced, touching the Mediterranean and splashing each other in the warm morning sun.

I spread out a blanket, content to gaze at sea and sand. Across the water was Capri; down the way was Positano. But we were in the earthy heart of the bay. It was peaceful in early April. Even the gulls were finding their space in the air stream far enough away to lend only the circle of their activity to the tranquility of the seaside. I remember thinking, *the children are at last free to run. They glide, about, almost as effortlessly as the birds overhead. They need the freedom as we do. I am glad they are our excuse to rest.*

We put down the guidebooks, trusting nature and our intuition for the day's agenda. Even at lunch no one wanted to budge from our idyllic spot. I opted to stay with the children, while my husband went out to purchase our lunch from the market.

Spiced prosciutto and sardines caught his eye, and he returned with a feast wrapped in white paper. Vine-ripened sweet tomatoes doused in the oil of olives from the nearby ancient groves was balanced with the sweet fruits of the south, pecorina cheese, and freshly baked crusty bread. We spread out the bounty and dined with the Bay of Sorrento in the distant horizon.

It had been an intense week of touring, a saturation of art and history. The day was balm to our tired bodies, our souls.

After lunch my husband leaned back on the blanket, keeping his eye on the boys prancing around like little pups. "Take a break," he suggested. "There are just a few lire left from lunch, maybe you can barter for some souvenirs."

"I'll take Thomas," I said, scooping him into my arms, deciding he would rather stroll with me. While the other children continued to play with their father in the sand, I discovered that in an Italian marketplace, bartering is easy with a baby in your arms. Thomas beguiled the shopkeeper and I walked away with a hand-panted pitcher, its green and pink flowers destined to be a happy reminder of the seaside city and its ceramic bell tower.

"It could have been a day just like today," I heard my husband say, as I returned, the pitcher stowed safely in the wagon. He was pointing to the smoke issuing from the mountain in the distance. The children were all around him on the blanket. There eyes darted back and forth from the mountains to the bay. Volcanoes hold a fascination that is seductive to any age, I realized. This was a cue for drama, I realized.

"Yes," I chimed in, "and children probably were playing on the beach with their hoops." With the profile of Vesuvius in the distance, the audience was captive to history and the infamous erupting volcano. "Until it grew dark, darker than night in the middle of day."

"Vesuvius spewed its lava all over the city of Pompeii over there," Dom continued, not missing a beat, "sealing it for 18 centuries, like wax over an anthill." He continued, "When it was excavated, they found a woman with a vase in her hands, a man with his coins. They must have been terrified. I am sure they thought it was the end of the world, and for them, it was."

Picking up on the human side, I added, "People came from Rome to Pompeii for a rest, like we are visiting Amalfi. Pompeii was a lively city. The mountains look rather harmless, don't they, boys? They did then, too. The people living on the slopes of Vesuvius had no way of knowing that there might be fire far beneath their homes. They had no way of suspecting that their mountain, peaceful for 300 years, would explode. That is, until it grew strangely dark in the middle of day."

We had a captive audience now, everyone close on the blanket, sitting comfortably in squats or poised with face cupped in hands. So, I pulled out a more accurate account than either Dom or I could conjure from memory. Pliny was one of the few historians who saw what happened and survived. Pliny's uncle, known as Pliny the Elder, was a commander for the Roman fleet. "The uncle lived across the bay in Misenum," I pointed.

According to this book, the young Pliny said that his uncle regarded the large clouds that burst out of Vesuvius as a novelty. As an officer, he ordered a ship to take him to the site to investigate the phenomenon. That was the fatal curious step for him. Pliny the Elder died in the eruption. But Pliny the Younger wrote exactly what he saw in chilling details.

"About 1 p.m. on the afternoon of August 24, 79 A.D., Vesuvius roared like a monstrous cannon. Dawn broke on the morning of August 25, yet Pliny found this day blacker and denser than any night. Wild waves made it impossible to escape by sea. Pliny the younger, 32 kilometers away from Vesuvius, saw a fearful black cloud filled with quivering bursts of flame, moving across the bay. Eventually the cloud lifted and the younger Pliny saw everything had changed, buried deep in ashes like snow drifts."

"Mr. Kay told me we could still get ash from the mountain," Mike said excitedly. "Could we, Dad? Could we? Could we?"

Dom looked at me and I returned the glance above their heads with a grin. What gluttons we were when it came to history. This was to be our day of rest. We were all enjoying the holiday spirit, picnicking, playing in the sand, shopping for crafts and relaxing. These children had had enough of museums and regimented tour guides. On the other hand, we were about 50 miles from Pompeii. We could be there in an hour and then on to the South. Todd groaned. He and Dominic were enjoying the sand.

"Why don't we just walk around by ourselves? We could see just how people lived 2,000 years ago, maybe play in their back gardens and have a picnic tonight somewhere along the way," said Dom.

Before making a conscious decision, we gathered the bread from our lunch, wrapped it carefully for the evening picnic, and headed to the car. I caught Phil and Mike darting glances at the brooding mountain in the distance.

Like most tourists, we entered the city through the old sea gate and headed for the forum, where carefree Italians continued to picnic in the ancient coliseum. I wondered if what the ash and pumice had protected for almost 2,000 years would soon be polluted by 20th-century revelers.

Pompeii had been a prosperous town; trade was good. In her prime, the population ranged from 10,000 to 20,000, and a babble of languages from German to Hebrew had mingled in her forum. They still did. We caught sight of bilingual tour groups, listened to a word or two as we passed, but did not join in any lectures. It was our day of fun. The streets were full of people as they might have been in 79 A.D., and the homes were without a doubt the most interesting focal point to us. The atriums, the back gardens, the courtyards, the faded mosaics; we absorbed them all.

On one street front we saw what looked like a sink or basin outside the main door of a residence. We were told it was a bar. This was a fun city, a thriving, trading mini-Vegas. We were given one of those rare journeys of a thousand years, a personal peek into life in ancient Pompeii.

The countryside at the foothills of Vesuvius were made fertile by the spill of the volcanic residue. Umbrella pines lined the road. The landscape of green, rich, rolling land beside the cement autostrada was beautiful. With one last surge of experimentation, we headed the blue Cortina up the

side of Vesuvius itself, winding around the road and enjoying the view from the top. About halfway down the volcano, we stopped for a peaceful evening meal. Mike got his ash to take back to school. Simple clouds hovered. No terror or earth-shaking action paled our place of scenic splendor that April day, only the faint smell of burning brakes as smoke drifted from under the car hood.

## Southern Italy

Smoke continued to issue from the hood as we re-entered the autostrada, heading south. In 1969, the roads below Rome were not heavily traveled. As dusk came on, we felt we were leaving the civilized world. For the first time in our travels, we began to question our ability to solve the normal problems that one faces traveling with children. What if this smoke amounted to a serious problem with the car? Would we manage in some isolated village? I was running out of disposable diapers. Would they even know of them in the south? How would we improvise with a poor command of the language? Even with a meager command of classical Italian, there were dialectal differences in isolated areas, we had been told.

The plunge into the South at dusk seemed risky. What did we expect to learn from this much-maligned distant cousin of northern Italy, anyway? What can one see in a land aban-

doned by its own people? Would we have a better understanding of the Italian personality or of ourselves? What did it
matter? Again, I asked myself *"Why does man even want to
return to the land from which his seed descended?"*

"You know, we are just 500 miles from the villages we
might have lived in and died in," Dom was saying out loud.
His touch with the south was one generation closer than mine.
It was as if he would be insulting his parents by not going.
"But we have seen Italy at its best," I thought. With all of the
references to the mafia, superstitions, and the cultural numb-
ing of third world life, I began to worry again about the dis-
appointments we might feel by going farther into the south.

Our banter became crucial. Both of us were intensely curious. Both of us were looking at the situation pragmatically. We
had with us five very young children. Were we being irre-
sponsible, taking undue risks with them, heading south? We
included the boys in the discussion.

"This part of the trip could be tough, boys. We don't have
recommended places to stay, and tourists are not common,
may not even be welcome. In some areas, the houses will have
chickens living with the people on dirt floors, and no plumb-
ing."

None of this seemed too bad to little boys. "What are you
afraid of?"

We pulled over to a rest stop; my husband lifted the hood
of the car. The smoke had ceased; he couldn't see any real
problems. The children were quiet, snug in their niches.

"Which way, folks? We could go north, visit Siena or
Milan or we can go south."

It was unanimous. We headed south.

After making the group decision, we decided it might be
wise to have the engine checked by a mechanic. The towns
were sparse, untrampled by tourism, or for that matter, local
traffic. The Autostrada de Sol was already a little eerie. We
finally found a garage in a drab little town in the middle of
nowhere. According to the mechanic, we were at the border of
Calabria. One of Dom's roles as a child had been to translate
the newspaper to his Sicilian grandfather, and now he pulled

from memory what phrases he could remember. His confidence grew as the words tumbled out. Although a Sicilian, he was sure he could improvise in the south. The boys were impressed. They had never heard him speak this language.

The local mechanic was not impressed by Dom's innovative spirit. Neither of them could explain to the other the common term for "burning out brakes." The mechanic was tired, annoyed, and as he put it, "Stuck with a man who might be speaking Japanese for all I know!" Dom had no trouble understanding that remark. He came over to the window to relate the story to us. We all laughed, and the local village people who had gathered around the hood laughed, too. While the mechanic ranted and waved, the crowd gave their support to the disgruntled impresario. The brakes were checked, found to be safe, and we were much obliged.

It was by that time pitch-dark, and we all felt the weight of our decision. It had been a long day. We were ready to stop. The mechanic pointed to the only hotel in town. One look at the building assured me this was no charming albergo. The front was drab, the lights dim. But we were in no mood to continue in the dark. We had just left the masterpieces of the Renaissance, a voluptuous coast in Amalfi, but this hotel spoke of a crumbling civilization.

Weary and worn, we grabbed our bags and headed down a hall to our room, glad to be out of the car. One naked bulb dangled from the ceiling of our room, a straight-backed, beaten chair, and a small table were at one end and two iron beds lined the other wall. Underneath, a cracked linoleum covered the floor. The richness of the inlaid mosaics in the homes of Pompeii was a world apart from this place. All that invited us into the chilly room were crisp, clean sheets. The beds were firm and comfortable. We put four boys together and took Thomas in our bed before we turned the little black switch at the neck of the bulb.

I lay in bed that night uncomfortable about our decision. What could we hope to gain from this isolated, barren land? A million little associations with a culture that was both beautiful and banal were surfacing within me. Images of visits as a child to the Little Italies of my grandparents were floating in and out of the room; the simplicity of the linoleum, the same chairs against the walls, all seemed remotely familiar.

But where was the laughter, the smell of bubbling sauce on the stove, the people who would open the door wide to anyone and love and hug and eat with such confidence and gusto that you knew they had the secret to life's greatest joys?

There were no relatives to meet me in Calabria, no one that night but a disinterested innkeeper. He seemed joyless, and his inn was devoid of beauty.

I must have tossed and turned half of the night, for when a pink streak of morning came through the window, I was still tired. The children had no such uneasiness. They had slept soundly. I was so anxious to get out of that hotel that I roused the group and headed down the hall to the toilet. There was a rusty latch, which I secured immediately, closing out the light of the hall. With the click of the latch, my eyes were drawn toward the crack of light in a small window. Peering straight at me were the beady eyes of a rooster. He flapped his wings, I jumped, and we parted company as quickly as I could get the latch open. My nerves now jagged and my privacy invaded, I acquired a new resolve. "We can admit this mistake and turn back to Rome if things get worse."

We drove silently into Calabria, choosing an inland route, a road not commonly used by tourists. Even local traffic was sparse. "We are in Calabria," I said to myself, quietly, "where my family comes from." My paternal grandparents were from the mountains, my maternal grandmother from nearer to the coast. We headed down the center, planning to touch what we could. Every mile, every scene was forever etched on my mind from that moment on.

There were remnants of the great civilizations, come and gone. Past Pompeii, we had seen the signs to Paestum, where the Greek temples of Magna Greca were reputed to be beautifully preserved. But there was no time to stop at each known site of history. The remnants of other cultures that have touched this Provence were now scattered, a column, a shell of a castle on the hill, here and there a few crumbling stones at the edge of a precipice, and a deserted shell of a building out in a field. We tried to put together the history ourselves. The villages were scattered along the hills like pebbles thrown against the incline and caught.

The remnants of buildings closer to the road lacked architectural interest. Wet clothes drying in the early morning sun stretched everywhere. The morning sun cascaded down upon the children bouncing their balls into the road and the fruit stands heavily laden, but without much business right then.

Along the side of the road, people lugged their carts. They moved slowly and automatically out of the way as we passed, as their ancestors had through the centuries, out of the way of the conquerors.

Near the sea, the towns seemed to be doing a little better. Little fishing marinas were scattered at the sea's edge. Unlike the well-developed, lush towns around Amalfi, these tiny villages were quiet, untouched by billboards and Cizano umbrellas. We drove in and out of new stretches of autostrada, where the little villages hugged the sea. Their names read like a litany of charming people, Pre Maria ... Paulo ... San Giovanni.

In places, the mountains dropped boldly down to the sea. The bay of Naples had seemed lively, lush, even gaudy in comparison to this stretch of land and sea. This coastal drive was sparse and peaceful. As I gazed at the sight of the Mediterranean in the morning silence, I began to unwind. I realized it was one of the most extraordinary sights I had ever seen. No one could have passed this fresh, untouched coast without a sense of its eternal solace. The blue of the sea was hypnotic at the edge of the rocks, the sea-washed sand and the striking light that permeated the coast had broken my tired,

glum mood. I looked in silent wonder at the mountains and rocky promontories jutting into the sea.

Wildflowers edged the rocks and the sun bounced off the water, making the morning light almost ethereal. The scene was so intense, so absorbing, I almost missed the sign, the sign that stopped us all. As my family put it, it was the sign that put a smile firmly on my face. In bold letters I saw "Marina of Fuscaldo." None of us had noticed it on the map, reading in the dusk the night before. Fuscaldo was my maiden name, the name of my paternal grandparents.

"I thought your grandparents, Fuscaldo, came from the mountains," my husband quizzed me. "Aren't they from San Giovanni in the Sila mountains?"

I took the crumpled note from my wallet. "Yes, I am sure that's true. Maternal grandmother—Nicostra, paternal grandparents—San Giovanni in the Sila Forest. But here it is. Fuscaldo."

We quickly pulled out the Italian blue book. No mention of a marina, but a short description of Fuscaldo: *Ancient noble city*. The city was nestled on the hill, the new little marina by the sea struggling to open businesses.

My family was at some point in history "of Fuscaldo," from Fuscaldo, I conjectured. Now I was intrigued with the mystery, a mystery that could be savored, knowing that my seed had been in this soil at some time in history. Something awakened in me. My senses become involved and I began to observe the terrain in even greater detail. The modern and ancient parts of the city were divided only by the autostrada. We stopped for some ice cream and talked briefly to the shopkeepers. Tourism had become their recent hope. The modern marina, a newer appendage, was defending its fishing industry, and a new Jolly Hotel was in the proposal stages for seaside accommodations.

It occurred to me that I might be able to locate some disposable diapers in this town on its way to modernization. Armed with one of my last English nappies and a few newly learned Italian phrases, I found the local pharmacist. No trouble with the magic word, "bambino." We were relaxed, comforted by ice cream, nappies, a city with my name and the Mediterranean beside us.

We continued to follow the coastal road for a while, and another familial association, another part of the search unfolded. Nicostra, 10 kilometers, the sign read. Nicostra, a word once so distant was the city of my grandmother's birth. We turned inward. The dusty road was lined with olive groves, anciently cultivated, yet still producing. Goats were herded across the bridge ahead.

The medieval town with its baroque churches and yellow stucco city square was still dressed for Easter. Lights were strung across the narrow streets. There was a newly built department store and some modern low-slung apartments. But many of the facades of the older buildings had been repainted to replace missing plaster or iron trim. A Norman arch here, some masonry there, the resources, all pale substitutes, only hint to their past beauty. There was festivity in the air. Banners, meant to imitate the rich tapestries of the middle ages, gave an air of celebration.

In my mind, I was swept back to my childhood, walking hand in hand with my grandmother to the little courtyard of the Italian church in her neighborhood. The feast of St. John the Baptist called forth banners like these, swagging from the windows and the stands. I had loved the feel of it, the sound of the accordion, the smell of the roasted peppers and fresh bread, the excitement of fresh flowers strewn as the statue of John the Baptist passed by. Carried on the shoulders of two of the eldest parishioners, the patron saint was the focal point of the annual procession.

I was a child of five years when my grandmother first took me to the splendor of the celebration. And my doting grandfather had bought me a popsicle as we entered the grounds. I could remember it so clearly, my grandmother reaching down gently and pointing across the crowd. "Break your popsicle in two, there is a little girl watching you. You must never eat in front of anyone who is hungry. God will not be happy with you."

"When there is but one loaf, you must split it." She had done so, many times in those difficult early years in America.

She smiled as I shared the popsicle. And as if the nobility of good manners were not enough, she rewarded me when we reached her porch at the end of the day. "You see this comb?" Lifting the comb from the gray black bun in the back, she let her twisted hair fall to her shoulders. "I wore it when I was a young woman in Nicostra, and my hair was shiny. On St. John's Day, we danced in the streets. You have it," she offered. "It will hold your hair back when you dance."

We drove around Nicostra, wondering which of the seven churches had been hers, and in which of the courtyards she had swirled with her shiny black hair.

From Nicostra to the tip of the boot, we passed through the varied terrain of Italy. There were no great art cities, but the treasures, the relics of a tumultuous history were scattered along the way in this stretch of coast.

The ancient road that we were touching had been used for six centuries by the Greeks. In the colonies of Greece, Pythagoras had codified mathematics, Zaleus had worked with law, and Homer had written some of his greatest poetry. In its Golden Age, Calabria, Bascilacata, and Sicily were the glories of Magna Greca. The cities lining this coast had hidden treasures scattered along and under its soil and sea.

When Greater Greece fell, the road was rebuilt by the conquering Romans, but later barbarians under Alaric used it when Rome fell. This route had opened the multi-colored grandeur of the fertile land to one conqueror after another. Here ideas had been born, seeds planted, but the drained and dry area had failed her people in later centuries, forcing them to send seed to more favorable climates. My grandparents were in that exodus.

Not more than a hundred kilometers beyond Nicostra, we began to feel the crystalline air of the mountains. As we drove along the ancient road, the trees were cool and full, the ground fuzzy with its new spring growth. The pattern of the pines changed with wildflowers underneath, making the scene lighter.

At one breathtaking turn we caught sight of a young, tawny-skinned Calabrian woman who wore the black velour skirt and bodice native to the region. On her head, balanced perfectly, was a pot of oil. Behind her was a burro laden with twigs, no doubt scraps from the chestnut forest. The sun caught her in a sharp beam through the trees, and the picture clicked immortally in my mind.

The forests of the Sila, where my paternal grandparents had lived, were also intriguing and I really wanted to see it all, but we decided the Sila would have to wait until another journey. We continued to follow the coastal road to the tip of Italy's boot, stopping only in Reggio, where in its small museum we saw an amazing collection of remnants from Greek life in the province.

The museum condensed the history of the Provence, a history that my grandparents had not shared with us, a history of the Provence from pre-historic times through the Greek, Roman, Norman, and Swabian cultures, through deforestation and drought, through war and feudalism that had drained the coast, sending its people elsewhere for their livelihoods.

There were signs of reawakening of the coast to tourism. I was not sure this would serve the people. Would this be one more exploitation of the coast, I wondered. I hated to see the beginning of what would soon change the quiet beauty of this whole, glorious coast.

The drive along the Autostrada del Sol from Sorrento to the rock of Scilla at the tip, where we could look across to Sicily, had been a revelation. A curly-headed boy directed us to the castle perched on the rock, where I could gaze at the sea and imagine the grist of the Iliad, where boiling waters could lie in wait at the crossing. I looked back with a ripeness of history. We stared across the straits with the spirit of Hercules, ready to cross.

I had not come looking for a coat of arms, even the family tree, only the soil of my ancestors. I found the stilled history and the beauty of a rich culture. There rested in my soul a completeness that I had not anticipated.

# Sicily

The ferry across the Straits of Messina from Calabria to Sicily was a relaxing break after the long coastal drive. The children had been troupers, not in the least affected by our adventurous scheme nor our frugal methods of travel. They trusted us implicitly, complaining only when we pushed too far or restrained them in confined halls. Along the coast we continued to picnic by the sea, letting them run in the sand and stop for ice cream or a stretch.

I was beginning to relax. The tensions of facing the mysteries of the south were diminished. The coast of Calabria was an enlightening surprise. My notions of the terrain and village life were blind concepts. Neither the tour books nor my family had prepared me for what was there. Our introduction to Sicily was more graphic, as my husband's family attachment was more recent. Both of his parents were born in a village near Agregento. His father had lived in that same village until he was 16. There would be relatives to meet us.

And so we landed in Sicily. We came not as the invaders of centuries ago, but with directions to a village in the southeast, a village bearing the name of the Prince of Aragon.

Until 1860, when Gherbaldi marched into Sicily claiming it for the Italians, Sicily was bounced around and used by the

Greeks, Romans, Byzantines, Arabs, Normans, Frederick the Second and the House of Anjou. Thus, it had become a melting pot of cultures and had organized its homespun form of defense, the mafia. Established originally to protect peasants from overbearing conquerors—a defense for the defenseless—the mafia grew powerful and corrupt. Its counterpart in America remained a source of embarrassment to both Old and New World Italians.

The city of Aragona was a reality to my husband. His father had described it well. When Dom's father was eight years old, his parents sailed for America, but an eye infection caused customs officials to revoke his health certificate, and he was left behind. Staying with a cousin for eight years, Dom's father earned his keep by sweeping the floor of a barber shop. At eleven, he became an apprentice and was a barber when he finally landed at Ellis Island. His tales of the poverty in the village were matched with tales of the grandeur of the Palace of Principality and the magnificent city square that had kept the tone of the Spanish occupation of Sicily.

Dom's father had never returned to Sicily. We would be met by his cousins, the first contact with the family from America in 50 years. As we neared the village, I asked Dom to pull over so I could clean up the children. "No, that won't be necessary. We don't want to go in as rich Americans." He even rumpled his hair deliberately. "There may be chickens and

pigs in the house. Don't comment, boys. It may be different from anything you've seen. We'll dress up when we go to the Palace. Grandpa used to love to stand and look at it."

The village, a cluster of simple stone houses nestled together under a clear blue sky, was now graced with laundromats and shops, TV antennas, and a few automobiles. We drove through cautiously. There were animals crossing the narrow streets. We had the address of a butcher shop, but Dom was more intent to find the barber shop where his father had apprenticed.

Following directions, we finally arrived at his cousin's butcher shop. Letters had passed, and we were "Family," the all-important word in Italy. The distant relative was quick to show us the interior of the family business, which had been modernized with refrigeration. He then graciously led us upstairs to his roomy apartment where we were introduced to his rather retiring wife and their lively young daughter.

Dom was attempting to speak his best Sicilian. We will never know what was lost in the 50-year transition, but they loved him for trying. I could feel the bond of blood that would easily overlook any shortcomings. Unable to understand a word, I silently observed my surroundings and the people. Perhaps my senses became even keener in the situation. My boys, also silent, were glancing surprisedly at the marble floors, wondering where the chickens were. The dichotomy of the Italian family in transition was noticeable. TV and the mini skirt had arrived, but not inside this apartment.

We were brought basins of water to wash and then served our evening meal, each of us grinning across the table when words were not discernable. Afterward, we visited another distant relative, and my husband whispered to me, "He says I should comb my hair." I smiled.

To each relative I was introduced as "Rosalie, the young, lovely mother, so blessed with five sons." A son-in-law to be, who was planning to take his bride to England soon after their wedding, spoke excellent English and became my friend and translator. As Dom tried to connect sites with tales and to re-establish names that his parents had told him to touch, I probed the young Sicilian for history and information, ancient and present. Thus, I was not left out as might befall a wife in Sicily.

The grand tour of the village was led by the senior male cousin with others indicating notable points of interest. Goats and chickens crossed with an air of owning the street, dodging small cars which were a recent part of the city traffic. Seven little churches took care of the population of Aragonese. The churches were still dressed in Easter pageantry, tiny lights adorned a church yard, and papier-mâché statues of St. Peter and St. Paul, the patrons of the city, were perched along the aisles of two prominent baroque chapels.

With the help of my translator, I envisioned the recent parade, reminiscent of the parades of Seville. Peter and Paul were recreated to lead the parade. On Good Friday, a statue of the Dolorous virgin, tears visible, was carried on the shoulders of penitents behind Peter and Paul. On Easter Sunday, a risen Christ was taken from the Church of the Resurrection and paraded triumphantly through the streets. The final parade ended in the city square, where the entire village gathered as we had at St. Peters in Rome.

We wound around the village following the parade route, ending our tour in the city square with great anticipation. The civil buildings which had been built under the Spanish domain were the most magnificent memories of my father-in-law. I noticed the startled look on Dom's face as we approached the diminutive buildings. They were simple by any standards except his father's, whose memories had been formed in a child's mind of limited measures.

Almost as an afterthought, our guide pointed to the hill beyond his village and mentioned the temples that the Greeks built were there in Agregento. His son-in-law would be our guide if we wished to see them on our way out. We ate the traditional Easter dish, a ring mold of pasta, broth, and eggs baked in a cake-like mold. The congealed Tiano seemed to represent the melting pot of cultures that had touched, ruled, and plundered the strategic island. The saffron spoke of Spain's influence, the cinnamon was an Arabic reminder, and the pasta and eggs suggested eternal life.

The next morning was insatiably beautiful as we drove toward Agregento, where we would visit the Valley of the

Temples and see the influence of the ancient Greeks. The colonization was well documented. The Greeks had ruled over Sicily and southern Italy for eight centuries, leaving behind some of the finest examples of their civilization, many with finer settings than in Greece.

For an island which becomes parched in mid-summer, no indications of this future doom were apparent. It was Sicily's glorious season. The rich tints of Italian heaven bathed the scene in bright, sharp tones. The English-speaking son-in-law was eager to lead us to the summit of Agregento.

We followed cautiously behind him weaving through seven miles of countryside, seeing in the distance villages clustered on the hillsides. "The city of Agregento is now a bustling town of 30,000," our unofficial guide offered as he pointed to the buzzing city. The new city was of little interest once we saw in the distance the Valley of the Temples. The Temple of Concordia stood high on the hill facing the modern city. As we stood in awe before the Greek temple, he pointed to where the fallen stones of the temples of Juno, Hercules, Jupiter and the Tomb of Tero, tyrant of Agregento, made up the valley. We expressed our gratitude and waved goodbye, then turned to meander through the ancient ruins alone. Almond, mimosa and olive trees were all in bloom, creating a garden of sweet fragrances.

In the midst of the elegant, massive structures, I tried to open myself to the antiquity of our surroundings. I stood before the evidence of a culture that wound back almost 3,000 years. The remnants of that ancient civilization made everything else we had seen seem like recent history. The site was not a busy tourist center as I was sure the Parthenon in Athens would be. In fact, we were alone in our visit to this ancient world. The boys wandered in and out of the columns in their usual adventurous spirit. They stumbled over stone mummies in the spring grass and shouted for us to admire their discoveries. There were over 100 monuments and temples. Alone, in the silence of centuries, I relished the experience. We were transfixed as we left the cream-colored Doric columns, bathed in warm sun and the  fragrant scents of the Sicilian spring.

The ancient culture continued to speak to us with the powerful impact of the Greeks who had created it. And voices of other cultures—Roman, Byzantine, Arab, Norman—silently told their stories as we crossed the island to the Arab-Norman city of Palermo. Rolling pastoral landscapes decorated with wildflowers and cities nestled in the hills dotted the route from Palermo back to Messina. Palms, red and white chrysanthemums, and orange groves made it a verdant garden. It was a spring paradise of color and light.

On our last evening, passing through a very small village near the beautifully laid out metropolis of Cantania, we looked for an inexpensive accommodation. By now my husband had begun to think that he had gained full command of his early childhood Sicilian. Convinced that he could fool the natives, he wanted to try to bargain as a native for a better price than an American tourist would get. He parked the car a little distance from the hotel and wandered alone into the lobby. He returned to the car with a grin on his face. "I rumpled my hair, spoke only in Italian, and tried to get him to lower the rate," he recounted. "Back and forth we bantered until, frustrated, he called his manager on the phone, saying, 'Antonio, un Americano...' and I knew I hadn't fooled anyone."

While he was gone, I observed men wandering—young men, old men, men in groups. They wore black arm bands. Is it a meeting of the local mafia they are headed for, I wondered. Finally we stopped a passerby.

"Where are the women in this city?"

"The women?" the cynical Sicilian answered. "They are all home in bed."

The Italians, never quite able to come to grips with any change in the order of their private beliefs and customs, were watching the world change on TV, but the women were "protected" at home. I remembered Berzini, who wrote openly about his people: "Believe not in the government or invaders; lie and placate and believe only in the family. They alone you can trust. Protect the women against plunder; the family is the core of life."

Our family was intact and safe, snuggled in our little blue

Cortina as we left Sicily. We gazed back with misty eyes. Dom had tales of his own to take home. A part of his life had been resurrected. His past belonged to reality. His pilgrimage was complete. It was the almond blossoms and the mimosa, the blue sky and the light of centuries that we saw as we left.

# It's Your Turn, Chickadees

# Chapter 4

# Solace By The Sea

*"No man will unfold the capacities of his own intellect who does not at least checker his life with solitude."*

—de Quincey

Climbing among the rocks, I could glimpse the Irish Sea. For one brief moment there was silence. It was solitude, space for reflection and the vistas of the sea that we craved on our last weekend in the British Isles. Except for the whisper of the wind, I stood motionless, wholly removed from the world. Far away from the sound of the city, the blare of great castles and ruins and prosperous principalities of Europe, I waited with my family at the edge of Wales, ready to cross to Ireland.

The year of study in England had been full. By this last bank holiday, I was saturated with the art and history of the world. What I craved was silence and some space, some quiet time to integrate it all. A weekend in Ireland sounded right for such a break.

My hopes for solitude were shaken as we boarded the ferry at Holyhead. A rowdy group of Irish school boys returning from a tour of England was running about the deck, making our little group look tame by comparison. Well into the night they romped and wailed, weaving in and out among the passengers. Their schoolmaster's warnings never seemed to register above the shrieks, cries and shouts of the boys.

The silence the next morning was all the more striking as we entered the car again. Following the Ring of Kerry on the western tip of Ireland, we had hopes of touching the sea at its outer edges. Not far from the port where we had bedded, the mist began to lift. The day was gentle, and the Wicklow Mountains soon unfolded a hundred still-life portraits as we drove into the countryside. The children were unusually quiet, as if the rolling hills were lulling them into a subdued state. It was a day of contemplation and lazy, gentle exploration.

Our drive took us first through country rich with thick pockets of yellow gorse. On hills dotted with little white cottages and stone fences we saw every shade of green—kelly, emerald, hunter—and when dotted with sod, drystone and slate, a veritable patchwork quilt in the distance.

The lay of the land put us to rest, and the process of emptying our busy lives began. Twilight plunged us into a deeper silence near the sea. The sparseness of trees and occasional rocks spoke of a less fertile part of Ireland. Narrow roads wound up and down the gentle hills. A single goat passed at one turn and then, at another, an old farmer crossed with his cart. In the distance, mountains were capped by the mist. Everyone in our car was still as we watched the distant sea come into focus. Its powerful beauty ahead muted the earth around. It was dark and bare and elemental.

As we came to the end of our first day in Ireland, with barely enough light to see the horizon, solitude took hold, playing out the scene with its captivating magnitude.

When the sun arose on another day in Ireland, we re-entered our little blue Cortina with a new sense of openness. The simple cottages by the sea, sparse and white, suggested a slower pace of life.

Carried by the wind, the gulls overhead seemed to follow a pattern in a stream, and we, too, let our spirits be carried into a stream that regulated our speed and direction. Off in the distance as we drove farther from the sea, we could see hamlets and glens, small houses built from the natural stones that surrounded them and crags that jutted out into the sea. The brilliance of a blue sky was interrupted with clouds that emptied gentle rains from time to time. The land around was all quiet.

We slept well that night, snug in a solid B&B. In the homey atmosphere we felt a certain peace, though fog still shrouded the drive in the morning. It was with a sense of intrigue we stopped at a small glen, where the Celtic crosses marked the lives of monks who lived there in the sixth century. So quiet was the land that when the hum of the car ceased, we could hear only the rippling of the brook that cut through the center of the glen. I sat on a rock that morning basking in the warmth of the sun. Bright flowers mingled with the ancient Celtic crosses, completing a mystical aura.

As I watched the children play among the rocks in the water, the soft tones of filtered sunlight played games with the ripples. A sunbeam darted here and there, occasionally sending a sparkle back to us. Gently and slowly I was taken into the otherworldliness of the land, and I really didn't see the old man slip up beside me as I sat on the rock, mesmerized by the darting light.

"The water stills you, doesn't it?" I heard him say. "It doesn't change. Ireland doesn't change. Kevin the monk came here to be stilled in the sixth century. You have to be quiet, open, emptied out to find yourself. In the stillness of the wind, gently blowing it will come. Inspiration is that way."

Inspiration had come. It had been there as we walked in the footsteps of the great poets. It had been behind and beside us when we viewed the art of the Renaissance. It was in the spirit of the ruins and the wonders of Western civilization that we had visited. Like the Grand Tourists, my husband and I had capped our education. Now in the quiet of Ireland by the sea, there were insights coming from a rich experience. An understanding of history was taking shape in a new step-by-step sequence. Human beings from each culture had touched us. In a full sense, we were now open to the world, and the world was now opened to our children.

In a personal sense, our own history was complete. We had touched the soil of our ancestors. Even if we were to be clueless about our future at that moment, we knew where we had come from. We were full with the ripeness of our past and the beauties of the cultures that had made us what we were; it was almost overwhelming. We had seen so much in so short a time that the sea was a balm to our fullness. It gave us space and time to absorb the amazing revelations of our journeys.

Perhaps the last little trip at the end of May was what prompted us to return to America by sea. It would have seemed almost too abrupt a jump to return to the world we had left a year ago in one short flight, in one short night. And, we reasoned, we had a year's luggage and accumulations to send home, so we purchased tickets on the cheapest ocean liner between America and England at the time, assured also that our trunks would go with us free.

As fate would have it, the Queen Elizabeth II was being built that year, and somewhere within our planning it occurred to us that a berth on the very bottom of this new luxury liner might be the same as a higher one on the Holland Line. It was. With a twinkle in his eye, my husband set out one night with new resolve. He returned with tickets on the lowest berth of the new ship built to perpetuate the old tradition of Britain's best. We sold our faithful Cortina and headed to South Hampton. With the time on board, we would contemplate and prepare ourselves for the realities of work and life ahead in America.

Walking up the gangplank seemed part of a fantasy. We were returning to America in English tradition, slowly, and civilly, as the British would have preferred. We had changed. We were now dressed as the British dressed. I had shortened my skirts as the mod world of Liverpool had introduced. The boys had short pants and English sandals, our last purchase at the local Marks and Spencers.

Underneath us in the hull of the boat were the artistic acquisitions and mementos of a year—a watercolor of the

English lakes, little demitasse cups—though only seconds, they were proper bone china cups with little roses—found on my weekly escapes to Liverpool. There was a Wedgwood vase, some brass candlesticks, and a carousel of slides reminding us of the landscapes and architecture we had grown to love.

In Phil's satchel were sketches, as an eight-year-old would see it, black and white renderings of Tower Bridge and watercolors of castles. There were Crayola versions of British soldiers, small match box cars, British red buses and lorries.

Michael had lost his teeth, acquired new ones, and was espousing British history with knowledgeable confidence. Todd, at five, was reading, and along with Renard, he carried a series of puppets and tin soldiers. Dominic's curly ringlets were longer, perhaps more like the Beatles, and he had in his pocket the favorite English candy, a tube of Smarties. Thomas was walking or waddling in long white leggings in his flat English shoes; he could have passed for an English toddler.

There were audible signs of change. The boys had acquired accents from their school year. They asked for a "bit of cheese" or a "biscuit" in a cadence that was more familiar to their friends at Thingwall Primary.

The voyage was almost a graduation. We surged forward, with due ceremony, on the decks and in the shiny new ball-

rooms. There were parties for children and movies to keep everyone duly entertained. I viewed the family with visible pride. They looked smart, finished in some ways. My husband had a sense of relief, even looked the conqueror. We had done what we had to do on a student's budget. We would not enter America in debt, and my head was filled with matters of history and art, the wonders of the world in my notes. Leafing through my journal at night in disbelief, I could hardly comprehend what we had seen and felt since we left home a year before. It seemed equivalent to a master's degree in art history.

Then things British gave way to the land across the ocean. The children were invited to watch the take-off of Apollo on satellite TV, and we were whisked into the wonders of American technological success. For a year we had been hearing about our own country from the British point of view. Now the news was coming from our presses and interpreters. The TV commentators spoke in familiar glowing terms of life in America. In spite of the Vietnam campaign, cries for women's liberation, and the racial riots in inner cities, theirs was a familiar confidence, a tone of self-sufficiency in their comments.

Midway in our journey across the Atlantic a storm stirred the waters, and many people headed to their berths, uncomfortable. Even the sleek Queen Elizabeth II could not steady the journey. I leaned over the deck as the sea swirled around us; I could see nothing but black waves. England was far from my grasp, and America was not yet in sight. The wind was increasing, and for a while the air became cold and fetid. I was not dressed for the change. I was not ready for the shift in the wind. My little family and I were between two worlds, with a black and tossing ocean all around us.

At dinner on our last night, the announcement over the loudspeaker seemed muffled at first, but slowly I began to see people leave their places. "It's the Lady," I heard a British gentlemen repeat. "We're approaching the Statue of Liberty," the urbane waiter at our table reported, almost in disdain for the rush from the room. "The Lady" was waiting in the harbor for us, the symbol of hope to thousands, the symbol of refuge to my grandparents, the symbol of home to us.

Without any hesitation, our whole family left the table, the food untouched on our plates. "The Lady" would welcome us home.

But even though "The Lady" stood there, torch held high, a once familiar world looked strange. Family had come to meet us, piling our trunks and our children in wide American cars. Driving from New York to West Virginia was a slow revelation. We had sold our little house on a university campus and would begin life in the capital city of Charleston, West Virginia. Home now was elusive.

The hospital where my husband would be seeing patients offered temporary quarters. We were put in an apartment building designed for residents and interns, a high rise on the grounds of the hospital complex. Ours would be a unit of three small rooms with asphalt tile floors, steel framed doors, and sterile walls. We took from storage bunk beds, a foldaway sofa, a table and chairs. Even with only the essentials, there was little room for five young children to move about.

I helped my husband open his office, taking out a few familiar artifacts to make it homey. Plans for schooling were difficult with only a temporary address. I found a parochial school that accepted the boys, and I began to see the complexities of transitions.

There had been five moves in our family's short life, the last to England, a complete break with permanence. I began doing the necessary purchasing of school clothes and supplies for the boys, and the apartment was already becoming overcrowded and disorganized. Some days, the exhaustion seemed to blur even my vision. This transition seemed overwhelming. While at the laundromat, as I would try to wash clothes or buy a soft drink, I would reach for a coin and wonder, do I put in a sixpence or a dime?

The school year began for the boys and the hospital work for my husband, giving part of the family some routine, but the small apartment seemed impossible to keep organized for seven people. My heart was yearning for some security at home, and my head was full of history and bits of new-found knowledge. There was no energy, no space, no time to put it to any use. The sabbatical was over, and my role reverted to caregiver only.

My husband was excited and anxious about his new practice, his time in the small apartment was limited. He reasoned that housing could come later. His plan was to begin work and, in his mind, to provide greater security for us. I could not even explain to myself that my security as a mother of a big family depended on space to think and organize, and freedom to create a nest that would give order to our lives. But the transition had played out its course, and I was slowly becoming too tired to reason.

I did realize as the three older children left for school and my husband left for his new office, that I was left to pick up the pieces and paste together a new life for everyone at home. The division of labor was clear in those years. My lot was the home and the children. I was a fierce mother in every respect of the word, but I clearly needed some stimulation beyond the daily demands of the children, and the adventure in Europe was meant to prepare me for an outlet in writing. I intended to continue at night if I wanted to make something of it. And as I stumbled through a new routine, I could not figure out how to meet the demands of seven people living in a confined area with no space or time for anything beyond survival.

The walls began to close in on me. There was no space to think. The boys were on the floors doing their homework, on the bunk beds jumping for exercise, and there was nothing but bare essentials to create any warmth. I could not write, and I could not put my stamp on the temporary quarters. The walls were sterile, the floor a tan tile, and noise bounced off the walls.

"As soon as we get on our feet, we can think of a home," my husband said encouragingly, still proud of never having created debt. In his mind, the nesting would have to wait. We had chosen travel and education. It seemed now we would have to pay the price for our choice.

But it was virtually impossible to keep the apartment organized with five boys literally climbing the walls. I tried to escape one night to my writing, getting a sitter for the boys. Concentration was becoming difficult, but my drive for some expression was real. Later when I read what I had written about England, it seemed more home than where we were. I missed the stimulation of our walks into history and the touch with a broader world.

As I was invited to welcoming coffees and PTAs, I found I was out of sync with the local problems. My interests in one year had shifted, and my new discoveries must have seemed remote to the people I met. There was no satisfying outlet for the wealth of knowledge swimming in my head.

Talking to the children at night, I found they were as lost as I was. Once more they had to adapt. The emphasis at school was no longer on reading or literature. The talk was about soccer and shoes, again. It was a whole new world once more. They soon learned, as I did, to tuck away their insights, hide their new-found interests. Adapting was a process we should have understood with five moves in ten years, but exhaustion had blurred all reasoning.

One night as the boys began arguing over who could use the table for his homework, I opened the door to the apartment and gasped for air. The night was pitch black. I went out into the night, not caring whether I could see or not; I needed space and silence. I suddenly realized as I walked alone that I didn't want to re-enter the apartment. Inside was noise and chaos.

What was the matter with me? I questioned myself. I was fortunate. I had a husband who was a doctor, five beautiful sons. What else did I need? I was confused and exhausted.

From nearby cities our families called, realizing a crisis was building, and no one seemed to understand how to avert it. Of course, everyone had opinions.

"She's tired. She needs rest," I heard. "Too many babies, too many moves, too many transitions, too Catholic, too Italian, too American, too intellectual. All those fancy ideas from Europe. She needs a home, where she can decorate, throw some pillows. He should ... she should ...."

And then one day, as fragile as Humpty Dumpty sitting on his wall, I felt I was coming apart. Like falling into quicksand, I began to sink into an abyss of nothingness. I would feel a wave of anxiety at the sight of strange artifacts on the shelf. Then it was terror at the sounds of the children in need. And finally I gave in to total despair. The boys were calling for me from every corner, and I closed my ears. Everyone wanted a part of me, and there was nothing left to give. Broken and terrified I stared into the darkness.

I remember trying to reach for a pan to make an egg. I could see the round instrument with a handle and I could see the children who needed to be fed, but my arm, my hand could not move. I was totally debilitated. I could not think, I could no longer make decisions, and I could not even cry.

"I brought this on myself," I kept thinking. We had a normal family in a normal neighborhood in our own country. I wanted adventure. Wanderlust had been the cause. Now I was not content with life as it was for other housewives. Why hadn't I left well enough alone? Adventure is for the single and the young. Education and growth, for husbands and sons. I am a mother.

A home with space was a noble start, but I was not yet free from the confusion in my mind. What was my role to be in this new life? Would the home in a suburb define my role? Was I to return to the routine of life for women of the '50s at home? I had grown to like the touch with a broader world, the stimulation of continued growth. I had liked being a student again. I had felt alive even though it meant extra work nightly, reading, learning, studying. This kind of stimulation was tapping something left dormant for a while, and the children were tapping my heart, but what was my work now? My husband and I had shared the experience of growth in Europe with the children, but at home the children's care was clearly on my shoulders.

I would soon be back to car pools and extra lessons for the boys, a home to decorate and PTA with expected community participation in the American style. Football games and the neighborhood Halloween was almost upon us. My head was reeling. Which direction do I go? There were clearly two roles to assume. Motherhood with five sons was a job; creative writing would be equally consuming if I were to continue research and completion.

And if I gave up all aspirations of outside work, and directed the growth of children, would that work alone be enough? Certainly it was physically demanding and emotionally rewarding, but what was tugging at me before we left for England would surely come back. There was something missing in that routine, as much as I loved the children. I knew I would have to deal with the monotony of daily work at home in order to nurture and oversee the needs of the five children. And many asked of me what I dared not answer: Are you going to give up all your dreams? Are you going to become sterile and only an echo of others' aspirations?

The tedious job of balancing motherhood and personhood was about to begin, and the dreams of doing both at the same time and doing both well seemed impossible. Did my work define me? What was I expected to be? Slowly I withdrew into the house and into myself, retreating into an abyss. The coping or non-coping was a stall for time, time to figure it out, and yet, I did not even understand that. I began to feel hopeless, confused, worthless.

I could not make rational decisions. I was alone, afraid, betrayed by my own dreams. I felt let down, defeated, confused, stymied. I knew I could not choose between a family I loved and work that took me from them. But to be fully alive I needed both. Men, it seemed, did not have to make this choice. I was confused, and as a woman taught to repress anger, I became instead totally functionless.

"I am a failure, a total failure," I kept telling myself. There is no hope. I'm a failure as a mother, a wife, a daughter, wanting more than is good for me. I continuously flagellated myself for my selfishness. There was no sleep. Days and nights became one long nightmare. Waiting for dawn was as horrible as waiting for the night. With dawn came the stark realities of life. I ran from them, hid from them like a scared kitten.

My husband was bewildered, confused at first, and then blatantly angry. I had always directed the home, why should it change? He found refuge in his work, and his hours at the hospital grew longer and longer. I felt totally abandoned. The world for me seemed to be way out there out of touch. Nothing would pull me back to reality except the faces of my children.

I saw them grope for life as they had known it. And I saw the luster go out of their eyes. As I withdrew, the younger ones withdrew. The change was almost a clinical experiment going on in front of me. That was the one reality that stirred me. The children were human beings who needed to be nurtured. Under all the confusion and disappointment for my own life, I was still a fierce and loving mother. I knew if I did not hold on, no one would really care about them the way I did. As for the children, they were amazingly sympathetic. You cannot deceive children. They knew under it all I dearly loved them. Now they were the thin thread that kept life in me.

One night I saw Mike, who was only eight years old, lift Thomas, an eighteen-month-old, into his bed, knowing full well Thomas was still wetting the bed and that his bed would be soaked in the morning. Philip, merely nine, struggled to teach, igniting his inventive ideas to the younger bewildered ones, creating farcical creatures at Halloween, but the spirit was one of desperation. There was no center, no direction for their tender souls.

Groping in the dark, I had no choice but to begin the toughest journey of my life. Out of desperation, I began a journey that would take me to the center of my very being. It was the journey that would take me through the dark crevices of my own psyche. A journey of self discovery, the psychologists would say. A journey to chemical balance, the medical world would say. *The Dark Night of My Soul*, the mystics would say.

Who would guide me on this trip? The tour books of the times were prolific. There were the current theories to explain old problems ... *I'm O.K. You're O.K.* and *Transactional Analysis* were explaining how we are a combination of our own wishes and what our families and our cultures expect of us.

There was *Future Shock*, which described a society in constant transition, without any roots, and the disorientation it causes. There was *The Peter Principle*, which stated that ambitious people who are never checked would eventually rise to the level of their own incompetence.

There were the histories of civilized people who had fallen simply out of exhaustion. The history we had just reviewed in Europe told time and time again of the fears and torments that come with the daily battle of survival of peoples in every age. The great history lesson of the fall of Roman Empire had graphically showed what happened when the Darkness took over an exhausted empire, and plunged civilization into its sterile period.

There were the classics like Ibsen's *Doll House* which were re-examined in the light of women breaking out of traditional roles. There was the not-too-distant comparison of Sylvia Plath, the young poet whose own story is told in *The Bell Jar* and whose journey to England with children ends with a final odyssey to suicide. There was *The Cracker Factory*, a story of a modern young mother who ended up in an asylum. There was *The Awakening*, another classic which expounded the dangers of women with children seeking a creative expression in spite of the culture's thinking. In this classic, the reader is made aware of the final demise, in the tragic loss of the heroine's children.

There were the more current books on the same subject, *The Feminine Mystique*, with its strong warnings that life in the "suburbs" and a life of subservience were lethal to one's identity.

There was the ancient wisdom of the Proverbs, illuminating the consequences of faithfulness, and the passionate pleas of the Psalms, extolling God's presence in times of need, and there were the poignant examples of sacrifice in both Old and New Testaments.

At first I was too tired to concentrate on any book or thought for long, and none of it was exclusive or comprehensive enough, but as always, it was the desire to be a good student that pushed me on. I began to grow, first by listening and then absorbing as my mind would let me. It was the hardest course I had ever taken. The subject was me. I thought I knew who I was, even where I had come from, but the subtleties of the cultures of both my husband and my family had to be understood again in the light of the times and place we were re-entering.

The broad cultures of America at the time and the particular culture of our region were there to influence our thinking as a team. Around me was a new age of women who were not only burning bras, but who were angry that they had lost their self-esteem through years of subservient positions. There was a strong call for identity. Women were rebelling against being called ministers' wives, doctors' wives, presidents' wives; they were declaring their names and keeping a distinct identity. "Who am I?" they asked, and no one seemed to have the answers." Do you work?" they would ask. And the question, of course, did not mean, "Do you get on your knees, iron, cook, or clean?" It meant, "Are you paid for your services? Are you a professional, do you have a right to a name?" Change, change, change was the call.

Around me were people from Appalachia who were by nature fatalists, whose cry was what had been good enough for their parents would be good for them, and to change would spoil the system, ruin the continuity, corrupt the young.

As our families offered help, and they came in loving visits to help, I heard also many dictums that had always sailed over my head. I realized that the two cultures from which my husband and I had come seemed the same, but in reality, there were many variances that made it difficult for us as a team to figure out our own destiny. The tapes from our childhoods were playing loudly without us knowing it. We had never really examined what pulled us along toward our goals. We had not yet assumed what would be our "song" as a couple.

There were the confusing dictums from one family to be secretive and the constant wish from the other to speak my mind, to free any anger or confusion. I was caught between one family who believed in the value of acceptance, that we should accept life as it came, and another who thought anything could be conquered and changed if one worked hard enough. One who believed that achievement and honor brought happiness, while the other thought security and sound investments would give peace. Both knew hard work as the key to success.

It was profoundly clear, in the midst of all the confusion, however, that there was one value upon which both families agreed: *Family is the center of civilization.* Both families from which we descended wanted our nuclear family to survive intact. Under stress, that would take work.

Work seemed to always be the defining word. Work had always defined my life, but looking at the children, I knew it was not work alone they wanted from me. They needed a center of love and stimulation to be *alive.*

As I looked out the window one day, I saw Thomas stumble on a rock. He was in real danger, I ran to catch him. He was alive and I was alive. I began to cry real tears. They were feeling tears, healing tears. I knew who I was at that moment.

I knew I was a woman, full of ideas and dreams myself. I had chosen to be a wife, and always I would be Mother. I was certainly influenced by the cultures of my Italian Catholic past, and I was open to the valid new ideas of my times, but the decision to integrate them was ultimately mine. As I returned to the house, I looked again at the window that had guided me to my son. Light was pouring in. It was my mother who had cleaned it and set a card in the corner.

The card read, "The longest journey starts with but a single step."

When my husband returned from work, I showed him where Thomas had fallen. He looked at a back yard he did not even know was there and began to plan a sandbox for the children.

The insights were all around. I was saturated with words of wisdom. It would take the hound, the Holy Spirit, to help me integrate them.

"Come away with me and I will tell you of love," I browsed from Hosea. Maybe we didn't understand that piece of advice either. "Come away to the quiet and I will lure you to your first love," the prophet had said. His song of love, had not only been good advice for rekindling a love of man for woman, family for their children, but for the great love of God for his people. Stillness was the first step, the prophet had said.

I did go away for periods of rest, for solitude and stillness, first as a break each Friday morning, then for the peace of a day's excursion, every few weeks. And slowly, the words I had been hearing began to sink in.

Step by step, I grew stronger, began to have a laugh with the boys, a light lunch with friends, a dinner with my husband. I began to relearn work habits and, starting with small ventures, picked up my life, beginning like a child with small steps, until I was more sure-footed.

As a family, we were able to go to the sea in time. This time we went for rest and recovery. There were gulls overhead, and the pace was now in a new rhythm, slowed down. At the sea, I saw a glimpse of peace in the waves and the quiet of the non-world, and it was with the Holy Spirit that I began to integrate what insights were coming. The waves began to lap at my toes, and in the wind I could almost hear the soothing spirit of God, enticing me to listen. I remembered the wonderful trip to Ireland and how the children had played on the rocks. The sea had given such solace, then. It had slowed us down, given us time to integrate what we had seen.

I thought of Hosea and his call to come away to learn of love. Even love would be investigated in this dark night we had known. Of love I learned much by sitting in the solace of the sea. Love, I realized, is not a feeling. Love is an action, a child teaching his brother; an action of day-to-day giving; an action of committed perseverance. For a mother, a father, it means giving, giving, giving. And in giving it means ensuring unconditional security to another. In the peace and freedom of the sea, I felt the wistfulness of a child myself, and I felt overwhelmed with gratitude; that somehow we had been protected with unconditional love.

As the children played by the sea, I watched the waves come and go, and I realized that waves of possibilities would come and go. There were glimmers of the culture from my past that I would treasure and empty shells that I would discard. There were gems of the new ways of expanding life's possibilities. I would have to examine carefully what would be truly valuable to me in the light of our large family.

While the cultures from which I had come and from which my husband had descended spoke of service, they often failed to explain a low self-esteem that can permeate the roles of women. While liberation screamed for social justice, its early emphasis was a total concentration on self. I was already committed to six people beyond myself.

Now the real test of motherhood was to come. I had begun to cross the sea, and I would see the family across. Every fiber told me that there would be no peace in bringing a soul into this world and neglecting its growth. But I was one of those souls. I came to include myself, and my growth would have to continue as well. We all wanted to be fully human, fully alive.

My dreams were real, and should not be dashed. I was pregnant with word and ideas, but the times were full also of possibilities that would not come again. The children too were full of new ideas, and although I had always thought it was my role to teach them, their very lives were teaching me new things. Each day there was something new to share, an idea born of our togetherness, a moment of joy, of fun, of spontaneous happenings. We would not be able to repeat the moment. The children were also part of a dream. I had been pregnant with them, and they were with me. They would ripen now only with sacrifice and love.

Slowly, other insights began to take hold. Instead of just keeping my head out of a sinking mire, I began to tread water. There were moments when I felt almost human. I ventured out on a shopping spree or joined a comfortable group of friends, a book club for stimulation, a prayer group for spiritual growth. I began to write again, first as catharsis, and then for enjoyment. And I could see that as I evolved, the words evolved.

In time, I would see the wisdom and the folly of advice that had come to me in this most difficult journey of my life. Was the terrible dark night of my soul the result of wanderlust? Perhaps the physical journey to England had brought the watershed to a more striking head. But I felt lucky. I could have gone through life never knowing why I did what I did, nor taking rational command for my life decisions. As for the journey to England, there would be enough knowledge and insights for a lifetime from that journey.

Wanting to grow, to seek a life that was fuller, is natural. Would it ever be simple for mothers?

I had no way of knowing, but I do know that Motherhood is a noble role in any age. The sacrifices are real, as is true of any worthwhile gift and goal. I made my decision that I had started a course that would be finished. This journey of self discovery had been the toughest of all and the most liberating. For I knew in the end who I was and what I should do with my life. I finally understood the reasons behind my decisions, and I knew that I had traveled with my family because I could not travel without them. It was as simple as that.

But the exhaustion had taken its toll. I began to see the need for space, not only physical space, but mental space from the children. I learned to schedule time alone. As we had set up our work at the time, my nurturing was a daily part of the role, and it could be exhausting. I would learn compromise and balance. The intensity of the role was absorbing; the children were young, the family was big.

Some of the goals of longer pieces of writing would have to wait. But I was no longer in such a hurry. I began to see a beauty in the process. I saw beauty in the slow mature growth and the simple exquisiteness of each day. And it finally made sense to "Look to this day, for it is life." I did not give up my dreams for quiet creative work in the future, nor was I willing to give up the major nurturing role of the children, although I had no way of knowing if in the end there would be as much time to do an equal amount of creative work as there was for children.

I knew I must ask for my daily breaks, for my peace. I needed to keep growing and to seek stimulation beyond the home. I took classes, became a free-lance writer, and then later began the work of compiling a cookbook. I embraced the community that I feared would trap me and found in it an added family. The histories and cultural wonders of Europe would weave themselves into my work in the community in a hundred ways. Nothing had been lost that was seen on our journeys together. And everything was to be gained from my journey to know myself.

It became a yearly trek to go to the sea for rest, renewal, and vision. For in life, sheer exhaustion mars vision, and compulsions return. The sea gave space and forced me to see what was tugging and pulling. The sea had given solace in Ireland. The sea, with its balm, its quieting spirit, was where I could hear best, too. There I would get the bodily rest that I needed and a total break from life to see more clearly what was pulling in our present culture, what was obsession, what was culturally good and what was valuable to life.

As the years passed, I began to seek out a different spot each year for our family to gather by the sea. I looked for coastal areas where each of us could relax, rest and be alone with the sea. We investigated beaches in Virginia and

Delaware, in New Jersey and the wonderful, rocky coasts of Maine. Once there, secluded and unwound, we walked the rocky edges listening to the sounds of the gulls in their stream, first unwinding our tired bodies, then letting the hum of the car and eventually the sound of the motor within my mind to cease.

We looked at our tired bodies, our puffed eyes and then slowly at pre-dawn as the sun came up, we looked at the world in new light. For light is always striking after the darkness. I had learned that work and growth can be exciting, but the motives must be examined. And that, I have found, can be done best in the quiet.

There was a pattern in these yearly trips. I would leave home wound up from life and especially the last days of preparation. But I would think of the Ring of Kerry, how being a part of a more simplified life had once slowed our pace. I would think of how, as the old man had said, "in the silence inspiration comes" and how one is forced in the quiet to listen to the small voice within.

Relaxed and open, each year I would listen to that voice within grow louder. I would question myself, assess the world's ideas. Is it the world's ideas? Who do I have to please, who do I have to be? I would see that each of us was growing. The noisy toddlers had turned into awkward, lanky pre-teens and somewhere along the way, the teenagers became young men. My husband and I, growing with them, had learned much.

One year, on our drive to the sea, eager as the boys were to arrive, they took turns driving. The older boys were beginning to test their wings with new driver's licenses. Without checking the map, the driver had sailed on, missing a turn. For an hour no one had noticed we were going north instead of south. Once we turned around, we realized that we had lost two hours. It would have been easier to check the map. I equate our yearly ventures to the sea as good map reading lessons.

As the boys learned to appreciate the solitude as well as the beaches, we began to go to spots that were more remote. There was an island in Maine and the end of Land's End in

Hilton Head. Once at the sea, as the gulls swayed overhead, we learned to let the wind take us along and be renewed in the peace of the sea.

There the boys had learned to spread out, some using a deck, some the beach, some the screened-in porch to be alone, to be quiet as I, their mother, had done. They often watched the dolphins dancing at sunset, and then followed the sun going down, gasped at the sunrise and felt the light pouring in. I, in turn, have watched the children, uninhibited, running, and learned what they, as my sons have given me. And I watched the gulls carried by the wind, and learned what they were teaching. I would wade in the water, and let it climb to my calves, and I, like the children and the gulls, would become relaxed, relaxed by the water and the sea. Perhaps the boys were listening too, learning, remembering. Perhaps the sea reminded us all of our journey of joy to England, Italy and Ireland and the journey that taught me who I was. For all of us there is, indeed, solace by the sea.

# It's Your Turn, Chickadees

# Chapter 5

# Sound Of Music In Vienna

*"And the night shall be filled with music*
*And the cares, that infest the day*
*Shall fold their tents, like the Arabs*
*And silently steal away."*

—Longfellow, *The Day is Done*

Our train followed the Rhine, that brown meandering waterway that winds through the soul of Europe. With his coat around his shoulders, my husband dozed on the aisle seat while I fixed my gaze out the window on Austria. It was June, but the air in Germany was cool. As we rumbled past wooded banks lined with sloping vineyards and green gorges capped by turreted castles, I wanted to awaken him. But then we entered the industrial pockets, dreary and drab in the distance, and I let him sleep.

There was little indication of the life that awaited us in Vienna. The train droned on much as my life had for the past 10 years, steady, directed with few surprises. In that decade since we lived in England, our lives had taken on a monotonous permanence.

But wanderlust, calling in the night, had won again. Approaching my 40s I could see the end of the tunnel for my parenting, and I was feeling stirrings of the soul, almost as adolescent as the boys.

My husband was just entering a very difficult time of parenting. He was facing the financing of college educations for five boys who all had aspirations of professional education. We were out of sync in our timing for an exotic kind of a trip, but he thought the idea of travel still worthy. It would be good to see Europe again. We had never been to Vienna, "if it could be done on our frugal budget . . . ."

On a dreary day in February—that time of the year when the soul longs for light and when the sounds of Tchaikovsky soothe the savage mood only temporarily—we had signed up for a Friendship Force exchange. Sight unseen, our capital city in the Chemical Valley of West Virginia would be matched with a similar town in Europe. The purpose was for peoples from different parts of the world to exchange ideas for living.

In March, having made a minimal down payment on a 12-day adventure, we heard that Gelsenkirchen, Germany, in the Ruhr Valley would be our sister in the exchange. The visit would be simultaneous. A plane would take off for Gelsenkirchen and return with passengers to Charleston. Each participant was asked to provide a home for the visitors from the exchange city. Instead of asking a friend to house two guests while we were gone, we thought it would be a wonderful experience for our boys to have the German guests in our home.

I imposed on the goodwill of my mother, who would be babysitting. As our boys were in junior high and high school, I requested teenagers from Germany to keep them company. When we boarded our charter in Pittsburgh, a friend who had placed the guests assured me she had honored our request. Two avant, gorgeous 18-year-old ladies would be staying at our home. Needless to say, the boys were ecstatic, and my mother has never forgiven me. To this day she reminds me that it was she who dealt with their rites of passage while I was gone. There were secret keg parties, Erica and Marian and five sons growing up overnight. Even little Tommy fell in love with blonde Erica from the start.

Once aboard the plane, though, I could do nothing about the problems I anticipated at home. It was escape I sought. According to the exchange plan, we would be the guests of a family in the Ruhr Valley, and then it would be our option to travel on our own for a few days. We were in our early 40s. We needed a change and a little romance. And I had set my sights on Vienna.

As the plane took off, we let the magic of travel take over and focused on the fun of the happy group of Charlestonians headed for Germany. The Friendship Force was comprised of an interesting cross-section of people with a wide representation of the work force of our valley. Each was to be placed with a family who shared occupations or similar interests. Crowded into a stretch "eight" plane, the boisterous group took off singing "Country Roads" and didn't settle down until we landed in Düsseldorf.

Gert, a gentle Ph.D. with twinkling eyes, met us with flowers. "Perhaps you expected to be with a medical doctor," Gert apologized. "I am sorry, I am a chemist. The best technical journals are in English. I asked to have a guest so that I might improve my English."

We had little command of the German language, but we smiled at each other and threw our bags into his little Volkswagen. "Ulla, my wife, has two brothers who are doctors. She will take you to meet them. You can see their offices."

We assured him we were happy just to see Germany. "I would like to see the cathedral at Cologne," I requested. Then I divulged a hidden dream: "The bust of Charlemagne at Aachen is on the cover of one of my favorite books. Would it be possible to see that golden image?"

"You can do both, I assure you," Gert said emphatically.

Ulla, a social worker with red hair cut straight around her square features, and Millie, their seven-year-old daughter, were waiting in their flat in a quiet village outside of Gelsenkirchen. Ulla and I shared many social projects and a love of history, but she was adamant that Dom should meet her brothers, the physicians.

We would see the ancient beauty of the Ruhr Valley first, she assured us again. We seemed to fly through the country-side in Ulla's little Bug, passing open fields with wildflowers and small factories, until the town of Aachen was ahead of us. As the sun went down on the medieval town, we entered the ancient Romanesque church that replaced the rubble of the dark ages. We gazed at the simple church where Charlemagne had firmly established the First Reich. Here, I realized, Western civilization had been given a new life. The crude throne and the amazing golden reliquary were the symbols of the light he wanted to bring once more to the Western world. I knelt in silence, walked in awe, my pilgrimage complete.

History reckoned with, Ulla swung over the back roads to Dülmen, where we met the elder Pringkerhoff, her brother. Joseph, an obstetrician, considered our visit a healing balm, a pleasant exchange. He related a wonderful story as we sipped tea.

"We kept prisoners of the Second World War right on our farm. With strict orders, we were warned not to invite them in, but they ate at our table every night. My parents could have been punished; still we ate together as we do tonight."

It was a wonderful little tea we shared, fruits from Israel, cheeses and firm dark bread with jams and strawberries.

Ulla's younger brother was an internist with a young family and a growing new practice. He was proficient in English and intense about his ordered day. It was obvious that his sister's Friendship Force guests were somewhat of an intrusion.

We met the young doctor in his home, where we were served a rather ordinary table wine. Then, as if duty required, he took us to his new office.

On one wall was a picture of the village of Dülmen, ravaged in the pursuit of the Third Reich. All around the office were the signs of a proficient, growing practice. Again, we marveled at Germany's ability to bring order out of chaos time and again throughout history. When we praised what was beyond belief—the renovated city, the advanced technology, the incredible architectural design of the office—we were invited to return to his home.

"You don't make house calls any more, Dr. Gaziano?" he asked.

"No," my husband answered. "Your proficient method of technology and home care is amazing. I see how you do both here."

"Nothing replaces the personal care." I added.

Back at his home, the young internist brought out a finer bottle of wine. And by the time his attractive wife arrived, we were well into the second round of drinks. With pictures of their four children all around us, I pulled out pictures of our boys, and we began comparing notes on adolescence. "We have always wanted a girl," I noted, and looked again at the children's faces on the walls, their golden hair crowning them like cherubs.

"What a beautiful family you have!" I sincerely asserted. A third bottle of wine was uncorked. Its quality and bouquet was unsurpassed. As we drove through the fields of Dülmen, Ulla smiled, "He had been saving that wine for his feast day. They liked you. You are as much as family, with us all."

It was not easy to convince our host family that their hospitality had lacked nothing when we told them we would be going on to Vienna. I tried as best I could to explain my heart was set on a little private excursion. Reluctantly, our hosts helped make arrangements for our train to Austria.

Gelsenkirchen in June is chilly, and we buttoned our raincoats as we boarded the dreary train that would transport us to Vienna. Waving our goodbyes from the window, we settled into the coach, not sure what was ahead.

After 12 hours of rumbling track, the train finally arrived at Westbanhof. The pavement seemed an oasis. Wearily, we hailed a taxi which promptly delivered us to our pension. It was the usual frugal plan we had learned while living in Europe. I had searched for an inexpensive pension with a little history of its own, in a nice location. This time we would be staying in the shadow of the Hapsburg complex.

"Vienna is Hapsburg and Hapsburg is Vienna," came back to me as if in some dream sequence. The imperial palace was ruefully impressive even from the angle of our titled glance. The enormity of the complex and the dynasty that had established it surrounded us. I was still looking up as the cabby drove away. He had made a complete circle, leaving us in a rather small courtyard of what must have once been a lively manor. Our suitcases had been dropped on the stones in the very center. Not a sound could be heard in the cobblestone enclosure. Not a person could be seen. We stood there for a moment trying to adjust to the darkness of the enclosure. The number on the iron gate matched our booking. Silently, we entered the palace. Inside, an iron cage lifted us to the apartments used for tourists. Down a darkened, narrow hall a porter directed us, and our key opened the door to a bathless, spartan room with high ceilings.

The weight of the search and the long train trip showed in Dom's eyes. This drab little room did nothing to kindle a spark. He flopped onto the bed, and I went to the end of the room and opened the shutters. In the distance a flute piped. I leaned on the window pane and strained to hear the refrain of the melody. A piano from a nearby bar was tuning up. Something stirred in me that had not been tapped in years. I was hungry for the romantic sounds of night.

I thought back 10 years to our travels with the children. At the end of those long days of holding five sets of hands and winding in and out of museums and cathedrals, our bodies had been tired and ready for rest. There had been no night life for us then. Now, I was alone with my husband in Vienna, but our moods were not synchronized. The intensity of my caregiving role was being relieved. I craved light, music, excitement. He was tired, caught up in his career and the awesome burden of financial planning for the boys' education.

"Can you hear it? The music—can you hear it?"

"You mean that racket from the bar down the alley?" Dom mumbled. "I sure hope I can sleep with that noise." He turned over and attempted to cover his ears with one of the pillows.

I joined him in bed, reflecting on the past 10 years. I had been on a high when we left England. A world had opened up to me and yet was not to be mine. Coming down from my almost exotic high sent me spinning into a devastating depression as we settled into the realities of life with a large family. My dreams of writing about our trip were dashed by the real needs of five little boys. The only writing I could manage was some free-lance articles and the histories and newsletters for organizations I had joined.

Now in Vienna I wanted a little fantasy, some music, and some romance. I listened to the revelers in the streets below. I merely had to set my feet in Europe and my imagination soared with the richness of history and the beauty of the surroundings.

I went to the window and leaned out. There was a group of happy young people singing as they passed under our window. They followed a long tradition of music in the streets of Vienna.

"I'd really love to hear the Boys' Choir tomorrow," I muttered aloud in the darkness, not even knowing if Dom was still awake. "You rest," I whispered. "I think I'll ask the concierge what the chances are of getting tickets for the choir. It won't hurt to try."

Two months before leaving home, I had ordered tickets for an opera in the State House and two tickets for Mass in the Hapsburg Chapel. The opera tickets came, but I had received no response from the Vienna Boys' Choir.

"June is a popular month," the cautious proprietor explained. "But there are often cancellations. If you present yourself at the Hapsburg gate at least one hour in advance of the Mass, Madame, you might get in. Mass begins at precisely 9:25 a.m. At worst, you can stand outside in the courtyard and watch the television monitor."

My husband could not see the point of trudging out so early on such a slim chance of getting in. "Besides, we've seen the choir in America. You go if you want. I'd like to sleep."

Early the next morning, I slipped out of the little pension, trying not to disturb my sleeping partner. It was quiet outside. The click of my heels was the only sound on cobbled alleys leading to the massive home of the Hapsburgs.

As I stepped into the courtyard, I saw the sign go up "Standing Room Only, Monitors Overhead." I knew I did not want to be in Vienna watching TV. I wanted to be in the chapel. A new line was forming for the reserved tickets to be picked up. I quickly joined the queue, hoping for a cancellation at the last minute.

I realized I was being watched by the clerk. As I approached the counter, the urbane Austrian looked over his glasses and whispered a promise, "There will be a seat if you stand aside and wait until the Mass is about to start." I obeyed, still anxious. At exactly 9:24, the gray-haired gentleman handed me a ticket to a prized aisle seat near the front. He waved away money. "It is my pleasure, Madame. Clearly you want to attend Mass."

At the Vienna court of the ruling Babenberg dynasty on July 7, 1498, Hofmusik Kapelle Wien, the Imperial Court Music Chapel of Vienna, was founded by Emperor Maximilian I. The little Gothic chapel had many times been embellished with timely changes. Now, amidst a backdrop of red and white rococo, with the glow of candles on the altar and the sparkle of an 18th-century chandelier, the Kyrie was being intoned for a myriad of visitors where once the imperial family had prayed alone. I took my seat on the aisle very close to the front.

An almost forgotten sound of Gregorian purity was chanted in answer to an adult male choir. It was like some celestial sound from the past. There is a honeymoon period in mystical union as in marriage, and then life goes on. When God calls us back to that first love, it is ecstatic. The Gregorian chant was calling me back to an ancient beauty.

The utter simplicity of the chant was balanced by the pomp of Palestrina as the Mass progressed. I had listened to tapes of choirs, symphonies, but never had I heard music like this, nor in such a setting. The chapel was more like what I envisioned a Viennese Opera house to be: embellished with thick, floral carpet, chandeliers, and tiered boxes. It was as rich as a sacher torte, but a prayerful reverence came through. The Mass was celebrated by two priests. The Introit and Kyrie were answered by adult voices. Then there was a pause, a hush, an expectant break just before the boys' choir was to sing. Those innocent charmers burst into praise, and it was as if heaven had opened its clouds for the angels to be heard.

Four choirs gave concert tours around the world, but there was no counterpart to hearing the boys in the Imperial Chapel. I was transfixed from their first note. A light flicked on, illuminating an empty spot in my soul and an awakening of all my senses. It was in that tiny chapel that I began to understand the mystery and wonder of music. The joy I felt was unabashed, exhalant joy. Before the Mass was over, I brushed away the tears, wondering if this were a foretaste of heaven.

There was no holding me down after the choir sang. I had been introduced to a level of music I had never heard before, and I wanted more. Anything Vienna had to offer was bound to be special. From the alley I could see my husband leaning out the window as I returned.

"I got in!" I shouted triumphantly from below.

Back in the room, he could see the glow on my face and he knew immediately he was going to regret not going with me. "They sang like angels," I bubbled. All through our coffee and croissants, he would hear the details, and even as we entered the precinct of the Hapsburg, I was still chattering on.

Entering the St. Michaelplatz Arch was a dwarfing sensation, silencing me only temporarily. I took on a guide-like demeanor, pointing out chapel and chambers as deftly as a member of the royal family. The home with 2,000 rooms, housing a dynasty that had lasted 700 years, left an imposing mark. We meandered through the archways and a few rooms, but we really didn't want to be inside on that fine June day.

Vienna's history extends farther back than the Hapsburgs, back to Attila the Hun and swarms of invading Magyars and

Turks and back to the days when its noble river served as the frontier of the Roman empire, back still to when it was a Celtic settlement. There was history under every arch, down every lane, but it was the Vienna of the 18th-century that I craved to touch.

Flags waved in the breeze on the other side of the arch. The lavish gardens, speckled with Sunday strollers, took us back to the turn of the century when walking was a happy part of an unhurried lifestyle. Children played, light and happy; old men and women walked arm in arm; young, jean-clad students filled the gardens with happy chatter; the oom-pa-pa of a marching band filled the space with joyous sounds. The gaiety overflowed into the lovely wide Avenue adjoining the palace and creating a dreamlike waltz of bygone eras.

It was what some would call a mid-summer's dream, seeing Vienna at early mid-life. Vienna was full of surprises, a mixture of eastern earthiness and western vitality. She radiates an ambiance, alive and yet with a hold on the 18th-century. Palaces and shops, major avenues emanating from a central ring create an elegant facade. Renovated more than 100 years ago when Franz Joseph was desperately trying to enrich and hold onto his dynasty, the famous Ringstrasse gives a beautifully unique plan to the city. The dynasty is gone, but the face of the city has grown more elegant and mellow with time.

It was an elegant plan where the eye could feast on neo-Gothic city hall, neo-classic parliament, neo-early renaissance and neo-classic baroque, all studded with statues of Greek gods, musical heros and archdukes, all blessing the Avenue in marble. An elegant plan, indeed, we thought as we strolled along. A plan like no other in the world.

Vienna harbors a romantic paradise of avenues and alleys, warm lanes for strolling, gardens and parks for meandering, a wonderful place to be lifted by the joy and beauty of music. During our stay there seemed to be a wistful burst of gaiety in the air. A capricious mood surrounded us as if a burst of fireworks was suspended, filling the night with its dust. It was like a fantasy, an affair of the heart.

We strolled from the Hapsburg to the Ring, past the opera house and then we stopped for a light lunch of the classic

wiener schnitzel and apple strudel. After lunch, we sauntered into the Stadpark, that happy haven of birds and strollers. My husband was beginning to unwind, to put his responsibilities aside for a while. He was rested, relaxed in the outdoors, and I was exuberant with the scene around me. Students spread their blankets, matrons lounged on benches.

We meandered through the serpentine walkways, letting the morning sun warm us. Amid the lush green grass and the profusion of flowers, there was the image of Johann Strauss, gracefully memorialized in stone. With bow in hand amid the birds, he stood, adding his benediction to the people.

We lay on the grass and joined the Sunday scene. In a little gazebo at a far corner of the park, a small chamber group was tuning up. A pompous peacock strutted out of the bushes and spread his blue and white feathers. Little warblers hid in the bushes, satisfied to be relegated to the chorus. And then the timeless three-four beat of Strauss's waltzes floated out over the crowd, lightening our hearts. Johann never thought his music was a match for his classic Viennese predecessors. But if he could have seen the smiles on the faces of the people around us....

In this open air, I was beginning to understand the real beauty of outdoor music. There was something special about the combination of nature and notes. The birds, the abundant grass, the freedom of children running, the flowers and the waltz were a holy union.

Music is a common bond. It was lifting us all. A happiness floated through the park. I could not imagine that pleasant green without the three-four beat. It transformed the scene, brought us all back into a more romantic time, when people gathered spontaneously for entertainment.

Later that night we stopped by the pension for our sweaters. Just outside the city limits is another world, the world of the Prater. A red and white trolley transported us to the magic park filled with beer gardens, burgermeisters, and the largest fanciful Ferris wheel in the world. There we were surrounded by roundabouts, shooting galleries, helter-skelters and racing courses, and again music. The music was earthy, emanating from the people, and their own emotions, their own instruments. There was the accordion, the zither, the sound of maudlin dancers, and the melancholy lingering of lieder, mournful, yet pure.

Riding back in the trolley, passing the little cottages at the city's edge, I wondered how the myth of romantic Vienna, born in the coziness of flowered balconies and simple cottages, had survived war and political upheaval, the shrouded understanding of scientific probing. In the ebbing darkness it seemed so enchanting. Was it all a facade? Or was it a way of life that gave balance to sobriety?

Was this the balance I needed? The domestic of Vienna was idealized, and the imperial palaces were preserved. The domestic of my life was being brought to a level of fantasy. In Vienna, a facade of fantasy was still there. Neither plague nor war nor social upheaval had ever stopped the music. There was a marvelous tale of a piper who piped his way into his own grave at a time when plague ravished the city. "Oh my dears, no more money, no more fun; everything is simply gone." And his flute issued its last note in the grave.

Returning to our pension, we walked through the Graben, a chic city pedestrian walk lined with elegant shops. The shops were filled with ebony mannequins and spoke of high fashion. There were cafes where exquisitely dressed matrons sipped coffee and tasted delicate pastries almost too pretty to describe. And always there was music. Along the Karntnerstrasse we saw a guitarist drop his hat and play. From across the street, an accordion blended in with the sounds of the street. And then, as we turned into the alley to our little pension for the night, I heard the sounds of a flute,

that same flute that filled my ears with its poignant notes on the night of our arrival.

It all seemed part of a fantasy—what had stirred my soul in the morning was now there to finish the day. Something inside was tapped, released, unleashed. My husband would never understand what had hit me. He just began to relax and enjoy it.

As I browsed through shops the next day and listened to the outdoor music, Dom continued to unwind. But he wasn't so sure about a night at the opera. I wanted to see the famous Stad Opera House, and perhaps grow a little by seeing a production in such a special surroundings.

"Opera is so ubiquitous, yet so misunderstood," the little booklet I picked up had said.

"Formal opera is an expensive art form," he answered, and we are putting down a decent part of our budget for the tickets to the great opera house.

"It will be fun," I assured, hiding my own questions.

Preparing to go, I felt a little of the excitement of being in the 18th-century setting with the descendants of Viennese society claiming their boxes. I dressed in my favorite yellow summer dress, feeling the lightness of a fantasy. Arriving early enough to see the opera house, we mingled unaffected-

ly with an interesting mix of excited opera goers from around the world. The outside of the building was neo-classical. In the lobby, the gold and white whirls ran wild, producing an effect of drama, elegance, and sophistication.

The inside of the theater was a joyful foil of the flamboyant art form which took place there. Rococo ran wild. Shells in plaster decorated the walls and the tiered boxes, and overhead the chandelier lit the whole horseshoe interior with its diamond-like prisms. At a level above ours, we saw where one could, for a few dollars, view the performance standing. I saw students and lovers of the art of music wait patiently as the fire curtain opened on "Lucia De Lamamoor."

For the first time I saw this drama of passions sung in a grandiose setting and understood its own special lure. Maybe it was the setting. Productions in plain little theaters just couldn't carry off this feeling. Somewhere in the middle of the evening I realized, there is no explanation for the librettos or notes so exuberantly done. Some words, far too foolish to be said in drama, were being sung with serious seductiveness.

These were situations too complex to be expressed in any other form. I didn't know exactly why it worked in this context, and yet my Italian personality should have been able to understand this method of expressing emotion. There was a direct resemblance to the facial expressions of my grandfather when nine grandchildren ran around the parlor at Christmas, and the mournful faces of my aunts, wailing their dead, were no different than the leading ladies in front of me. That was opera. There was that beautiful connection now.

The intrigue of family feuds and family weddings would have made excellent librettos, now that I thought of it. I had only to see the production to realize the extremes on stage were a mere fanciful production, extravagantly embellished with wonderful music and artful backdrops. The Städtopera House is perhaps one of the most lavish, loveliest theaters in the world. My husband described me as a papillon that night, a butterfly coming alive. Music was touching us in every direction.

Just a trolley ride away at the edge of the Vienna Woods we found we could enter yet another small fantasy. There in all its brightness is the summer home of the Hapsburgs, the villa of Schonbaum. For a few pennies, we climbed aboard the green line to be transported to the belle epoch where Empress Maria Theresa splashed yellow everywhere, redecorating it happily for her 16 children. Now, there was a Viennese woman of whom to stand in awe. Running an empire, raising 16 children. I was eager to see how she threw her pillows, raised her roses, and just plain survived.

"For the first time in my travels I have been chided for not understanding the language," I told my husband as we climbed aboard. "I have a great little picnic for us, but finding the market almost cost me my pride. A policeman looked down from his horse, understanding perfectly well what I wanted. But before he would point it out on my map, he looked me straight in the face and admonished, 'In Austria you should speak German!' "

We were soon at the edge of the gardens. Manicured and symmetrical, the rows were a veritable paradise of ordered flowers and shrubs, carved and cared for. At the top of a gentle knoll at the end of the massive gardens, a hilltop pavilion commanded a beautiful view of the Vienna Woods. The climb had whetted our appetites, and the picnic I had procured at the Neuve Market that morning seemed like a banquet. Sweet miniature tomatoes, crusty rolls, little mushrooms in an herb-scented marinade, three cheeses and the most succulent peaches. I spread it out on a bench amidst the scent of summer azaleas and sweet roses.

The idyllic setting was not the backdrop for 16 children to run through, I thought, a little homesick for the sight of our own boys. When a house becomes a museum and the gardens are taken over by the National Trust, it must change the character of the home. The marbled halls and lush lanes had become only a painting to be glanced at, an empty shell. This summer home was silent, except for the guttural sounds of the guide announcing the tour as we entered.

Again, I wished I could understand the language, but no guide could capture the heart, the passions and the style of the complex family who had lived there. Here the tragic beginnings of aborted loves and suicides which plagued the ponderous line must have enlivened the halls with wild life. Here Mozart had played and Napoleon had taken over, and always orchestras had filled the mirrored halls with music.

I was glad to be without details of chamber rooms, walking silently with my thoughts of the fated Hapsburgs. I did not want to be obsessed with the political intrigues of its history, only. I gazed at Maria Theresa's family. The portraits of her children, one after the other, filling the gilded halls. The doors to the garden were flung open to let in the early summer air. The slate and marble floors shined. I could imagine the children running through, boisterous, lively; I could envision the glittering ballrooms and bedrooms of the extravagant, frivolous, frolicking romantic Viennese; the sparkle of diamonds and chandeliers at night as a Bach sonata resounded or a Strauss waltz conjured smiles of memory.

There were echoes of history, power, defeat, tragedy, love, and, of course, music in the palace of Schonbaum. It was Hapsburg, and Hapsburg was Vienna.

But Vienna was more. The next morning, our last in the city, I set out to bring back just a few souvenirs of our stay. The elegant shops on the Graben were chock full of expensive gifts, none of which we could afford. We managed a few unframed prints, a petit point for each of our mothers, and some coins and tokens for our sons.

Vienna would never have to be defined in artifacts for me. I slipped over to the Stadpark before returning to the pension,

bought an ice cream and sat at a little cafe table close to the music in the gazebo. The memory of the graceful figure of Strauss, blessing the park with his violin, and the faces of the people shining with joy was all I wanted to take home. It would be enough to visualize the never-ending three-four beat of his waltzes lifting the souls and soothing tired spirits as the not-too-blue Danube flowed gently by.

# It's Your Turn, Chickadees

# Chapter 6

# Mid-Life Journey

*"Midway in life's journey
I went astray from the straight road
and woke to find myself in a dark forest."*

—Dante, *The Divine Comedy*

It was a warm September day. The heat was giving way to the promise of autumn when we set out for a tour of medieval Italy. As I grabbed my last carry-on bag in the kitchen, I could see the garden framed in the large window, the morning sun giving it a mellow glow. Clusters of chrysanthemums that Mike had planted were golden in the morning sun. Ahead of its time, the crooked little Chinese maple was turning a waxy red, but the trees in the distance were giving only a hint of change.

The new white gazebo at the far corner still pleased me. It was festive even in the quiet morning with the sun filtering through the fretwork. Silent now, it would always be a reminder of the last summer that our children were home as a family. They had built it as their gift to us for our 25th wedding anniversary.

The project consumed all their free time that summer. Mike had taken the lead, as a full-time job, but everyone pitched in at night. The boys involved their friends, in a kind of Tom Sawyer spirit, innovating, learning as they went. We ate on the work site. I prepared picnics and checked their progress until the last pillar was in place.

The garden came alive that Saturday night in August with an outdoor Mass, music in the gazebo, tents framed with flowers and food. Little by little we had prepared all the food for 500 friends and relatives, storing our favorite dishes in neighbors' freezers. The same scrubby area that had been undeveloped when we moved in, used for years for football in the fall and snow slides in the winter, had become a garden, a wonderful site for celebrations.

It was silent as we left, the serpentine walkway empty, except for a few fallen leaves here and there. As I gave a last check to the house, it seemed empty too. The boys were well into their new semesters, the youngest in high school, two in college, two in medical school.

The quiet was a strange anomaly. How often I had screamed for silence during the noisy years of adolescence. A house that had always been so filled with life was now quiet. And I, who had given my all to my motherhood, was seeing the end of that job. At times I had become euphoric with the possibilities of new horizons: part-time work, small allotments of free-lancing, could now become a full-time commitment.

My first cookbook was out, and I had organized a local festival, an outdoor day of music, inspired no doubt by that wonderful combination of music and nature in the Stad Park in Vienna. My credentials were limited, in reality. I had some acceptance and limited skills in the work place, and so I began to attend workshops and conferences and spend more time at writing. As I went to the computer more often, I realized that the computer was exciting but it didn't love back. Strangely, how when the job was coming to an end, I suddenly saw what it had meant to me. I knew that nothing would replace being the hub of a family. The children, consuming though they were, had brought fullness to my soul, to my emotional life. They had been a tough challenge, but raising them had brought a purpose to my life that would outlast me.

"The boys have created your dream, the gazebo," my husband very boyishly began. "What can I give you after 25 years of marriage?" Need he ask? "Silver tarnishes...," I began.

The planning of this Italian journey began first with suggestions of cruises and romantic resort brochures, all of which I finally discarded. We both wanted to go to Italy, but we had done the Grand Tour, explored the Renaissance and its treasures, even seen the lush coast.

I knew I wanted something more from this journey than escape. I don't know at what point we ceased to be tourists and wanted to see with the eyes of pilgrims the sights we chose. At some point it became clear that journeys had marked the passages of our life.

Without realizing the connection at the time, I put together a tour of small medieval towns in Italy. Siena in the north, Assisi in the Umbrian heartland, and San Giovanni in the south. It was my writing that would benefit, I reasoned, denying there was more. "I would like to understand the medieval mind, for my research." I cited. That sounded all right with my husband. Italy was Italy. The smaller walled towns and villages would be good fun.

Along with *Michelin's Guide* to great art and *Fodor's* facts on historic sites, I tucked in a copy of Dante's *Divine Comedy*. Dante's allegory through heaven and hell at mid-life had always eluded me. I had agonized over his symbols when I was young, too heavy at the time to fit my blithe spirit.

I pulled out the gold-edged copy again as the plane soared above Kennedy Airport on its way to Rome. It was as though I read it for the first time. Who in youth, when introduced to such heavy lines, truly understands the impact of being caught in mid-life?

Glancing over my shoulder, my husband suggested I read aloud, and so we shared the introduction:

> *"When I had journeyed half of life's way,*
>
> *I found myself within a shadowed forest,*
>
> *For I had sought the path that does not stray."*

"You women think about life constantly, always trying to figure it out, " my husband said, glancing at my eyes, transfixed in the text. "I just get up in the morning and go to work, one foot in front of the other and day by day, life goes on."

I smiled. Then continued reading aloud.

> *"Ah it is hard to speak of what it was that savage forest.*
>
> *Dense and difficult.*
>
> *Which even in recall renews my fear.*
>
> *So bitter, death is hardly more severe."*

We landed in Rome's morning. Our sleep on board had not been satisfying, and we entered Rome tired but happy to be on ancient soil again. We headed for the familiarity of the

Spanish Steps, that happy haven of cosmopolitan life, cheap accommodations and English tea rooms, all near the American Express Exchange. With our children's final education still ahead of us, it would be another budget trip. After crossing on a cut-rate charter flight, we had planned to pick up a cheap Fiat rental the following morning and begin our medieval venture.

Our stay in Rome was to be short, an afternoon siesta, and then as evening came, we enjoyed a walk through the hub of happenings around Bernini's fountain; just enough time to feel and taste of Italy's hub once again. We were still reckoning with jet lag when the scents of rosemary in a trattoria enticed us. We sat in the open air and began to unwind. With a bottle of house wine and some roasted chicken smothered in rosemary, the Via Sistina began to look better, and before the sun went down, the joys of travel began to take over.

"Is there a box nearby, where I can drop these cards to the boys?" I asked as my husband drove up in the little brown Fiat the next morning. The boys had insisted that babysitters were no longer needed as we planned this trip. Three were away in school. The youngest, still in high school, could be under the wing of the oldest, Phil, a medical student.

Now, I needed to touch base with my sons.

"Where can I mail these?" I waved the cards at my husband.

"Get in!" he pleaded.

Quickly I tucked the cards into my purse and entered the world of the little brown bug.

"The stick shift is stuck," he muttered. Every muscle of his face was pulled tense, engaged.

"Maybe we should have gotten a better car," I ventured.

"Oh we don't need to waste our money on luxuries. The rental agency screwed up our name and our reservation, then when he found it, this was all he had. One of those smart young mechanics with a comb sticking out of his pocket, and other things on his mind, brought it out to me. He shows me how to put it in reverse, gives me the keys and tells me to back out of the garage. The garage is on that hill," Dom pointed to the snarled of traffic behind us coming down the steep hill.

"Here I am in the middle of Rome, and the car won't go into reverse! And everyone was watching as I left! Let's get out of the city."

Twenty-five years of marriage had sharpened my sensitivities. Quietly, I pulled out the map and helped him get out of Rome ... as quickly as possible. The traffic circles and convergence of vehicles traveling at unrestrained speed seemed far more chaotic than they had been that Easter almost 20 years earlier. We had driven to Rome that time in a familiar English Cortina. This time we had to adjust to everything in Europe quickly, and neither of us was ready to admit that our reflexes could be a little slower. The ubiquitous motorcyclists buzzing in and out around us had not changed a bit.

"Young show-offs!" my husband murmured.

As we drove from the chaos of Rome into the countryside, my husband began to feel a sense of relief. Then he realized a humiliating interplay of Italian protocol on the autostrada. A red Ferrari zoomed past, almost swiping the side of our bug. Then a Mercedes. There was no power in the little Fiat; nor respect.

I tried not to feel guilty as I enjoyed the changing terrain. I offered my mate an apple and some cheese that I had quickly procured while he picked up the car. He took the apple, keeping his eyes on the road.

"Siena," *Fodor* says, "is the finest example of the Middle Ages in Italy." I wondered rather blithely to myself what a medieval city had to offer beyond the beauty of its cathedral.

My images of medieval man were lost somehow in brief historic sketches and snatches of art meant to depict the times, medieval jousts, castles and walls, and perhaps a few renderings of man with a hoe, bent over the earth, beyond the walls. Art and architecture remain as testimony of the age. Charlemagne had been given credit in the eighth century for wanting to resurrect the written records, but records were still crude. Who was to tell us what subtle change between Dark Ages and Renaissance was really like?

My husband brought me out of my revelry. "I can park this vehicle," he yelped.

The sign clearly read: "No cars within the city gates." We pulled into a car park, and entered the Middle Ages.

Flags waved gently as we passed on the other side of the walls. The September air was warm as we pulled our bags from the Fiat and walked toward the little Palazzo where we were to stay. The 17th-century residence was in the center of the Tuscan town, not far from the gate, not far from everything.

We were escorted silently through a darkened stairway which wound through arched walkways and ended in a wing that seemed pleasant enough. The antechamber of our room was flanked with armoirs and chests. Without a word, our guide put the luggage down and handed us the key, pointing to the large chamber ahead—a spacious, well-appointed suite with a shuttered window that framed a well-ordered Tuscan landscape. The view was like the background of the Mona Lisa, serene, with vine-covered terraces spilling over the hillside. In the foreground was a little garden, where I saw guests having tea.

I turned to express my pleasure, and the old gentleman who had guided us up the stairs was gone. We were alone with the beauty of Tuscany in the distance and the ambience of a palatial room. A chintz bedspread covered two connected twin beds. A matching regal swag was draped between two Corinthian columns. My husband relaxed, congratulated me on the find, and dropped the car keys on the desk, relieved.

We were invited to dinner by a gentle bell. Young waiters, dressed formally, smiled and led us through the recessed arches. The quiet underplay was tasteful, the northern Italian cuisine superb. This is the way to see the Middle Ages, we both agreed.

It was a very good way to see the Middle Ages. We started on foot with the September sun bright overhead. I soon took off my sweater and tied it around my shoulders as we climbed the narrow hills over which Siena is spread. The walls that limited her growth have protected her character.

We entered the enclosure of the Duomo. The facade of this cathedral was Gothic. Begun in the 11th-century, it was embellished over two more centuries, changing dusty Siena into one of the most splendid and refined cultural centers in Italy. Inside from floor to ceiling was a masterpiece of valuable art. There were ropes marking off graffiti on the floor too valuable now to step on, but as we walked around in the September morning, 700 years after it was built, a bell rang, calling us to remember its purpose. In the silence, a chant began, and the Duomo again became a reliquary of poised praise.

It was easy to follow the paths of medieval man. The roads had not changed. We wandered from hill to hill, feeling the safety of limited traffic, and took in the subtle beauty of crafts and food, passed down with the tasteful pride of the Sienese. Peeking through an archway of a gate, I saw the wonderful style of these people. Looking into a shop window, I saw it in the pastries, the panforte packaged in beautiful wrap, telling us what a delicacy it was. There was style even in the paper doilies they were displayed on.

Art permeates every corner, a true mirror of the city's character. Even the usual trinkets for tourists were artful. Everything we saw was tasteful.

We came upon the heart of the city in mid-afternoon. The Piazza del Campo, Siena's center, is said to be one of the

world's most pleasing to look at. Entering it was like walking into a historical happening. All the hills converged to form a shell-shaped civic center, a place where life once beat with the fervor of intense conflict and vitality, where battles with Florence were proclaimed and where for 700 years, a continuous horse race has been held.

I recognized the sight of the famous wild horse race from pictures and news clips, but the sense of place took on a different feel stepping into it in the sunlight. I could imagine the fervor of a 700-year-old tradition in such a setting. The Palio, the oldest continuous horse race in the world, attracts a thunderous crowd of tourists. But it is the Sienese who feel the pitch rise for months ahead. Rivalry has existed through generations of the city's families, and they take pride in keeping alive a medieval tradition that has continued between districts or contrata of the city. Each district proudly maintains its own medieval flag, emblem, and colors. The prize, a Palio, or flag from the cathedral, is awarded to the fastest horse. The pageantry is planned all year, is visible a week in advance, and comes to a colorful pitch in July and August, creating an excitement unlike any in Europe.

It was peaceful and pleasant in September, a few souvenir flags reminiscent of the pageantry of the medieval joust, waved in the wind. Matrons crossed arm in arm. A young couple was having cappucino in the cafe. In the center, the Mangia tower cut through the horizon, next to the handsome publico palace and the civic museum. The piazza's base was formed of herringbone brick, representative of 24 members of the city's first governing body to include merchants with the nobility. The setting was extraordinary by anyone's standards.

There was a time before the conquerors razed nearly all of them when Siena had a skyline thick with towers. The tower of Palazzo Publico built in 1325 was rebuilt in 1345 as the concept of city government rose. A city as we know it was born, and the embryo of government was established. Here in the heart of the walled city, every conceivable ritual of communal and personal life was tasted.

Inside the civic museum was art which had endured like the architecture outside, as testimony to the happenings and beliefs and style of the people of Siena. We saw works of

Mantini, Sodoma and a whole school, come to be known as Sienese. Impressive and beautiful as the works of the masters were, to me the most interesting piece of art in the civic museum was a fresco of Good and Bad Government done by Ambrogio Lorenzetti. Here was my answer to what life was like in the 13th-century in this city.

The panoramic tale showed on one side, the many towers and buildings, with elegant riding parties parading up and down the streets and ladies dancing. Outside the city walls were verdant pastures, happy lords and ladies, castles, fine living. The other half of the painting, depicting Bad Government, graphically pointed out the vises of greed, corruption, poverty, neglect and descent. Tyranny astride a black goat and seated between cruelty, deception, defraud, fury, and discord, took command of the scene with the symbols of justice chained and trampled upon. The allegory inside the public building was graphic, memorable.

There was no doubt what life in Siena at the break of the Middle Ages had come to be. She had the benefit of good government. In spite of plagues, constant battles between the ruling classes of Guelf and Guibiline, the incessant competition with Florence for power, her natural containment had been an asset. Without access to water, she remained small. Her personality was formed around limitations of space and money, and she remained urbane. Everything we saw was beautiful and lasting. The taste in every detail seemed to be a part of the fiber.

As we were called to dinner again that night in our little palace with its sweet view, we thought again of the art, the creations of man in the 12th-century. The art was wonderful, but it seemed half the story. "We will know a time by its architecture, its deeds and its words," Ruskin has told us. We delved into the poet who recorded it as he saw it.

"Read me a little more of Dante," my husband suggested.

> *"Oh soul, self humbled for the climb to grace,*
>
> *I said, if it was you who spoke, I beg you,*

*Make yourself known either by name or place.*

*I was Sienese, she answered ...*

*Sapia was I though sapient I was not.*

*I found more joy in the bad luck of others than in the good that fell to my own lot."*

There was, of course plague and pestilence, conflict and financial failure. There was life, I thought, and today's Siena showed her best face. Dante had been a student here, in one of the world's first universities, another invention of the medieval mind. He would tell us while in his own exile of the corruption and the cost of government. A plaque would tell us he had been there.

We enjoyed a last walk around the city the following day, and passing by a side street came upon the home of another Sienese writer. By a tiny, unobtrusive portal a historic marker denoted the home of "Catherine of Siena," patroness of Italy, Doctor of the Church. Somewhere in the recess of my mind I remembered Catherine. Her image was another vague medieval symbol.

"Tell me about this Catherine," my husband plied, thinking I was sole expert in the medieval heros and heroines. Not to lose footing, I feigned a little knowledge, scanning my books.

We sat for a moment in the little entry, reading the leaflets about Catherine. "Her father was a dyer, it says here," I read aloud. "She was 24th of 25 children. Refusing marriage, she spent time in solitude, became a mystic and then a woman of active charity, dealing with death daily and the Plague."

"A medieval Mother Teresa," my husband commented.

"I suppose. But here it says she was consul to emperors and popes, dealt with Guelfs and Guiblines in their intense battles, advised, reproved and taught, and then wrote *The Dialogue,* a classic on the spiritual life. A self-taught illiterate,

her book came in a flash, the reports say, yet remains on the list of the best." I became more than curious.

"What were her credentials?" I said aloud, applying 20th-century thinking to the making of a medieval saint.

A nearby Englishman, in uncharacteristic English openness, answered my ridiculous question.

"Her credential was her blameless life," he said in customary English underplay.

We walked out of the house into the courtyard which faced a back street and brought us to modern Siena in a jolt. I ducked as a spitball came spinning toward me. Italian school boys were no different than ours, or their medieval counterparts, I learned. Dante went to school here. Dante had described it. Catherine had lived it. There were sinners and saints, then and now. There were palaces and plagues, saints and sinners. Good and bad government.

It seemed, however, as we walked back to our little pension-palace, that medieval Siena had discovered an art of living that would remain superior. Gifted in their own peculiar arts, the Sienese knew how to live well. It was a beautiful medieval city, a gem of artful life.

We were beginning to appreciate this urbane, beautiful life. Perhaps this was what our mid-life could be like, quiet and sophisticated. We had earned a position of conspicuous leisure if we wished. Cities like Siena could teach us how to enjoy possessions we were acquiring. We had learned much in the little walled city in the heart of Tuscany.

# Assisi

Keeping our itinerary, after three days we left Tuscany with hopes of entering Umbria, the heartland of Italy, before dark. Early in the drive we enjoyed distant views of hill towns and a pleasant rolling terrain. My husband was coping well with the autostrada as it moved through the long stretches of good highway.

As we turned to secondary roads that crossed the Appenese, the drive became treacherous. The scenery was magnificent, but my husband could not take his eyes off the road, and cars began to pass again, impatient with his caution. Our estimation of Assisi before dark now seemed off. But he continued to drive steadily, and I handed him a snack that would hold us until we arrived and again began reading aloud to pass the time. I had taken on the pleasure of pointing out places and facts as we drove along, and even continued to read snatches from the allegory of the supreme poet of the Middle Ages. But as we approached the brown hills of Umbria, I realized Dante could wait.

We had put Assisi on our itinerary to meet St. Francis, the medieval saint. Ahead of us were the hills that the saint had roamed. On the slopes of Mt. Subasio, the terraced hills, even in the semi dark, were soothing.

Driving on the Italian roads had frazzled my husband again, and he was grateful for the sight of a medieval town that didn't require driving. We had taken longer than estimated, and we were a little anxious, wondering if our reservations were still firm, having made no other contacts than a letter some two months previous.

"You did all right in Siena," my husband remarked. "What will it be in Assisi? Two beds and a cross?" he quipped, knowing full well I had succumbed to the enticement to see Assisi, not from a palace, but from a monastery turned pension.

"Take everything out that you need. We're not getting back in this car tomorrow," he pleaded. I silently prayed the room would still be ours. A tiny nun peeped through the window hole in the wooden door. Without saying a word, she led us down a dark corridor and turned the key to a clean, spartan room. I looked in ... two beds and a cross. I smiled. My husband was relieved. He was asleep before I returned from the bathroom down the hall. Through the night I heard him murmur, "Give me room. Don't push me off. I will not leave my carcass in this foreign land!"

Dawn broke before his rest was complete, and the cheerful singing outside our window was more than he could cope with. He put a pillow over his ears, and I went to the window to see who was serenading us. "Arise and shout your joy!" they sang with all their hearts. The young seminarians from the North American College of Rome had been set loose in Assisi. It was their first break from formal studies, and their energy was well directed.

"Wait until you see the view," I suggested to my mate.

Beyond the boys were round russet domes and small towers, crooked paths swooping down to the plains of Spoleto. "Oh, I think you can see Francis here," I said, getting right into the spirit of pilgrimage.

"You go and tell me what he's like. I just need the morning to unwind."

At breakfast, I met a kindred spirit. She introduced herself as a teacher from Germany who wanted to the meet the Francis of her studies. Phillipa, a retired school teacher dressed simply in a navy dress, heavy walking shoes and a hat to cover the crown of her white hair, introduced herself as a sociologist and a humanitarian. I related that I was a mother of five sons and found myself doting on my boys.

"My interest in Assisi is purely academic," she asserted. "I am not a spiritual person. Francis is one of those fascinating people from history who defied the times. I'd like to see Assisi from the hill, the hermitage, the plain of Spoleto," she continued, but almost in an aside, she looked at me, "Would you like to go with me?"

This is perfect, I remember thinking. Dom can have the morning off, and I can get an overview of the city.

"Yes, that would be great," I smiled.

The nun at the desk gave directions that seemed simple enough. The hermitage was two and a half miles. It would be a pleasant five-mile walk, to and from, or a short walk to the city center where cabs would be available. We decided to share a cab and walk around the hermitage.

"Every cab in town is engaged," we were politely told at the stop across from the Roman temple of Minerva. "The 'party' is going to the hermitage." A rally of the communist party, active then in every little city of Italy, was in full sway, and the cabbie knew the 'Italian way' of placating every invader of his city. "The cabs are all tied up for the 'party,' " he repeated.

I looked at my shoes and wished I had been as practical as my matronly companion, but decided I could make it. We set out on foot to climb Mt. Subasio.

"I can see why the ecologists claim this man as their icon, this man who lived with the birds," my companion remarked, "but the communists ... you can say what you want of a hero, I guess ... even the communists want to claim Francis. This is utterly fascinating," she added.

"They say the hippies claim him, too." I added, just having read that Zefferelli was interviewed by a group of hippies when he did his movie, "*Brother Moon, Sister Sun*." The young band of Francis did look like a commune of hippies in the movie.

"You have young boys," she plied me. "What do they think of him? Do they see Francis as the ultimate rebel?"

"I don't really know," I answered, going through the litany of the ages of the five boys, where they were in school, what their aspirations were. "Our boys are leaders like Francis was. They're all full of life. I think they could identify with him in many ways. They're at various stages of trying to figure out what to do with their lives and not wanting to do exactly what their parents do. Yes, some of our boys are rebelling, you know, long hair, loud music, they're groping as Francis did. But they probably see him vaguely as a statue in the park as I did for years."

"Maybe they could learn something from him if they understood his genius, but it isn't your boys that you're here for, is it?" Phillipa asked, cutting to the core of my search. "What is your real interest in him?"

Now she had me. I wasn't sure myself. This visit to Assisi had something to do with my mid-life search for meaning. I felt lucky as an American traveling to Italy, knowing I had a nice family, good friends, a comfortable home. Although I had had some repressed career goals, I was lucky, I thought. But every once in a while, I questioned what I was doing with my life. The days always seemed saturated, filled with too many activities.

"My life is good but complicated," I answered, still thinking aloud. "Maybe it's the nature of women to be pulled in so many directions. There are times when I just want to be alone. Once a year at least I go to the sea to seek some silence, but at home, I can't even free myself from daily clutter to be as creative as I would like to be. There are times when I crave simplicity in the work I do or hope to do. I know that I can't think with all this clutter. The mind has to be free and uncluttered, simple like Francis's, to be truly creative. He was probably one of the most creative people of the Middle Ages. He defied convention, defied his family's middle-class life, defied the authority of the church in its complicated style."

"Dante might have been the supreme poet of the Middle Ages, but this man's life was a poem. He lived free as the birds, with music on his lips, and simple as a child. I have read every author on the subject of simplicity, from Thoreau to Anne Murrow Lindberg. Each one of them experimented with time away from society, even gave us books on the subject, but Francis was the master of the simple life. He discovered it so young. Most of us have to have tasted everything before we realize we will want more and more insatiably, but he seemed to come to this knowledge so young. He found what every philosophy eventually arrives at: *that to free the spirit, we have to shed worldly goals.*"

"For 700 years we have been studying him because he lived what he preached. He lived the gospel as no other human being has done. 'The poverello,' they called him. Beautiful, isn't it? 'Poor in spirit.' "

"Do you think you could do that?" Phillipa asked me.

This woman cuts to the bone, I remember thinking.

"Of course not," I said honestly, "but there is always something to learn from these rebels, these extremes of humanity, these giants of history, these saints ...."

"I know I can't give up what Francis did." The sweat was forming on my brow and neck, and we were not even halfway up the hill. Taxis carrying dignitaries from the party passed us.

"I value the 'good life,' the pleasure of this journey; I value my family, the role of being the mother; but I will have to give that up as the children are spreading their wings, and I will have to learn to let go soon enough. And yet I don't know where to go from here ... I am almost afraid to be free. It is difficult to let go of familiar securities. More and more often I find myself asking: 'What's it all about?' ... this life of striving and achieving?"

"It takes a lifetime of acquiring and achieving before most of us even question it. Francis was much younger when he asked that question. He was at the height of his youthful attractiveness, in the vigor of his manly desires, poised to seek fame as a knight, when something struck him as wrong with it all.

"He knew there would never be enough treasures to satisfy him, not enough parties, not enough power. That's when he took to these hills, drank in the beauty of nature and the solitude that poets thrive on. Once he was alone, listening to his God, he made a momentous decision. He would have none of it."

The cabbie returned, and knowing how to placate everyone, rolled down his window: "I can take you up to the hermitage if you get in quickly." We were in before he could finish the sentence, viewing the sweep of the valley from a comfortable vantage point.

At the top of the hill we entered the quiet chapel erected where the saint had once knelt. My friend and I, too, knelt in silence. Solitude is a universal need. We both knew it. We both were seeking it in the footsteps of the simple man of Assisi. Coming out of the chapel and looking down at the plain below, the mountains in the distance, I felt refreshed by the quiet, far away from the noise of the world, far away from the confusion of my own inner world. Umbria was brown and peaceful, as peaceful a place as the famous saint who had inhabited it in the 13th-century.

The time had been most rewarding. Returning to the monastery, I found the morning had been pleasant for my husband, too. The nuns had packed us a lunch at his request, and standing firm on his decision not to enter the car that day, we set out on foot to see the city of Assisi nestled all around us.

It was easy to follow the life of the famous son, and it was easy to envision his medieval dilemmas as we walked the

steep, winding streets. The city's Roman history and Etruscan past offered but a few remains, the temple of Minerva, a few museum remnants. It was the 13th-century that had made the lasting imprint on the town. And Assisi remained medieval in spite of the heavy flood of tourists who had come to visit it in our century.

We passed the tiny home of the Bernadones, Francis's birthplace, shops that could be retailers like his father's business, taverns where he could have reveled with his friends as a young man, the courtyard where he tore off his clothes and gave them back to his father, declaring himself free of worldly possessions. And we saw the tiny church where he heard the message, "Repair my church."

We entered the huge cathedral constructed to commemorate the simple man. It was filled with frescos by Giotto and a myriad of vaults and chambers so complicated that we were at first turned off with the profusion of stimuli and the vastness of the memorial. And then in some awakening I had succumbed to the fact that this was typical of the world's way of remembering. We saw the tiny portuncula where the simple saint lay on a stone and died, later to be covered with yet another huge bascillica. The anomaly did not pass by my husband nor me.

There were also hills around all Assisi to be explored, hills untouched by buildings or people, hills appealing to a pilgrim bent on understanding the saint's love of nature. Heading upward, we wound to the top of the city where the castle built by Barbarosa commanded another fine view of the plains below. The ruins of the fort were mute. Below was the plain of Perugia and the rugged gorge of Tescio. Only parts of the castle wall, once linked with the city wall, remained; that day's only invaders were a few insects crawling over the stones. The clear blue sky and a warm sun were welcome enough for our picnic.

The freshly baked bread, fruit juices in cardboard containers, and cookies made in the monastery kitchen were a wonderful lunch, and with full stomachs, we stretched out on a blanket letting the warm rays of the September sun seep in, and we were grateful.

"Phillipa turned out to be a very interesting woman," I told my husband. "She had a different interest in St. Francis than I did. She wasn't interested in saints per se. She said she wanted to understand his genius from a sociological point of view, how he was such a happy person with so little."

"Being a practical man," Dom replied, "I really never saw the need to give away the family business. I can sympathize with old Mr. Bernadone. Can you imagine one of our boys coming home from medical school and tearing up his degree after all the sacrificing we did to help see him through? It even seems a little rude and dramatic."

I saw the grin on my husband's face as he thought of the well-known scene that had occurred in one of the squares of Assisi. The bishop and the father had been stunned as Francis threw off all his clothes and ran through the city in his birthday suit. "He was a rebel, and I never heard that he apologized to his father," Dom remarked.

"Well, part of that image is Zefferelli's interpretation," I answered. "But even the movie maker created a scene where he seemed to be looking back at his father's house as if reconciliation was in his heart. His break from his parents and the world had to be shown emphatically."

He was a scene stealer; there was no doubt, I thought as I lay there. My husband was right, Francis was a rebel to corruption and a cause that was based on love. He was a poet, a joyful, pure, childlike saint, still full of chivalry as he identified with the poorest of the poor, dressing simply, eating simply, living simply, so as not to offend those who were poor.

Everything he did, he did dramatically. I could almost see him dancing along the path below us, rubbing two sticks together, pretending he was playing a violin. I think that is what fascinated me most. He was not a dour saint. I loved the joy he exuded. How happy and pure was his fun. He was a man who lived his love until the day he died, not an idealist who talked, but a song who continued to be sung.

Our friend Dante had the greatest respect for the saint. Checking his *Divine Comedy*, I saw that he placed Francis at the highest pinnacle of Paradise. We, too, 700 years later, were still learning from him. The world goes through its cycles of power and corruption. In every generation, boys grow up, rebel, take their place in the world. We move on and let them live their lives; flowers bloom again.

Looking down the plain, the city spilled out in front of the ruin of the castle behind, the tall grass and wildflowers swaying in the warm fresh air. I felt like Francis still had something to teach us. His life was real; this city was real. It was easy to be caught in revelry as the trees around were motionless, gray and limpid. A lizard darted across the stones, and it jolted me.

Sitting on the hill with the gentle wind at my neck, I realized that in my secret heart beyond the bounds of hypocrisy, I had been forced to make an unprejudiced examination of myself while I was in Assisi. I knew I could never aspire to know the poverty, the humility nor the obedience of this saint, even though I saw his nobility. I was married and did not understand the rigors of chastity. But do we not grow by just touching the earth where such nobility flowered? Studying the saint, seeing the beauty of the land, the reality and the essence of a peace that still seemed to pervade the land, could we not absorb just a little of it? I hoped so. His life was all around us. It had been a pilgrimage to the center of simplicity. There was an unexplainable stillness that seemed to pervade the Umbrian countryside. Perhaps just a little would stay with us.

## San Giovanni

Leaving the heartland of Italy on a Sunday seemed a wise move. The autostrada was quiet. We bypassed Rome without any complications and headed south with a little more speed than we were able to accomplish around the larger metropolises.

Entering the Amalfi coast once more opened a flood of memories. The south was still both romantic and mysterious to me. We sailed past signs to Capri, Ravello, Pasitano and I sat back enjoying the wonder of this extraordinary coast. This part of the journey was meant to provide material for my work ahead. Hoping to develop some stories around the people of the south, I had begun to dig further into the history of the more remote villages in the mountains below Rome.

On our Root Search some 15 years before, we had skirted the coast of Calabria and found it to be surprisingly beautiful. The history was rich, but incomplete. There had not been time to investigate the mountains. San Giovanni in the Sila Forest was the home of my paternal grandparents. It would be a good destination for our medieval venture, a continuation of medieval hill towns of Italy. Siena and Assisi were both archetypes of the Middle Ages. San Giovanni de Fiore, translated, was "St. John of the Flowers." In Italian or English the village sounded quaint.

Passing Naples, we were relieved to realize it would be the last large city to circumvent. By late afternoon, the traffic was mercifully light and we began to relax a little. As we neared the sea at sunset, houses, rocks and trees took on the enchantment of twilight, seeming to shine with a light of their own. My first sight of ancient villages of the south perched precariously by the sea gave a rush of excitement. There were so many untold stories, so many unpainted scenes. This isolated coast of Italy was ripe with mystery.

The September sunset was a mellow benediction to the day. The fiery streaks from the orange orb lingered for hours over the mountains in the distance. Rocks and cliffs alternated with woods, olive groves and vines. We were soon surrounded by the Sila as dusk came on.

My husband seemed more at ease on this part of the journey, as traffic had been sparse and the drive quiet, but as we headed up the once-forested mountain, the drive became a little more difficult. The road was narrow, and there was no flower-bedecked median that we had enjoyed on the autostrada. It wound upward, circling the mountain with no view of anything but a rocky edge.

The Sila Forest, historically rich with chestnuts, was depleted. As we ascended the heights of the mountain, we saw the feeble attempt to replant. There were a few saplings here and there on the bare hillside. It seemed we were leaving civilization. The wind outside tumbled through the brush, sweeping a few leaves of deciduous trees, waving the limbs of sapling pines. The silence deepened, and I became sensitive to the desolation. An enormous, transparent paper moon hung in the rose-tinted sky over the few pines.

At the crest of the mountain, I saw it: the village of San Giovanni de Fiore. The 12th-century village of my ancestors crowned the hill. At first, the city looked like an impenetrable fortress, isolated on top of the mountain. On closer approach I could see there were no city walls as had surrounded Siena nor castles as had looked out of Assisi, no formal gate to this city in the south. Tiny houses clustered almost on top of one another formed the outline, a fortress hardly able to defend itself against the hardships of daily life.

Slowly we drove through the alleys and narrow streets. I noticed well-carved doors here and there and a fine window imposed on much medieval poverty. People were hanging from the balconies, eyeing us with uncomfortable glances. Chairs were pulled out in front of the buildings, people visiting as if the courtyard or street were their living room, glancing at the Fiat that was interrupting their privacy.

There were no families to greet us, no one to put on the pot of soup or pasta that I had been accustomed to smelling as we visited relatives in America. The only recommended hotel was Dino's, written up as a hotel-lodge, newly renovated for the budding ski trade of the Sila. The small lobby was virtually empty as we entered, except for two young men, one behind the desk and the other across from him, eagerly chatting. Their conversation came to an abrupt end as we entered.

"We have reservations," my husband said in English, without thinking. The young clerk's eyes were alert. He answered in quick, direct sentences all in excellent English, but gave orders in Italian to the younger man beside him to tend to our luggage.

"Yes, we have a very comfortable room for you on the second floor."

I looked at the picture of the village on a poster over the desk. Covered with snow, it looked better, much like an Alpine village in Switzerland. I had a strange feeling we were the only guests in the hotel this autumn day.

"Have you come for the archeological digs?" the clerk inquired, eyeing us with as much curiosity as we had for the people outside. "They find a few coins, some vases every time a new building goes up." I glanced at the work site of the plain, rather poorly constructed buildings going up across the street.

"No, I'm doing some research for a book," I answered, adding, almost reluctantly, "And this is the birthplace of my paternal grandparents."

"Ah, your grandparents no doubt told you about the Badia." He saw my puzzled look. "The Badia, you know, abbey, small church. It is not a Duomo, small church, but very old. It is being renovated, and a museum is going up next to it. Tourists will like it. The rose window is a perfect example of 12th-century Romanesque. For my part, it is the prophet that I find more interesting. Dante talks about Joachim, our Joachim of Fiore, in his *Divine Comedy*. Even though Dante puts him in Paradiso, the church has not canonized him. It would help us if he were a real saint."

"No, my grandmother never talked about the abbey, Joachim or Dante, I have to admit. She did have wonderful memories of the St. John Feast Day celebrations. That's in June, right?"

"Would you like to see the abbey?" the young man asked, coming back to his favorite theme. He seemed to be a coil of energy, a spring that might be released by one change of circumstance. He moved deftly, instructing his associate with a quick glance as he handed him a large key, reaching out to shake our hands at the same time.

"My name is Tony. I would be happy to show you around tomorrow, if you wish, perhaps take you to the courthouse for the records of your grandparents or the graveyard where your ancestors are buried."

We thanked him and followed the younger Calabrian. "I hadn't thought about going to the cemetery, but this young man could be really helpful," I told my husband.

"Dinner is at eight in the dining room." He pointed to the room down a corridor as we squeezed into the tiny elevator with our guide and our luggage. Our rooms were spartan, with a big comfortable sofa and large bathroom designed, I'm sure, to entice new tourists. Looking out from our window I saw a barren hillside, empty fields, a scarred mountain.

Later that evening in the dining room, we were the sole diners, as I suspected. Tony had told the chef of our arrival, and as we finished, he came out to greet us. His English was not as good as the younger Calabrian's. "I worked in Pittsburgh for a while, but I wanted to come home. Life was too fast. Here we take time for what matters."

"What does matter?" I asked.

"Family," he answered without hesitation. "In the end, that is all that matters. In America, everyone like to be big boss. I really don't care to be boss; I just want to cook and watch my family grow. Did you enjoy the veal?"

We assured him we did.

He continued. "My children weren't too happy to come back, but I didn't know where they were half the time. Here, if I don't know where they are, my wife, my sisters, my brothers do. The family is all around."

He offered us some more wine, insisted we have some of his dessert, free. I wasn't surprised. We left wondering how this hotel could continue and what his children would do for a living.

The next day, passing the desk, we asked for directions to the abbey. Tony was willing to show us. He quickly motioned for his assistant to come behind the counter, and we headed to the narrow streets. The houses seemed glued to one another, and nowhere in between did I see soil, even in the courtyard of the courthouse. St. John of the Flowers, I thought, and where are the flowers?

People crowded around the entrance of the public buildings in the center of the piazza. We entered a poorly constructed official building where people carrying out their business looked dour. Women with their poorly dressed children, waited on the benches. Dom broached the questions to an intent Tony as I looked up the family records. "What is the unemployment here?"

"High. About 7,000 in a village of 20,000 are out of work. The social system doesn't really offer much."

"How do they manage?"

"Oh, we help each other," he offered defensively. "I was lucky to get the job I have. I give most to my parents. My girlfriend understands. We'll wait a little longer. My brother is not so patient. He's in America, NYU."

"Really," I remarked, "and do you intend to follow him?"

"No, not me. Some go; some can't. My family, my ancestors are here. I love the village, the land. Do you want to see the graves of your ancestors?"

"Maybe later," I suggested, "but you told us about the abbey."

We passed only a few people on the street of the little abbey, a child with his mother, and an old woman in her provincial costume coming out of church. I started to get out my camera, and then realized it would seem offensive. Would I be one more foreign invader in a land that had seen people come and go, now seeing the antiquated ways as an oddity? I wouldn't chance it.

"Who was this Joachim?" I plied our guide.

"He was a 12th-century mystic, from a nearby province. Wealthy enough to travel the ends of the world, he had seen much, but he was touched by the lepers he saw, just as St. Francis was. After his trip to the Holy Land, he gave up his title, his worldly possessions and came home to find a spot in these mountains where he could establish a branch of the Cistercians. Climbing up the mountain you entered by, he was lead by angels, they say, until he found the spring, right here in this spot where the abbey is now."

The abbey in front of us was small and simple, as Tony had said it would be. There was one exquisite rose window that allowed a perfect light into the small building. The abbey was being whitewashed, and its simplicity was beautiful, the only touch of beauty in the drab street.

"Joachim's preaching was eloquent," Tony continued as we entered, "but he preferred to preach in the open fields. He spoke of three ages: the age of the Father, the age of the Son, and the final age of the Holy Spirit. When we reach the age of the Holy Spirit, we will not need churches at all. We will be one in spirit," he explained. "I think the medieval church was not ready to hear this," Tony interjected. "So Joachim is merely called Blessed, but the little abbey is a gem of peace."

I agreed. He pointed proudly to the museum next door.

"I'll leave you here. Angela will take good care of you."

Angela was a young girl of sixteen or so, assigned to the museum as its sole guide, curator, protector. She sat in the entrance, in a shadowy alcove, working on a piece of lace. With Tony's introduction, she quickly flicked on the lights, and much to our surprise, the museum was ours, all ours. There were no great pieces of art, in fact there was no art at all. The museum was composed of agricultural implements and a few cooking utensils.

Had I forgotten? This was the livelihood of most people of San Giovanni until the turn of the century. An area, stripped of its forests, had become agricultural for centuries and that, too, had been depleted. The medieval system of feudalism had sucked the land and the people of their very rich heritage. We were but 40 miles from where Homer had written, and Pythagoras had codified math, and where once the forests and soil were rich. The people were left to the plunder of feudalism from medieval times on. Feudalism had held its tight grip in strange forms up until the 1940s, when fascism tried its hand at control. Southern Italy had seen the great exodus at the turn of the century when my grandparents, with thousands of others, boarded the boats at Naples and left.

Angela, a pretty, brown-haired young woman, seemed intent on showing us every implement, but since she spoke little English, and I spoke little Italian, we groped for communalities in explanations. My husband began in his Sicilian dialect to bridge the gap, and she seemed to understand when he explained that my family had come from the area. "We live in America now," he repeated.

"I have cousins in America. They never write. We are forgotten people. It is the most terrible agony to be forgotten." When Dom translated that, I felt sick.

"Tell her I'll write," I said quickly, and I took out my little note pad for her address. "I'll send you a cookbook of foods my grandmother brought from this area," I promised. I flipped through my notebook, looking for a blank page. When

I finally found one, she became very agitated. "What is she saying?" I asked Dom.

"She says we should not waste a whole page on her."

The low self-esteem of generations of women of this region suddenly hit. My grandmother had assumed the matriarchal pride of the family with much verve, raising four children after my grandfather died, in a strange new land. She had been revered for her motherhood, almost to the extension of worship of her motherhood. But out of the range of motherhood, her self-image suffered.

My mother learned to drive a car in the '40s, only after much persuasion that women should be able to shop and go to church alone. I had been the lucky one to go on to an American college, with the goal that it would benefit my motherhood. I had seen the confusion of the women who dared to wish for both career and motherhood with full confidence.

I was sure my sons would marry women who would aspire to professions of art, law or medicine, to be followed along side their motherhood. They would see life as fully as possible, but this young woman spoke of the permeating lack of self-esteem that cut through the ages. The low self-esteem of all the people held down by the uncertainty of the earth, the imbalance of feudalism, suddenly hit me. What they had had to conquer staying in this ancient land seemed monumental. The history suddenly penetrated. This was the other side of the equation; the picture in Siena, Good and Bad Government, had told the story graphically. Here was feudalism at its worst and a government incapable through the centuries of facing the needs of the lower half of the peninsula.

And again, on this more personal pilgrimage, I was forced to make another examination. Even in America in the 20th-century, we ignore what we want to ignore. Both government and individuals have chosen to ignore isolated peoples. I have cousins in America whom I have forgotten. I know there are people suffering from want of a letter, a touch of love. Somehow in this little village, the desolation was so real.

Isolated, forgotten, a dreadful example of feudalism that lingered too long, of land depleted, of low self-esteem deeply

penetrated. The ironies of history, this land once rich with the poetry of Homer, the pillars of Greek temples, the rule of the Roman Empire, was now a lonely village devoid of even flowers.

As we left the next morning I bought one of the beautiful pieces of lace that Angela was working on. It would be a reminder of San Giovanni, the ancient city on the hill. "He belonged in Paradiso," Dante had said of the mystic Joachim, who came to the mountain to contemplate in the silence of the Sila. The silence of the Sila now penetrated me.

As we drove down the hill, the wind from the sea stirred and whispered through the roads. We headed back to Naples, where we boarded a ferry to end our trip with a short stay in Capri, a honeymoon cap to our journey.

Looking down at the Bay of Naples on our last night in Italy, we enjoyed a simple picnic, remembering our first trip and picnics with our children. The sea sparkled from Capri, and the day was filled with that incomparable light of the Mediterranean. It penetrated our skin and our thoughts as we tried to savor what we had seen. We thought of the marvels of the art and taste of the people of Siena. We were touched by the poet of Assisi, who chose poverty and a simple way of life, and we could never forget the poverty of the south. Now we understood better the dilemma of Dante who sought to figure out the many players in the drama that had produced all of this.

The book of Proverbs says: "wisdom is a gem to be sought above all other gems." And we had come to realize it was one of the gems of travel. The light that comes though painful searching shines like a diadem.

I picked up my gold-leafed copy of Dante's masterpiece and finished the last canto as the sun set on the warm September evening.

"Read aloud," my husband requested.

> *"I yearned to know how my own image*
> *merges into the circle of light and how it*
> *finds place.*
>
> *But mine were not the wings of such a*
> *flight.*
>
> *Yet as I wished, the truth I wished for came,*
>
> *clinging my mind in a great flash of light."*
>
> —Dante, *The Divine Comedy*

# It's Your Turn, Chickadees

# Chapter 7

# Peace In The Mideast

*"How happy are those whose strength comes from you, who are eager to make the pilgrimage to Mount Zion. As they pass through the dry valley it becomes a place of springs; the early rain fills it with pools. They grow stronger as they go; they will see the God of gods on Zion!"*

—Psalm 122

Mid-life was taking a new turn as we set out to see the Mideast. The children were at last all away, the youngest in college, the others in various levels of school or residencies. My husband and I were alone again, searching for a new balance in our lives. The house could be full at holidays—ringing with laughter and banter—and empty the next day, the refrigerator stuffed with leftovers no one would touch. "The children aren't ours anymore, are they?" a friend had remarked. "Just holiday visitors."

"It's what we worked for, isn't it, to see them grow independent?" I answered, not really sure myself, and with the children leaving, there were new horizons for me.

My involvements in the community were broad and satisfying, and finally more serious writing was becoming possible. My work could go in many directions, and there was much I wanted to do.

My husband had new horizons, too, especially with the financial needs of the children coming to an end. He seemed to have a burst of energy, with the weight of their education being lifted.

When he brought home a brochure announcing a medical meeting that might take us to the Mideast, I was once again interested. Tel Aviv, Jerusalem, places I had always wanted to see, "Why not?" I thought. "Another journey. I have always grown with these experiences."

Two days before we were to leave, the phone rang, announcing the death of a close friend, a sudden death brought on by a heart attack. There seemed to be little indication of disease. He had been a virile man, active and productive. The community was stunned. "It's bad enough to loose him," his wife sobbed, "but I have no idea where he is. Do you believe in heaven? And why? If there is a God, Why? He was in his prime, doing what he loved to do."

The words stung. He had been stricken like my own father, in the prime of his life. I had heard these questions before....

But that was my father, I thought, this man was our age. I didn't have to go far to see other radical life changes among my friends. Mastectomies and cancers were announced like a litany. There seemed to be a frenzy to preserve life; fitness crazes and new diets were the rage. We were surrounded by a bevy of symbols defying age—youth creams on the shelves of my female friends, sports cars in front of our male friends' homes. People flaunting and testing their sexuality. Among our friends there was a noticeable number of women intensely expanding their careers and men taking younger wives. It was becoming increasingly clear where we were in the aging process. Mid-life was taunting us.

Time was becoming more precious. It was ticking out. Perhaps the journey we had planned to the Mideast would give space again for assessing the changes my husband and I were experiencing at this new turning point. I knew I needed a plan that was centered in values that mattered. I could not fool myself; I could wear a sequined dress or my husband could put on a university sweatshirt, but underneath, the arteries were hardening, the skin, without estrogen, was drying. Yes, life was changing, and where would mid-life to death take us?

Journeys had clearly marked our passages before. With each life change, there had been a turbulent questioning and sometimes painful adjusting, and then abundant new life. Now it was more than balance and techniques that I needed. Life, itself, seemed tenuous. If there was but little time left, or if indeed half of our life was gone, then I wanted to brace myself for what was ahead. Should we concentrate on health of the body, or a sharpening of the mind? And what about after-life? If I had once found Dante's *Divine Comedy* a poetic mix of real and allegory, now I found Heaven and Hell uncomfortable words to contemplate. Were they real terms or allegorical? What of the soul? I could no longer rely on my childhood interpretations, limited by the simplistic explanations once given to me.

And yet neither did I buy the cynic's interpretation of "eat, drink, and be merry, for tomorrow you perish." I looked at the life of our friend now laid open at his funeral, his accomplishments, his relationships, entangled at mid-life were now exposed. There were at the funeral a wife and a mistress mourning his loss, each thinking he loved only her. I looked at his family, his friends, his relatives who were affected. The heartbreaks were compounded. His unfinished business and his legacies, both good and bad, would continue to be examined. Life with all its complexities seemed exposed, the negative and the positive mixed, and the emptiness touching us all.

"More than ever, we need faith," I heard as we attended our friend's funeral. "Would my faith sustain me, if I were in my friend's place or the place of his wife?" I was forced to ask myself. What of this business of heaven? I began to call on every resource to try to understand. It was all unexpected, this new concern for life beyond life. There was enough to worry about in the day-to-day questions of living. Mid-life most definitely had announced itself, if only through our friends.

Yes, I thought this journey to the Holy Land could give some space to think about it all.

"The meetings will be in Tel Aviv and Jerusalem," our notification suggested, "and travel throughout Israel is possible." The thought of a trip to the Mideast became more and more enticing with each new brochure. We signed up in October. By April, however, the bombing of an El Al airliner had alarmed the world, and terrorism was at a peak all over Europe. Three-fourths of the people who had signed up for the meeting canceled their reservations. We considered only briefly and then held firm with our plans.

From the very onset, we were made aware of the power of terrorism. El Al's security check at the airport was stringent. We were interrogated by two separate security guards. Did we speak Hebrew or did we know the Arabic tongue? Neither. We had no nationalistic interests. That was clear. Then why did we want to visit Israel? Too deep to answer, I thought, but I mumbled the acceptable answer, "My husband is attending a medical meeting. I intend to visit the Holy Land. Ancient history interests both of us. Here are the documents concerning the meeting." The guards examined the papers with scrutiny. None of the interrogators seemed welcoming.

Once on board the plane, however, echoes of "Shalom" filled the colorfully decorated jumbo jet. Announcements were made in Hebrew, and a decidedly nationalistic flavor ensued. I do not speak Hebrew, Arabic, nor Yiddish, but I do understand happiness. We were caught in a feeling of family fun. Many were headed home, and there was an air of heightened expectancy. We were headed toward a young nation in an ancient land, a land that had not only encapsulated 10,000 years of man's history but a land that cradled the concept of a single, caring God. We were all headed home.

Good food, a blanket, and night were dealt in that order. From JFK to Lod International Airport outside of Tel Aviv, we were waft as if wings of eagles had taken us silently from our Western smugness to the heart of the Mideast. Medieval man placed the Holy Land in the center of the world. A pilgrimage there was wrought with the greatest of perils, but honor and atonement were the possible rewards. The Mideast, when we visited it, was filled with tension and unrest. Pilgrimage to this center remains one of the most prized of all spots on Earth. Without defining it, we were seeking insights, even a vision of the ancient meanings of life or at least a glimpse of a cultural treasury that only that land could offer.

In our youth, our adventures with austere budgets meant accepting "hard-up" rooms and thread-bare pensions. Just landing in Tel Aviv at this point in history seemed adventurous enough. We welcomed the comfortable accommodations on the 11th floor of the handsome Tel Aviv Hilton, complete with a balcony view of the Mediterranean.

Tel Aviv was lively, throbbing with discos, condominiums, a center of commerce with all the Western amenities— hardly the place to complete a vision of ancient history, I thought on first sight. Our "eagle" came with jet lag. Without a word, we hit the bed and slept like babes in spite of the afternoon sun.

A few hours later the sound of Eastern music awakened us. The music seemed to be coming from the outside. From our balcony, the sea looked calm; evening had cast a bluish-green tone on the surf. At the beach's edge, a huge yellow and white tent had been erected. Thick clusters of potted flowers marked off the favored spot with a festive spirit. The music came to a dramatic halt. We discerned a rabbi, a bride and a groom. Again we were entering into family fun. It was easy to join in the wish of the guests who exclaimed: "To Life!"

Tel Aviv abounds in new life, having been founded by a group of brave visionaries in 1909. In spite of its newness, the city is part of a complex that is recorded in ancient history. Jaffa, or Joppa of the Bible, is the appendage city that sprawls along the Mediterranean. From our balcony we could see the edge of Tel Aviv-Jaffa complex winding around the sea's edge. Near to us were the high rises, and in the distance where the old port once buzzed with trade, palm trees shaded the edges.

Early the following morning, I walked into the ancient city, trying to visualize what it looked like 2,000 years ago, trying to imagine it as an active port, and before recorded history, when the Joppa of the Bible relates the disembarking of Jonah. Amid Turkish coffee houses, art colonies and busy bazaars, I felt the wonder of a continuing city, even its new crust was a bit touristy.

While Dom began his meetings, I attended a cinematic introduction to modern Israel and her bounty. The narrow streets, unchanged traffic patterns and layered ruins helped to sharpen an association with what was and what is the land of Israel. I was quickly becoming secure in my headquarters in the Hilton, and presumed it would be safe to hop onto a tour that followed the western coast of Israel all the way up to the Lebanon border.

The sun was brilliant overhead, and as we drove along in the coach I listened to the able, native guide, chatting sometimes with my fellow travelers but most often keeping a silent reverie along with my own musings. From the window, the view was better than the cinemascope the day before. Each of the cities along the western coastal border of Israel is washed by the sea and shines as a gem individually shaped by the tide of history.

Just 30 miles north of the active port of Tel Aviv, a sign announced one of the great cities of antiquity. CAESARA, it read in bold letters. "Events of impressionable magnitude happened here," the guide echoed as we approached. In its classical phase, its harbor was a feat of engineering genius. Under Roman rule, a few years before the time of Christ, a great surge of building took place.

Herod, the local tetrarch, was not only an amazing politician but an extraordinary innovator. Half Jewish and half

Gentile, with his eye on placating both his own people and the power of Rome, he often hedged his bets. For his Jewish subjects, he rebuilt the great temple of Solomon in Jerusalem. For Augustus, his Roman boss, he built a city of massive proportions, luxurious homes of gleaming white stone, an amphitheater by the sea, a hippodrome for racing, a temple for the emperor. He named it for Caesar. Building was Herod's passion, his glory, his god. The city was to make him immortal.

We approached the outskirts with great expectancy. From the bus I could see a silent golden beach. In the foreground a medieval fortress built by Louis XII was all that remained intact. The surf beat against its thick stones as the morning sun reflected in the foam. A respectful silence stole over the travelers. My eyes scanned the panorama. An empty beach had replaced a city that rivaled Alexandria and Constantinople. All that was left of its classical era—the age of building ordered by Herod—was the amphitheater in the distance.

As I walked closer to the empty theater by the sea, the genius of Herod's architectural planners came quickly into focus. Its placement by the harbor gave theater-goers a breathtaking view.

As our group wandered around rather pensively, putting history together in bits and pieces, a few remnants of other ages were pointed out by the guide: two headless giants, statutes of the Byzantium era built around 300 A.D.; a moat; a half finished cathedral built by the Crusaders some 1,400 years after Herod's gleaming city was constructed. References to Caesara meandered through my subconscious: "2,500 Jews were dragged through these streets as captives after Jerusalem fell," I had read and I knew that St. Paul had been imprisoned in this city for two years.

I stumbled on stones. From what age had they come, I wondered. In 1949, a stone with the imprint "Pontius Pilate" was pulled from among this rubble. Caesara's history and its beauty, now shrouded in silence, make it an incomparable site to visit.

I was reluctant to board our bus when our allotted time had elapsed. Glancing at the fortress, with that noble sea lapping forcefully against the stones, I was mesmerized by its melancholy beauty. The half finished Gothic structure looked nakedly undressed, as did the pagan statues of the Byzantium age. A city once gleaming with white marble was now covered with sand, but the aura of significant happenings remained a reality in Caesara. The call to reboard broke the spell.

## Akko

As I entered the bus, a young girl sitting alone toward the back caught my eye. Her straw hat was perched atop a head of long chestnut hair. She stood out strikingly among the average looking middle-aged tourists. I remembered her winning smile when the tour guide had made us introduce ourselves. She, too, had joined the tour group in Tel Aviv with the hopes of beginning a complete tour of Israel. When asked how many spoke English, the young woman had raised her hand, and again she gave an assent to understanding French.

At some silent moment on the beach we had bumped into each other, wanting to know some of the same answers to history's questions. She came forward as the bus started out, asking if I was traveling alone. "Yes, today I am. My husband is attending a meeting in Tel Aviv," I answered.

"Well, then do you mind if I join you?" she asked.

"I don't mind at all," I said. "Please do. Is this your first journey to the Mideast?"

"Yes," she proceeded. "I've been studying in Paris and decided it might be a good time to see the rest of the world before I settle down."

"Are you traveling with a group?" I asked.

"No, I'm on my own. My friends were heading to Spain, but I've seen enough of central Europe. I thought it would be interesting to see the Mideast. It's been incredible, a real awakening."

With that word "awakening," my mind reeled back to my own experience a generation ago. We had followed an opportunity to see Europe through my husband's training. I could have studied in Paris as this lovely young girl from America was doing, but I chose instead to marry. She was from California, I had heard her say. I was in college on the East Coast when Professor Manning of the French Department called three of us individually into his office to tell us we were qualified contenders for a Fullbright—Bonny, Maria and I. Both Bonny and I were engaged, she to a lawyer, I to a young medical student. There was no question for me; I wouldn't consider putting off our marriage. Bonny felt the same way, the same way most female students in the '50s felt. It was marriage and a family we wanted. Maria won the Fullbright and studied in Paris.

I told the young girl I thought she was brave to travel alone in this troubled spot and that I admired her. She responded with daughterly respect, and an immediate rapport was established. I told her of our awakening in Europe and how I had given up my chance to do graduate study on my own.

"Did you ever regret it?" she asked.

"Oh, no. I wouldn't have Philip, who was born the next year. He's much like you—a free spirit, an artist, and now a medical student."

It was becoming increasingly undeniable to me that a whole generation had passed. Phil would like this girl. As would Mike, Todd, Dominic and Tom. She was spirited and bright. Her long, shiny hair hung freely from beneath her hat. Her thin, long limbs spoke of youthful strength and the agility of a doe, well bred and well cared for.

She was curious about my note pad and questions. "Are you a reporter?" she inquired.

"No. I'm writing a book. Something I've planned to do since childhood."

"Have you published before?"

"Yes, I have a cookbook out. I do some free-lance travel writing. I'm working on a series for Family travelogue, but it's incomplete. The cookbook was completed while all of our sons were in their last years at home. My son Philip illustrated it, and the others helped prepare the food. Festive food is a family passion. We all like to cook." And then, as if in defense of my own life choices, I heard myself add, "I did my bit for Women's Liberation: I taught five Italian sons to cook."

She smiled, and I was more conscious of the years that separated us. I did not feel "old" when we set out for this trip, but suddenly my body next to hers seemed less lithe, my hair less shiny, my face less toned. The fading of vitality was perhaps not as apparent on vacation, as I am always exhilarated in travel, but I was gaining a keen awareness of my place on the passageway from birth to death.

As we chatted, the coast was unfolding in wonderful, breathtaking views. The light continued to give wonder, and we were awed by its beauty. The guide announced in German, French and finally English that we were approaching Akko.

Starting from the sea, scents wafted up from the fisherman's harbor and tempered into exotic notions of Eastern cuisine, convincing our group that the flavor of this city transcended Western influence. If the sailboats docked seaside and the indigo blue sea pounding on a sea wall and jutting bay hadn't convinced us, inhaling the tantalizing aroma of freshly prepared fish taken directly from the Mediterranean surely would. Shishkabobs roasting on an open grill carried us inward to the city with a Turkish imprint. I did not hide my hunger nor my curiosity.

"Have you eaten much Eastern food?" My young friend now had a chance to expound on her culinary knowledge, asking me if I had ever tried falafel.

I honestly remarked that I had not, and she gave me a new recipe. "Wait until you see them make the sandwiches. You won't be able to resist!"

We deboarded with new interest, the young girl with her flowing hair and I with my little note pad. We passed one of the vendors making falafel. I watched him take a pita pocket, filling it with lettuce and sweet tomatoes first. Then from the grill he took freshly fried chickpea paste formed into balls and freshly fried potatoes, adding them to the now tempting sandwich. Lastly he sprinkled it with tahini. We did not resist. Grabbing a pocket of exotic scents and flavors, we walked along the narrow streets feeling a part of the mystery of the trade and teaming streams of people throughout the ages.

Akko, like many cities of antiquity, found it wise to build directly on foundations of other cultures. We walked backward in history as the guide glided down past khans with mosques and palms into a great hall built by the Knights of Templer. A medieval city remained intact below. The digging continues, uncovering archaeological traces as far back as Canaanite life. They peel like the layers of an onion to the core of ancient history.

Up three flights of winding stone steps, out in the air, the sound of a muzzelin over a loud speaker called the Muslim to prayer, and the thick exotic smells brought us back to Turkish times. Coexistence wound through the people, the blonde of their hair with the black of their eyes; the bazaars, the khans and the hospitaliers of Crusaders are mingled. My eyes were taking in the mixture, trying to sort out the dates of happenings, but the strong smells took over my senses, and the glistening green minarets and domes by the indigo sea cleared the image. Akko remains Eastern. The Orient was tantalizing to the senses.

# Haifa

The last city along the western coast of Israel that we were to see was just nine miles below Akko. We had swung along the great crescent and headed back to Tel Aviv when another port came into sight. Its contrast to the ancient Oriental coastal town was striking. Haifa is an active port; life breathes heavily and boldly in the modern working port. The ancient dust of other civilizations has been stirred and propelled into a vital momentum. Haifa seemed clean, spacious, and well groomed.

Our guide, a Sabra, native-born Israeli, proudly directed the driver to the edge of the city that would give us a sweeping view of the harbor and gleaming city. In three languages she slowly and boldly pointed to the panorama which demonstrated Israeli efficiency. We disembarked in the bright afternoon sun with a new energy. Haifa's skyline was exhilarating. Cameras clicked and zoomed in and out in tribute to the wonderful scene, the blue sky and white buildings in perfect contrast.

The guide had everyone singing as we climbed back into the bus, singing along the way of life and love and the song of Solomon. The last magnificent visit caught us in a descending late afternoon sun—the glory beyond Carmel of the starker cliffs of Rosh Ha' Nikra. Chalk white, they jutted out to the sea. A blue Mediterranean, much as I had remembered it to be at Capri, completed a rapturous contrast. Washed by that sea, the cliffs had deep crevices. We descended alongside a group of schoolchildren to view at close hand nature's wonder, and again I was reminded of our awakening and the first sight of the Mediterranean with our little boys, a glimpse of the world a generation before.

It was peaceful in England when we first visited the island until eruptions broke out in Ireland. Now we were watching children on school break riding the funicular up and down to a spot so beautiful only God could have created it. But the sun not only glistened on the foam, it was caught on the guns of the sentinels of a border watch. We were at the border of Lebanon, and the quiet peace of Carmel and Rosh Ha' Nikra was shattered by the reminder of recent eruptions and silent guards.

We followed the blue of the Mediterranean back to Tel Aviv in quiet contemplation, the unrest of the Mideast foremost in my thoughts.

## Galilee

I had spent a full day surveying the western border, and Dom reported an excellent international presentation at his meetings. That evening we recounted our day's experiences over an exquisite Eastern meal. My enthusiasm built as I told him of my discoveries on the tour, including the young woman I had made friends with that day.

"Sign me up for tomorrow's tour," he said, "you've convinced me. I want to see Galilee with you."

I was delighted to have his company. We could share our insights of the fertile seas and plains of central Israel. His political banter would also be a point of introspection for our journey. Together we have pooled our sources of knowledge and shared the common treasury that our life together has lain open.

Early the next morning we boarded an air-conditioned coach en route to ancient soil: Galilee. The very name, full of musical vowels, sounds softly lulling. Ancient rabbis tell us that God made seven seas, then Galilee for His own delight.

The morning was bright as we approached the harp-shaped sea of Galilee, and our competent guide gave us all the facts: "Galilee is a provincial area. It is a fertile area. You will be driving along the lushest bread basket of Israel, a crossroads of cultures. No one can dismiss its historic connections. Of course, its most common association is with the person of Christ."

We were to visit the small city of his birth, Nazareth; the simple fishing villages where he gathered his followers; the Roman-occupied towns of Tiberius and Capernaum where he preached; and the hills where people listened to and learned from his words. Galilee at the time of Christ had become an outlet for produce and trade. The trade began on the sea route, continued here and was disseminated to the rest of the continent. Had Christ chosen this crossroads in culture and trade to begin his new work, or was it just another coincidence of history? I was growing excited about recreating history as only travel can do.

The bus was soon filled with passengers from all the Tel Aviv hotels, and on the last boarding spot I saw my young friend with her straw hat waiting to board.

Our first stop was in Nazareth, in many ways unchanged through the centuries. There were now monuments to Mary and the child Jesus and many tourist stalls with rosaries and the predictable kitsch remembrances, products of the cottage industries that have existed for thousands of years. Our young friend from California, expert it seemed on crafts of many lands, pointed out the beauty of a few truly well-done pieces of weaving by local artisans.

The city was mainly inhabited by Muslims and Christians. Some coexistence was experimentally possible far away from the inner intensity of Tel Aviv and Jerusalem, but how could we as tourists judge the day-to-day problems of coexistence in this unsettled land. Huddled around the bazaars and fountains, in a continuity of life altered only slightly in the last 2,000 years, the gentle hill people stood in sharp contrast to the bustling tourists with their cameras and trinkets.

It was a short stop. Next, the tour wound around the Horns of Hattin, the historic spot of Saladin's mighty defeat of the Crusaders. The countryside was lush, and there was evidence of local produce; abundant and succulent figs, melons, eggplant, being sent out to the capital for consumption.

Our diverse tour group chattered in various tongues as the guide explained the surroundings in three languages. Galilee was once a crossroads for the trade of Egypt, Rome and Israel; now it was a crossroads of thought and pilgrimage.

There was a relaxing openness within our group in spite of its obvious diversity. The area was cheerful, the air stimulating, the summer morning perfect. We stopped at the banks of the River Jordan, that old tributary that feeds the Dead Sea and the Sea of Galilee. In the tradition of pilgrim tourists, we stood by its banks, pouring its clear water over us in a symbolic baptism. Then we filled small bottles—available for only 35 cents at the convenient souvenir shop—with holy water from the Jordan. The pleasant marshy banks completed our first vision, interrupted only modestly by modern advantages of tourism.

With the morning's travel behind us, we were growing from a diverse group of travelers to a band of pilgrims sharing a desire to complete our visions of life in Galilee. At Tiberius, a much needed lunch break would allow us to enjoy a common meal.

The catch of the day was the catch of many ages: muscht, or comb fish, better known as "St. Peter's Catch." As we stood in line observing the bounty of the sea succulently prepared, my young friend approached, "Do you mind if I join you?" she asked. I was happy to have her company, but with my husband present, I instantly began comparing myself—my clothes, my hair, my age—to her. I couldn't help myself, and suddenly I was not certain I wanted her there. I wondered if Dom would be making the same comparisons.

As we partook of St. Peter's Catch, we knew it was a superb choice. The fresh water specimen was pan fried with its enormous head and comb-like spine intact. About six inches long, it lay crisp on the large plate accompanied by steamed zucchini and tomatoes, also native to the Galilean horn of plenty.

In Galilee, these human experiences of hunger and fatigue and the need for refreshment seemed to be treated with concern. Human needs, basic and simple, were what the Galilean Master had chosen to fill, and the sea before us now was the source of much of his solace.

Our stomachs more than satisfied, we shared a moment of conviviality with our fellow travelers. A tame goat wandered in and nonchalantly joined the group.

A breeze from the sea gave a coolness and refreshment to our pilgrim souls. I needed the balm. Our guide broke the spell of our reverie, calling us to the lake's edge, where we would board a boat to cross the Sea of Galilee.

The sea was calm, the day bright. We were reminded of the backbone of the area, the fishermen. The guide gave a simple introduction to the natural problems of the sea, "As calm as it seems today, storms come up quickly. Many of the local fishermen have been swept out to sea, ships lost and their day's work lost."

Biblical references to the historical spot could not elude me. The storm at sea, the catch of Peter, the charcoal fire by the sea, and Christ's clear words to Peter, who did not expect a catch. "Oh ye of little faith," I heard from memory. Was I like Peter? I wanted to have faith. I needed something. Was it to be found here in the Holy Land?

Would our young friend need much faith? Youthful confidence often blurs the insecurities that lurk within, and verve can temporarily hide the reality of traumas in life. There is the obvious reinforcement that energy, beauty and the world are theirs. But what about the time when youth and beauty has faded? Would she need something to sustain her in the years to come? Or is life to be lived, squeezing out every experience for its moment's joy? Or as Camus cynically suggests: "What more should we expect of life? When it is over, it is over."

I have lived fully, I thought, with travel, possessions, five children to perpetuate my genes. What more could I ask of life? I had met its struggles, suffered its indignities, loved and lived fully. Life had given me much, but that, it appeared, could be soon over, snatched as quickly as my friend's life. If there was eternity, I knew at that moment I wanted that, too. "Oh ye of little faith," I heard again as we grew closer to Capernaum.

A quiet had descended over our group. At close look, the waters changed from blue to green and tawny brown. The sea was still. Those around me were either pensive or full and resting after lunch. The sea remained calm as we headed to the center.

In the distance we could see Tiberius, laid in ruins, the city that had once gleamed magnificently by the lake with its white temples that would outlast their builder. Capernaum soon came into view. It, too, was a shell of an ancient town. As we pulled dockside, my reverie was put to rest. Scant ruins of a once-great synagogue, a courtyard overgrown with patchy grass pushing through a once-solid, pristine floor. By the water's edge a few tombstones remained. Long vanished was the home into which Peter, the fisherman, had welcomed Christ. It was here that Christ first made his invitation, "Come follow me."

The guide pointed out a tombstone with the name Zebedee. His sons James and John had followed, too. The guide quizzed us often, and my Biblical history was sharpened. I was answering with knowledge even surprising to me. I had not read the Bible in its entirety for many years. The young girl looked on with a certain amount of interest, I thought.

"Wasn't it here that Matthew the Roman tax collector looked on from a distance at the new Rabbi?" I ventured.

"Yes," answered the guide, "you remember it well."

It was a sense of deja vu that made the city a wonderment. We walked on the stones that once comprised the synagogue's base. A stillness among the ruins, recent and ancient, was beautiful by the sea. Dom stepped away from me to capture the scenes with his camera.

The young girl observed us both—I with my pad, he with his camera. I wondered if she perceived us as aging travelers, squeezing out something extra from our lives. I glanced at her watching me and wondered if she guessed she was the topic of my scribbles. Why did this girl intrigue me?

A gentle wind tempered the tropical climate. While we had sailed across the sea, the bus had wound down the road to meet us. At the next stop a mosaic depicting bread and fish marked the spot where Christ miraculously fed the multitudes. Here the base needs of a simple folk had been paramount. I loved the miracle of the loaves and fishes. Working with community festivals, I had often found myself in charge of feeding the masses. Not knowing how to predict their needs, I often wanted a miracle.

As our bus ascended the last hill, the final vision of the topography and spirit of the area came softly into focus. Ahead of us was an unpretentious octagonal church perched atop the mountain. We were on what is now called the Mount of Beatitudes. Inside, on the walls of a church built to commemorate Christ's sermon on that spot, were eight thoughts, one on each wall, inscribed simply. There was little adornment, and the edifice was open to the elements. It invited a walk outside. From all vantage points outside, the expanse of sea and earth were as provocative as the inscriptions. This vision was now complete. I saw in my mind's eye a sea of people spread out comfortably enjoying the view that I was now inhaling, and I heard with them a summary of principles of compassion as they were uttered by Christ: "Blessed are the meek," and "Blessed are the poor in spirit, for theirs is the kingdom of God."

Never had I understood how rich in treasures and yet lacking in these principals I could be. Suddenly, as the breeze from Galilee blew through the valley, I knew how noble it was to be "poor in spirit." And I knew I wanted to possess these ideals of faith, faith in the dignity of all men, faith in a God who would guide us so eloquently and yet so simply.

"Blessed are those who mourn, for they shall be comforted. Blessed are those who hunger and thirst for righteousness, for they shall be satisfied. Blessed are the peacemakers, for they shall be called sons of God." This then was my inheritance, the legacy I could claim.

## Deserts

The Judean Desert, just southeast of Jerusalem, is one of the hottest, most desolate spots on Earth. Its lunar emptiness is a stark contrast to the lively, industrious Mediterranean coast and the tropical climate of Galilee. Out of the bleak desolation of exile in the mountains and caves of the deserts,

Israel's greatest insights have come. Her prophets have come forth from this burning expanse with concepts more valuable than trade and pleasure.

We were prepared for the bleakness of the desert experience but not for the 104 degree temperatures. Travelers who want the full experience of desert crossing can join a tour on foot or caravan. We were quite content to descend to this lowest spot on the earth's surface in the protection of an air-conditioned vehicle. Even so, we could not escape the barrenness.

Death penetrates the silent land. Even a brief stop in Jericho—a tropical respite—is but a quick break in the parched plain spread out in the vast enigmatic emptiness. Dom's meetings were over, and so he joined me once again to see Massada and the Judean desert.

About 20 miles outside Jerusalem we saw a streak of water. Given its name by medieval pilgrims who noted the complete absence of life, it is universally known as the Dead Sea. With a salt content six times that of the ocean, no vegetation nor living creatures reside within; no sea gulls circle its length. At 1,300 feet below sea level, this was the lowest spot on the Earth's surface.

Following the roads along the Dead Sea gave little relief from the hellish heat. Miles of bleak desert continued with brown domed hills devoid of vegetation. The Mountains of Moab to the east cast a stamp of solemn erosion of life. The silence penetrated the coach, giving ample time for meditation. Here was where the devil had come to Christ, telling him he could have the world. Power would be in his hands. He was hungry from 40 days of fast, and here the devil had promised food. I looked into the plain and saw only rocks and dry dust. My thoughts went back to the young girl I had met along the way. Had she been sent to tempt me, as Christ was tempted in this very spot? Or was she an angel sent to warn us that life is short and we are not in its youthful phase? Was she speaking to us in the silence? Or was it neither? Would we see her again in the desert?

Ahead of us was a mountain jutting starkly into the desert. Thirteen hundred feet above sea level, bleak and ominous, loomed the fortress of Massada. The drama that had occurred 2,000 years ago on that mountaintop had been confirmed by a massive archeological dig in 1964 and 1965.

Pottery, architecture, everyday utensils and scrolls were uncovered. It was, however, the ashes and remains of humans who had died ignominiously rather than accept slavery, that spoke to those who dug. Since then, Massada has become a place of pilgrimage, especially for young Zionists. It has become a symbol of resistance of few against many, a harbor of hope for freedom fighters. It is, however, a tragic tale of death. I was glad we had a Hebrew guide to tell us the story with his passion for its significance to his people.

According to the able historian Flavius Joseph, the fateful revolt set off by Jewish zealots in 66 A.D. in Caesara had ended when Titus captured Jerusalem and destroyed the temple in 70 A.D. All hope for freedom seemed dashed except for a small band of 967 men, women, and children who headed toward the desert and the fortress of Massada. Originally built by Herod for use as his own hideaway, the fortress was a luxurious structure, complete with Roman baths, cisterns, and palatial mosaics.

The refugees divided the fortress into small family dwelling spaces. Records indicate a frugal lifestyle of rationed food and water. They held out for two years.

At the end of 72 A.D., Procurator Silba set out with 10,000 members of the Roman Army to take the fortress. In massive strength they pushed through the desert and encircled the fortress. With engineering skill, they constructed the necessary rampart up the steep hill. The fate of the Jews would be sealed when the wall was finally breached.

The night before the Roman attack, a leader arose among the zealots and made the fateful decision for the group. "We shall die before we become slaves. Long ago we resolved to serve neither Rome nor anyone else but the only God. Now the time has come that bids us prove our determination by our deeds. At such a time we must not disgrace ourselves." His words were met with acceptance. In the morning, as the Romans burst forth, they found only an eerie silence, families embraced in death. Nearly 1,000 Jews had committed mass suicide.

Five witnesses, two women and three children, had hidden in a cave to report the details to the Jewish historian.

Our guide was decidedly affected by the story. He seemed to see no other answer. Silence fell over the rapt group on the bus.

"But people have been enslaved before," a gentleman from Philadelphia inserted.

"Why would anyone with children make such a decision?" one woman offered. "Of course, two years in this desert would confuse anyone."

Ascent to the fortress could be accomplished on foot, via cable car, or a combination of the two. The guide warned all walkers to cover their heads from the heat of the sun.

The 1,300 foot climb looked foreboding to me, but Dom was caught up in a spirit of adventure. A gust of sultry air hit us as we left the comfort of our air-conditioned bus. A souvenir shop waited conveniently on the plateau, with a stunning array of sunglasses and safari hats. Dom, who never wears a hat even in the bitterest cold and who would resemble a "godfather" in a fedora, gladly purchased a khaki colored safari hat. He would have outdone Bogie. He was caught up in his new self-image, surveying the ramparts and calculating the depth of the cistern. I was caught in the philosophical banter still being conducted in my mind as he chose the "combination" trip to the summit.

The park authorities had very wisely chosen not to reconstruct the massive fortress in contrived resemblance to its original design. An empty shell remains, just as the workers uncovered the dust. Reasonable guardrails and walkways had been constructed for safety. We walked to the edge of the precipice and surveyed the situation from many angles. The Dead Sea came immediately into view in the distance, miles of desert stretched out beyond sight. The earth was hardened and cracked.

From the ramparts, my husband was fighting the battle from above and below. His eyes quickened at the ramp. We walked along the areas marked on our map as "the palace," examining the intricacies of poignant mosaics. We sat in the synagogue and faced Jerusalem.

A fellow tourist who had refused to buy a hat at the souvenir shop looked peaked. I offered her a scarf, and she took it gratefully. I felt my hair, ringing wet on my neck. As we gazed down one last time, the terror of approaching soldiers gripped me.

"There will never be another Massada!" I heard a youth cry out.

There, in the presence of the spirits of those who had died at Massada, my heart ached and I longed for peace.

## Jerusalem

*"He took me to the top of an enormous, high mountain and showed me Jerusalem, the holy city, coming down from God out of heaven. It had all the radiant glory of God and glittered like some precious jewel of crystal clear diamond."*

—The Book of Revelation

No one enters Jerusalem without an image, a preconceived idea of what the city is like. Nor did I. Jerusalem has

been idealized, sought after, and longed for more than any other city in the world. The hope, "Next year in Jerusalem," raised by Jews after every Passover since the first diaspora, has sustained a race of people. She is envisioned by Christians and Muslims as the site where all humanity will gather for final judgment. Jerusalem has been described in glowing idealism as the epitome of peace, justice and beauty. Those who crave her spiritual essence know they will be comforted in Jerusalem just as Isaiah promised long ago.

Archaeologists have found Jerusalem a constant surprise as bombings uncover more layers of ancient civilizations that await their scrutiny. One million pilgrims visit daily, meshing their concepts with reality. I was just one of many thousands with questions to be answered, some very deep within me.

We were told the best way to approach the city would be from the Mount of Olives, and our coach drove up the not-too-high mountain in the early morning. The atmosphere was penetrated with an unearthly light that I will forever refer to as "the Israel light." It penetrated the indigo blue sky and lay its glare on the muted brown of the dust below. The hill we ascended was congested with tourists and a strange mixture of camels, barkers, and barefoot children eager to beat the buses up the mount. As we pulled into a spot already crowded with roaming visitors, an amalgam of flowing gowns, goats, camels, and hawkish guides, the congestion diverted me momentarily.

The postcard stands and milling crowds faded quickly into the background, though, as I gazed at the city that some say is suspended between heaven and earth. It was both a heavenly and an earthly sight that I saw. There, spread out on its rolling hill, was the history of 3,000 years, mixed and scarred in such a way that no one could deny its brutal history. The Turkish wall, marking it off from the modern city, followed the line of the earlier Roman wall. Turrets and domes, citadels and minarets, spread out in a conglomerate of buildings and stones so diverse in style and structure and yet all belonging. The sight was both stirring and revealing.

From the time the Hebrews first took her from the Canaanites until they retook her 2,000 years later, 12 civilizations had brutally claimed and reclaimed her. Three religions fought for the right to know her as their holy center. Yet history tells us that before religion was codified, Jerusalem was. Somewhere in the midst of antiquity, Jerusalem came to be.

"What you have come to is Mount Zion and the city of the living God, the heavenly Jerusalem, where millions of angels have gathered for a festival," rang clear to me. The sight in front of me was indeed heavenly too. But, out of its fierce dramas had come earth's scars, the reminders of other prophetic warnings: "Jerusalem, you that killed the prophets and stoned those that were sent to you. How often I have longed to gather your children like a hen gathers her brood, but you refused to listen."

Would man ever listen? What was religion for? I had always felt religion was meant to lift man above his base animal reactions, to bring him to a higher way of thinking and acting. And yet here, in the name of religion, half the world had been fighting for centuries. Why? What blind walls divide us. We are searching for a City of God, to dwell in His temple, for peace. In common, we say we want peace, but do we ever understand and respect the differences? It was not consoling to see. The composite before us of the city and her history was so profound, so inclusive, it created its own illusion. Was it necessary to continue? I felt no other detail could touch me more. The hubbub of the inner-city life might even mar this vision. The city from the distance in the ethereal light of morning had revealed enough. Need we see more?

With the struggle still in my mind, we headed for Jerusalem, driving past the Kidron Valley and the Garden of Gethsemani, reinforcing in my mind the agony, suffering, and death of this eternal city.

Even among the tombs, archeology, religion, and politics were mixed here. The graves, ancient as Absalom, son of David, have been consecrated, desecrated, cherished, and hoped for as burial sites for Jews, Christians, and Muslims. The visions become blurred with brutality and banal remembrances. Prophetic reminders from the Old and New Testaments sounded in my mind, "Oh, Jerusalem, if I should ever forget you...." "...We cannot play our tunes in a foreign land."

We entered Jerusalem via the Dung Gate. Immediately in sight was the vision that had sustained a race for 2,000 years:

The Wailing Wall. The laments rang clear. It was the retaining wall of the Temple of God. A gyration of swaying movement accompanied the deep lamentations:

> *"For the temple that is no more,*
> *we sit in solitude and mourn,*
> *For those who no longer revere God,*
> *we sit in solitude and mourn."*

Hasidic Jews, dressed in black Eastern European attire, hugged the wall, oblivious to the Western pilgrims with their cameras, clad in comfortable jeans and tennis shoes.

A bar mitzvah was in progress nearby, adding shouts of joy from youthful candidates and parents to the cacophony of noise. And over the ramp, a muzzelin was calling Muslims to prayer at their holiest site.

We chose a Hebrew guide to take us through a medieval synagogue, and as he pointed out the balcony where women were constrained, I teasingly questioned him, "Why?"

"Why not? You can hear the word of God just as well up there," was his witty but sharp reply.

Before we could approach the Arabic section of the city, we had to pass through a sentinel of soldiers and another security check. No orthodox Jew would be following us, for we were about to enter the area of the Dome of the Rock, a mosque built over what is thought to be the site of the holiest of holies of the temple of Solomon. To Judeo-Christians, it is known as the spot where Abraham was willing to sacrifice his son Isaac to God.

The overlapping of religious significance continued through the colorful Muslim section surrounding the Dome and winds into the Christian section where on Fridays, on the Via Dolorosa, laments are heard for Christ and his passion. Pilgrims traditionally follow the path marked by 14 stations of the cross, partaking once more in the pain and death of Christ.

The old city of Jerusalem is divided into four sections: Armenian, Jewish, Christian, and Muslim. The pressure to understand and respect each culture became paramount as we crossed from one section to another. As Dom and I held hands and wound our way through the colorful Muslim market enjoying the sea of people and pungent smells, we slowly became aware that we were doing something wrong. In this culture, any touch or show of affection was disapproved of, even between a married couple.

There were sharp contrasts between the pristine appearance of the Cardo shops in the Jewish section, newly built since the bombing of 1967, and the lively open stalls and crowded living conditions of the Muslims. In both sections, as we wandered through in obvious Western attire, it was difficult to pass the barking cries of children who were selling everything from art prints to stems of olive branches for only one shekel (around 60 cents). There was an uneasy tug of conscience that the delicious falafel we bought for $1.35 represented a good portion of the Muslim's income and that our comfortable room in the Jerusalem Hilton could accommodate his whole family better than his present home.

The mariet called the Muslim to prayer. We saw hundreds of Muslims follow that call and in their mosques, they called to Allah with deep reverence, but as is common in Jerusalem, the throngs of Muslims returning from Friday's sacred service made it almost impossible to browse and added confusion to the Christian service of the "Way of the Cross."

The passions and diversity do not end with allegiance to major religions in Jerusalem. Within the Jewish section, there are many different sects. In the Christian's Holy Sepulcher, six sects divide the holy spot of Christ's crucifixion and entombment, each jealously guarding its own portion.

From one section to the next—and within each section—I was awed by the divergent tongues, the varied styles of candles and icons, as well as the different methods of in worship.

But with all the diversity, the faith of the pilgrim seemed untouched. Passions run deep and faith was and is intense. From the wailing wall, tears of joy and praise mingled with laments. The muzzelin calls the Muslim to prayer fives times a day and heads bow intently in response. So, too, within the Tomb of Christ, I heard a litany of laments so palpable, belief was reinforced. I saw in the eyes of a Liberian ambassador an intensity of faith beyond any I had ever experienced. I could

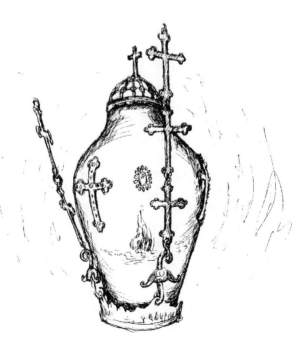

not account for my own feelings at this mournful spot. As a Christian, I felt the presence of Jesus as I came out of the tomb. There was an unexplainable essence there, an intangible reality.

There was a newly understood, ancient context that came to me. "Faith is the substance of things hoped for, the evidence of things not seen."

Outside the old city sprawls a growing international capital, with an extraordinary hospital, a medical school, museums, parks, and condominiums. We could see the touch of God's work. There are those who will always say Israel was meant to be a holy nation, and Jerusalem a holy city. It was long ago proclaimed: "The Lord your God has chosen you from all the nations on the face of the earth to be a people peculiarly his own. It was because the Lord loved you and because of his fidelity to the oath he had sworn to your fathers, that he brought you out with his strong hand from the place of slavery, and ransomed you from the hand of Pharaoh king of Egypt," A land promised, a land loved by so many. From Jerusalem to the nation's borders, I was touched by her tradition, her hold on life, and her diverse beauty. But more than anything, I was moved by her faith. The faiths of many; the faith in one God. My own faith was revitalized.

## The Red Sea

It was at the Red Sea on the seventh day of our journey that we finally rested. From the top of a bus, leaving Jerusalem, an image went with us. We had noticed a man walking to his temple of God. The rotund father walked briskly, almost as fast as our bus. He walked purposefully, his prayer shawl waving in the wind. Behind him were two spindly legged sons following as quickly as they could. Mama must have been at home, preparing the shabat. I was sure, as the guide had pointed out, that she could hear the word of God there as well.

On Sunday, as our bus pulled into the beautiful resort in Eilat, I inquired about Catholic services. The cabbie answered my inquiry with an apology. "It is a new resort and there are no Catholic churches yet." I knew that the Sabbath could be kept holy in many ways, I had just seen so many prayers offered up on three "Sabbaths" but I was a little disappointed that in so sacred a land, I would not be able to give my petitions and thanks at a Sunday Mass. I remained silent.

We were early for check in, so we dropped our luggage in the magnificent lounge. Only a wide glass window separated us from the beautiful blue sea, that "Sea of Reeds," now called the Red Sea. Someone was practicing on the piano, and the sounds of Chopin quieted us as we sat on the comfortable sofa, waiting for our room.

From our room's balcony we could see the wonderful beach and a swimming pool in the shape of the star of David. The sea was a turquoise blue at the edge but faded into a royal blue and then a green. A tent of bedouins serving tea was colorfully erected beside the pool, and a tame camel caught Dom's eye.

As in Vienna, Dom and I seemed once again to be out of sync. My nurturing role was lessening at that time, and I was ready for light-hearted music, and he was concerned about his responsibilities. In Israel, things were reversed. He was seeing an end to the financial burdens of raising children and he was ready for some fun and adventure. I was caught up in mid-life contemplations and the uneasy task of planning my future.

On our way to the beach, we stopped to have tea with the bedouins. Dom seemed to want to climb on the camel, but resisted. He grinned at the size of the exotic animal and settled for taking a picture.

I looked around at the young people on the beach. There were no topless bathing suits, but an abundance of bikinied sun-goddesses enjoying the gift of the idyllic setting. With my shirt over my bathing suit, I vowed to lose a little weight.

At the edge of the beach, I spread out a thick terry towel that the hotel had provided. Things were quiet, tourism having been curtailed by the spring's sad bombing. The sea was majestic, deep, the sun penetrating and warm. In the distance, just beyond our sight, was Mount Sinai, where God had made

His covenant with man, handing it to Moses. Here, He had reminded His people: "I bore you up with eagles wings; and brought you here to myself. Therefore if you hearken to my voice and keep my covenant you shall be my special possession dearer to me than all other people, although all the earth is mine. You shall be a kingdom of holy people, a holy nation." *A holy nation*, I thought, *and a beautiful land.*

It was a breathtaking view. I took my own small Bible out and read quietly. Peace finally crept into my whole being as I lay on the beach.

It was there, in the peace of a Sunday afternoon, as the music wafted over the waves of a clear Red Sea, that the Word came alive for me. Ancient words made real for having seen a need for them. Words we had touched in so many ways in Israel. The words of Isaiah, the words of David, the words of Christ. Sights floated back. Massada, Caesara, Akko, Haifa, Jericho, Emmaus, Galilee, Capernaum, Nazareth, Bethlehem. With all of the tension and beauty, the ground underneath remained holy.

It was now clear that I had come to that heavenly city of Zion, the city of the living God, the heavenly Jerusalem. But even here, there were continual battles, as in my mind there were continual battles of values and battles of the soul and body.

In the name of religion, people have placed the differences of liturgy and tradition above the love of God and each other. I, like millions of pilgrims, had no explanation for it. But my faith had increased as I walked in the lonely desert, entered the temples of worship and sat by the quiet sea. I could still hear the cries of the Muslims, the laments at the wailing wall, and the tears in the tomb of Christ. The borders in the near distance reminded me that life would continue to present its constant battleground. There were battles in my mind that would probably go on as long as my finite body existed.

It is not unorthodox that all religions wanted to claim the city. It is the inheritance of those who listened to God's promise for them. It was clear, God had told us through Moses, that the Lord our God is God indeed, the faithful God who keeps his merciful covenant to the thousandth generation toward those who love him and keep his commandments. In the hearts and minds of sincere idealists, we all crave that city of God with temples of our own liking. Yet the temples of worship throughout history have crumbled. The gleaming temple built by Herod in Jerusalem was but one example. Our bodies, which are the real temples, will also crumble.

I only had to look down to realize my body was slowly changing. The young girl had made it clear to me. My body was not lithe, and its ultimate decay was a reality. But I heard clearly as I read the text in front of me: "I will put my laws into your hearts, and write them on your minds." Those words, written 2,000 years ago were still alive for me.

At that moment, I knew my happiness, my peace, was not dependent on any physical temple. The domes, the spires, the skin—may fade. Somehow it became as clear as the sparkling Red Sea in front of me that the city of God is made up of people who simply crave and suffer for peace and love. The possibility of that city being formed is within us, within our decaying temples, in that sacred spot called our souls. It is an old principle that became startlingly clear that day.

Mankind fails to live peacefully, but the means have always been there. They are still there, inside us. At the heart of our temples is conscience. At the core of our souls is the possibility to love, to forgive, to show compassion, to feel union,a union with God and man.

The way to inner peace would not be easy for me, nor for the warring people around me in that hot spot of the Mideast. But wisdom was there for the asking. It was reachable for the seeking. And faith? The substance of things hoped for, the evidence of things not seen, it is a gift.

By faith, Abraham had obeyed the call to set out for a country that was his inheritance, without knowing where he was going. By faith Moses was hidden by his parents and by faith he had crossed the Red Sea. By faith he had waited in the desert and had been given a set of dictums that were the basis of a peaceful life. And greater still was the purpose of His laws, His dictums for peace. God had done all of this so that we would know Him, and in knowing Him, know love. For God is love.

Love in marriage and love in friendship can be sublime, but it can be rejected, it can be neglected; and the passion, the flame can grow cold. Even with God, love must be acted upon, the flame encouraged, or it will go out. Time together, understanding, caring and forgiveness are integral parts of the flame being recharged. "Seek Me and you will find Me," He promised.

I realized God set laws not only for the understanding of peace and justice, but mainly so we would all know love. Some had listened and understood. Some had mouthed but not acted upon their knowledge. Love would not come to those who see a brother or sister hungry and without clothes and say: "Keep warm and well fed. Good luck and goodbye!" But the kingdom would come to those who love and act, who crave the kingdom. The people of God have failed as individuals, as partners, and as countries time and again. And yet God has taken us back time and time again throughout history. He has, indeed, through history reminded us:

"When the Lord corrects you, do not treat it lightly, and do not get discouraged. The Lord trains the ones He loves as a father reprimands and trains his sons. Do not spurn the community. Pray together. Love one another. Know Me."

For 25 years I had been seeking knowledge through travel. I had traveled with my family in search of the civilities of life, a sense of history, culture, a search for richness of life. I had traveled with just my husband in recent years in search of wisdom. Travel had been one of my best teachers. Travel had served me well as a mother, as a wife, and as a woman searching for life's greatest treasures.

Journeys had always enriched my understanding, and the insights from this journey were profound. They were life-giving at a time when death and aging had sent us into a search beyond our normal comprehension. There are times in life when a door opens and the world comes in. I had experienced that on earlier journeys, journeys when culture and beauty had been opened to me, but in the land of Israel, a door had opened and heaven had been revealed. And heaven, yes heaven, had been there, if only in a brief glance.

I knew I would lose that vision without renewal. I knew I must continue to read the Bible again and again. But I was now convinced that there is a heaven, where failure and tragedies and lessons learned and then forgotten, where love and warmth and energy will be put to rest. And I knew heaven could begin wherever we were, and are. Change would come as it had come to us as a family.

Since we began traveling, the institutions of mankind had changed. Religion, government, business had all been examined in different terms. The family as an institution had been threatened and troubled. People are no longer willing to suffer for family or for love of God. Covenant is not even a word understood by many. The desert, too, has ceased to have meaning in our culture. It is no longer a desirable place to grow strong or to learn discipline. And the family of man had been threatened by war, by nuclear annihilation, by cynicism and self-seeking remedies.

Had my search brought me any closer to the answers? I asked myself that day by the Red Sea. Yes, I had grown, as I had on previous quests. The Holy Land had compelled me to examine myself and to try to see the bridge between the real and the ideal. It had been a catalyst, as all travel is for me, a stimulant to continue learning and growing. Am I finished, satisfied? Of course not; I am still on a journey, with perhaps one of the toughest climbs ahead. I have seen enough of life to know that there will be a battle within until the last breath.

The snatching of life so unexpectedly of a dear friend had been a warning and a blessing to those of us left behind. None of us knows the hour or the day. But my faith had been renewed in the Mideast in spite of all the crises around and within me. A covenant is two-part, renewed by repeating the sacred words and renewed by reliving the sacrifices it entails.

The covenant was clear that day:

"Continue to love each other like brothers, and remember always to welcome strangers, for by doing this some people have entertained angels without knowing it. Keep in mind those who are in prison, as though we were in prison with them, whether that be prisons of mind or body. Remember those who are being badly treated, since you too are in one body. Marriage is to be honored by all. Put greed out of your lives and be content with whatever you have."

God Himself said, "I will not fail you or desert you and so we can say with confidence, 'with the Lord to help me I fear nothing; what can man do to me?' Do not be led astray by all sorts of strange doctrines. Keep doing good, and sharing your resources, for these are the sacrifices that please God."

Somewhere not too far from me across the Red Sea on Sinai, God made a covenant with man. And within this Holy Land, He had renewed that covenant, time and time again. He had made that covenant with me. My faith had convinced me. It became so strikingly clear, as clear as the sparkling water in front of me, that the covenant God had given us could be reduced to the simplest of terms. Love your God with all your heart, and love one another, as I have loved you.

# Epilogue

Returning to England with the family was more than another journey to see the land of low skies and high teas. It gave us one more chance to gather as a family and to realize what these journeys had meant to us. Journeys had clearly marked the passages of our lives.

We found that the world was open to us as we were open to it. Wanderlust had called to me as a young mother, telling me my life was not complete. England had been the first step out of a limited world. And each journey that we took as a family, as a couple, and I as a woman and a mother, from that time on had been not just an escape, but a chance for a creative change, a chance to look at ourselves and our world in new light.

The journeys themselves took on a life of their own, and the places became holy ground because of what happened as we let ourselves be touched. The act of making a journey was the awakening of dormant possibilities. Seeing things from new angles, seeing ourselves in new frames, we acquired different perspectives on life.

In certain special places, when all the elements of peace and beauty touched our souls, there was a communion of holy people, those who had walked the paths before, still showing us the light on the path, and those who might follow, those to whom we might show the way.

In some humble way I wish to share this vision, that it might light the way for those who want to step out of the ordinary, who want to take a leap of growth, whether it be to far-away places on this earth, or to the deep crevices of their souls. And if the light makes life's long journey a little clearer, then I will feel that sharing my own personal odyssey will have been worth the writing.

Travel has changed me. What will aging bring? I suppose the last epoch will be as full of surprises and snarls and joys as the earlier ones, but somehow I know we will keep on traveling. The earth is still exciting. The sky and the sea are open. We will trust with wings of eagles the words of the prophets who have journeyed ahead and proceeded to the eternal light.

And who will ascend to the final hill and stand in the holy place? Those who have pure hearts and know themselves, those who know that though the world has many temples, many cultures, and many remembered deeds, the holiest temple is within them. The journey to know what is within us is the toughest and most satisfying of all journeys.

As I sat by the fire in Oxford, having let jet lag and reverie play out their course, I felt exhilarated with the thought of seeing England again. There would be new lanes and old haunts. Tom was already talking about the sawdust-filled pub where we might all go after decorating the tree. I looked over at my daughter-in-law, carrying our first grandchild. I was glad Anne had been brave enough to travel with child. For to travel with children is not simple. But I knew the journey would enrich her new family. And I wonder if my grandchildren will hear me when I tell them, "It's your turn, Chickadees."